COMPETING ON
QUALITY
AND
ENVIRONMENT

Competing on Quality
and
Environment

Christian N. Madu, Ph.D.

Research Professor and Chair
Management Science Program
Co-Editor, International Journal of Quality & Reliability
Management
Department of Management and Management Science
Lubin School of Business
Pace University
New York, USA

CHI PUBLISHERS
FAIRFIELD, CT

A C.I.P. Catalogue record for this book is available from the library congress.

Library of Congress Catalog Number: 2002 190126
ISBN: 0-9676023-1-9

Published by Chi Publishers.
P.O. Box 1171, Fairfield, CT 06432

Sold and Distributed by Chi Publishers
P.O. Box 1171, Fairfield, CT 06432
Telephone: 203-261-0739
Email: chipublishers@aol.com

First published in the United States in 2004.

To my wife Assumpta
and
the boys Chichi, Chike and Chidi

CONTENTS

PREFACE

This book is based on the author's experience in teaching courses in operations and quality management and conducting research in quality and environmental management issues. Through these exposures, it has become clear to the author that high quality and environmental quality are intertwined and that one cannot be achieved without the other. In quality management, there is increasing focus on creating value to the customer, doing things right the first time, reducing waste, and increasing productivity. These are the same concepts that are shared in sustainable manufacturing. Here, the emphasis is on how to minimize environmental burden by using renewable resources and adopting strategies such as recycling, inverse manufacturing, re-manufacturing, reverse logistics, and so on. All these focus on resource conservation, protection of the environment, and creation of value to the customer. Therefore, there is a need to have a book that will unify these topics and bring to focus what corporations need to do in other to create value to customers.

Corporations today, develop their quality practices around satisfying the needs of the customers. They pay attention to what really matters to the customer. It is by understanding what is important to the customer that a corporation can begin to address how to create value to the customer. The use and practice of quality function deployment as a tool for understanding the customer requirements and satisfying such requirements through design strategies is increasingly important. It is also, clear that what matters to the customer could be both intrinsic and extrinsic in the product or service. Thus, a more holistic view of products or services is needed. Customers today adopt a much broader view of quality. Such views look beyond the direct value created by the product from its usage but may also focus on how the product or service impacts on its extended environment. Many corporate advertisements today do not focus only on "product quality" as commonly understood but also tend to show that the corporation is environmentally friendly and responsible. This strategy of corporations show casing their environmental practices is in response to the growing demand of customers on corporations to adopt environmentally friendly practices hence the growing importance of sustainable manufacturing.

This book views product quality and environmental management as two important strategies a company should adopt to remain competitive. While product quality management has been in vogue since the 1970s and has been widely treated, corporate environmental management issues started gaining in popularity since the 1980s. Yet, many continue to perceive environmental management issue as an esoteric topic that should remain in the domain of the sciences. There is in fact, a growing focus on environmental management. It is important to understand that top management must buy into the idea of environmental management as it relates to the bottom line. Otherwise, it will be difficult to justify its value to the organization. In this book, quality and environmental management are viewed as closely related and achieving a common goal of helping the organization to produce high quality and environmentally friendly products and services while remaining competitive. It is our contention that customer requirements include a significant component of environmental quality and since customer loyalty and retention are necessary for an organization to remain competitive, it is important for corporations to address both product quality and environmental management issues that are of concern to the customer. This book therefore, treats topics on quality and environmental issues from the perspective of how they could help an organization to continue to meet the needs of its customers. Important chapters on the practice of quality and environmental management are presented, and a chapter on "Competing on quality and environment" that aims to integrate both topics that form the theme of this book.

This book is a basic book on the topic of quality and environment and it is targeted to academicians and practitioners. It could be used as a text for introductory classes in quality and/or environmental management in both undergraduate and graduate classes in business, engineering management, and industrial engineering. Practitioners could also use this book as a good reference manual.

This book benefited from the suggestions and recommendations of Chu-Hua Kuei, Pace University. I also thank my graduate research assistant Ozgur Pehlivan for his efforts in organizing the final manuscript.

Christian N. Madu
Lubin School of Business
Pace University, New York

CHAPTER 1

●────────────────────────────●

INTRODUCTION TO QUALITY

The concept of quality is not new. Historically, people have been preoccupied with quality. People are interested in the quality of food they eat, the quality of shelter they have, the quality of their relationships with one another and the quality of their life. Gitlow *et al.* (1995) traced the history of quality as far back as early 2000 BC. They note the Code of Hammurabi, Item 229 which states, 'If a builder has built a house for a man, and his work is not strong, and the house falls in and kills the householder, that builder shall be slain.' Obviously, the builder is being made accountable for his/her job. This sense of responsibility for the performance of the work forces the builder to inspect every part used in the building construction and assure the quality of the work, otherwise the consequences will be grave. This prehistoric concept of quality remains unchanged. Quality has the same meaning today. What is perhaps different today is the focus on a structured quality approach, that is, a quality plan that is well articulated, included in operational strategies and integrated in a decision making framework to attain some predefined goals. Keeping this in mind, quality becomes a powerful tool through which organizations can achieve competitiveness and survival. This structured approach to quality has been credited to having helped many leading corporations such as Xerox, Motorola, IBM, Harley-Davidson and a host of others survive and thrive in their competitive environment. But what do we mean exactly by quality? Quality may mean different things to different people. It deals for the most part with people's expectations and perception on how such expectations are satisfied. For example, a customer at a bank may have different expectations of the quality of service he/she is receiving. If the bank teller is courteous and appears to be friendly, the customer may overlook other factors such as the time it took to provide the service and the errors that the teller may have committed in providing the service. Conversely, if the teller was quick and swift but does not appear to be friendly, the customer may not be happy with the quality of service. Obviously, there are several attributes that can contribute to what a customer perceives as quality service and quality cannot be achieved until we understand the importance of these attributes to the customer. The bank example illustrates the difficulty in assessing quality for the service sector because aspects of quality in the service sector are often intangible, indirect and difficult to measure. Furthermore, these attributes of quality may have different priorities to different people thus making it more difficult to analyze.

When we deal with tangible items or products, quality can be measured differently. Garvin (1988) identified the attributes of product quality which are briefly defined:

- Performance — deals with operational characteristics of the product or service. For example, a car attaining quality for performance would be 33 miles per gallon.
- Features — these may be secondary characteristics like dual airbags, leather seats, eight-speed CD changers, etc.
- Reliability — deals with consistency of performance over time. How long will it operate before failure?
- Conformance — does the product meet its design specifications?
- Durability — what is the useful life of the product?
- Serviceability — what is the ease of repair of or obtaining service when needed?
- Aesthetics — deals with sensory attributes of the product such as feel, sound, look.
- Perceived quality — deals with customers' perception of quality (i.e. how do customers perceive the quality of a Mercedes Benz compared to that of a Volkswagen?).

DEFINITION OF QUALITY

Having discussed these attributes, we shall now proceed to define quality. We shall start by noting the quality definitions provided by the most influential quality scholars in the United States quality movement. Philip B. Crosby defines quality as conformance to requirements (1980); Joseph M. Juran (1988) defines it as fitness for use; while the late W. Edwards Deming (1993) defines it as a predictable degree of uniformity and dependability at low cost and suited to the market. The definitions by Crosby and Juran focus on designing products and services that meet customers' needs and expectations. They presume that it is possible to identify customers' needs and then develop quality guidelines to satisfy such needs. Although this may be possible for products, it is often difficult to measure quality or identify quality attributes in service. As we discussed above, perceptions play a large role in determining quality for the service sector. The definition by Deming seems to be appropriate since it allows room for variations in quality while guaranteeing a predictable degree of uniformity and dependability. However, attempts should be made to minimize the variation in quality. These definitions do not completely capture the focus on Total Quality Management (TQM). Evaluation of the three definitions presented above will show a focus on the more technical aspects of quality. For example, the issue of conformance to requirements and fitness for use address design issues. Simply, quality is achieved when customer needs are designed into the product. On the other hand, Deming's definition of quality focuses on achieving a stable process. If variations observed in a product are within the normally established limits, then the process is stable and can be considered to be predictable. None of these discuss organization-wide changes. Not surprisingly, W. Edwards Deming is considered the father of Total Quality Management. While his earlier definition of quality focused on its statistical component, in his later works he viewed quality from both statistical and management perspectives and argued the need to revolutionize the management practice so that quality can be viewed from a systems perspective. He strongly argued that quality should be an organizational-wide effort and is the responsibility of everyone with management providing the leading role. Since then, several definitions of TQM have emerged, but we shall define it as an organization-wide quality program to continuously improve products and services delivered to customers by developing supportive organizational culture and implementing statistical and management tools. TQM is a holistic concept that considers the improvement in all organizational activities and processes. It is through joint collaborative efforts of all functions and members of an organization that the totality in TQM can be achieved. This new focus of quality can be differentiated from the traditional view of quality where the responsibility for quality is entrusted to inspectors or inspection stations. With TQM, every employee is an inspector of his or her own work and all employees work for the common goal of the organization. Maintaining inspection stations at the end of the assembly line leads to suboptimization since it encourages the production of defective items. Thus by requiring everyone to get involved in the quality process, less defect is produced thus leading to less waste and increased productivity for the organization. A more expansive view of quality was provided by Madu and Kuei (1995) who introduced strategic total quality management (STQM) as a reflection of the overall performance of a firm. This is a strategic and holistic view of quality by defining the focus of a firm on its stakeholders rather than customers and defining quality to include environmental quality and social responsibility issues.

LEADERS OF QUALITY AND THEIR CONTRIBUTIONS

As we mentioned above, W. Edwards Deming is the father of TQM. He developed many of the major management principles that today guide the practice of TQM. There are however, other major contributors to the TQM movement including Joseph Juran and Philip Crosby. Their contributions are briefly reviewed.

DEMING'S APPROACH TO QUALITY

Dr Deming's work on quality started in the late 1920s when he worked as a mathematical physicist in the US Department of Agriculture and was exposed to the work of Walter Shewhart on variations within the manufacturing process. Deming expanded this intriguing concept to what is now known as the theory of variance. Deming later applied his expertise on sampling and statistical control in his work at the US Bureau of the Census. Deming focused primarily on identifying sources of variation in processes and eliminating or controlling them. Unfortunately, he could not get enough US managers to heed to his call on this new wave of managing quality. Deming participated in a team to improve the quality of the products produced for the Allied Cause during World War II. Nersesian (1993) pointed to the problems of quality then when he noted that 'Bombs did not explode on impact. Torpedoes made a full circle and struck the submarine that fired them.' Deming's approach to solve these problems was to change certain principles of management. At that time, Taylorism was widely embraced in the US. Deming called for a change in worker motivation as a means of influencing productivity and was fiercely challenged by both management and organized labor.

In 1950 after World War II, when Japanese products were the scorn of the world, Dr Deming was invited to Japan by the Union of Japanese Scientists and Engineers (JUSE). Japan was in desperate need for a messiah to solve its quality problems. As Nersesian (1993) noted, in opening a Japanese car door, the entire unit would pull out underscoring the low quality associated with its products. Thus Japanese managers were more willing to listen to any new philosophy of quality. In a stroke of luck, for Deming, Kaori Ishikawa, a famous Japanese professor of management, was present when Deming delivered his lecture. Professor Ishikawa was so impressed that he organized his ex-students who were then holding high-level management positions to come and listen to Deming. Deming's message was subsequently put in full practice by Mr. Kiichiro Toyoda — president of Toyota Motor Company. Dr Deming in his seminar emphasized the use of statistical methods and a systemic approach to solving quality problems. He blamed poor quality on the system and not on the workers. He stressed the importance of basic statistical tools now widely known as the seven quality tools. This list of basic tools includes histograms, scatter plots, Pareto charts, fishbone diagrams, control charts, flow charts and check sheets. His seminar was repeated several times in Japan.

While working with Dr Shewhart, Dr Deming was introduced to the plan-do-check-act (PDCA) cycle. Dr Deming used it extensively in his seminars to illustrate how statistics could be used to control processes. He emphasized the need for every employee to be involved in the application of statistics to improve quality. His contributions to the Japanese quality program were so immense that the most coveted quality award is named after him — the Deming Prize. Deming made an enormous contribution to the quality movement. Deming's recognition in the US did not come until late 1979. Since then, his management and quality principles have been applied by several corporations in the United States. Dr Deming died in December 1993 at the age of 93. We shall briefly discuss his management and quality principles.

A SYSTEM OF PROFOUND KNOWLEDGE

On reviewing the Western style of management, Deming insisted that it must undergo a transformation by adopting a system of profound knowledge. The system of profound knowledge offers a new way to understand and optimize the organization and through this, the whole country can be uplifted. He identified the foundation for a system of profound knowledge on four interrelated parts, namely:

- Appreciation of a system
- Knowledge about variation
- Theory of knowledge
- Psychology — of individuals, society and change.

He noted that his 14 points for management offer a natural application of the system of profound knowledge necessary to transform the Western style of management to one of optimization. He referred to profound knowledge as knowledge for leadership of transformation. In this system of profound knowledge, he frequently reminded us that knowledge is built on theory and without theory; there will be no knowledge, nothing to revise and nothing to learn from. More directly, he states that 'Without theory, experience has no meaning. Without theory, one has no questions to ask. Hence without theory, there is no learning. Theory is a window into the world. Theory leads to prediction. Without prediction, experience and examples teach nothing. To copy an example of success, without understanding it with the aid of theory, may lead to disaster (Deming 1986, p. 106).' Keeping the importance of theory in mind, we shall now review Deming's 14 points for management.

DEMING'S 14 POINTS FOR MANAGEMENT

Deming's 14 points for management are adapted from his famous book *Out of the Crisis* (1986). These are:

Create constancy of purpose to achieve continuous improvement of products and services and survival of the firm

This point stresses the importance of leadership. Management must have a vision of what it intends to accomplish, how it intends to satisfy its customers and how it intends to provide quality services or products to its customers. This vision must be clearly stated and understood by employees. There should be a long-term focus to continuously improve and achieve the mission and vision of the organization. Overly focusing on short-term goals may derail the organization from its long-term goals and may become disastrous. By developing a long-term view, the organization is able to study changes in its environment. It is able to hear the voice of its stakeholders and know when its market segment is changing. Adapting to such changes, allows the organization to improve, compete effectively, stay in business and continue to provide jobs.

Adopt the new management philosophy where Western management must respond to challenge and lead through change

The new management philosophy calls for understanding of a better way to manage people and processes. People need to be motivated and challenged. Management should develop an atmosphere that motivates employees to enhance their performance. Management must also be innovative in today's competitive environment. Being able to manage change and respond to challenges ensures the survival of the company. The emphasis of business should not be to maximize stockholders' wealth but to maximize stakeholders' wealth. There is a need to share managerial responsibilities and get everyone involved in problem solving and decision making. The functional departments and the organizational layers in an organization are interdependent and should operate to achieve total system optimization. They cannot be treated as independent units because that will lead to suboptimization of the entire system.

Cease dependence on inspection and build quality into the product

The traditional view of quality is that inspection at the end of the assembly line is necessary to identify defective items and then move them upstream for rework. This point argues that dependence on inspection encourages the production of poor quality products because the emphasis is on quantity and not quality. Thus a worker's productivity may not be linked to quality since it is not the worker's responsibility to take care of his of her quality problems. By ceasing dependence on inspection, it becomes the responsibility of every employee to build quality into his or her work. This will ensure the production of high quality products, elimination of waste and a reduction in the cost of quality. With that achieved, everyone benefits. Customers will receive high quality products, workers will take pride in their work, the organization is able to compete effectively with high quality products and society as a whole benefits from increased productivity. In other words, no one loses. Everyone wins. It is a win-win situation.

Cease the practice of awarding business contracts on the basis of price tag alone

It is a mistake to award contracts to suppliers and vendors without a total cost assessment. Often, the bidder with the lowest cost may not offer the best quality. Cost should be related to value and quality of work. It does not make sense to award a supply contract to a contractor who will supply a high proportion of defective items which will either have to be replaced or discarded. By factoring the cost associated with waste and loss of customers' goodwill, that supplier may in fact be the most expensive bidder. Emphasis should be on quality rather than cost because in the long run the overall cost will be less due to high quality. So, an overall cost assessment of each bid will identify the quality of each supplier and link it to the quoted cost before contracts are awarded.

Continuously improve the system of production and service to improve quality and productivity

An organization is viewed as a system of interdependent units. These units interact and exchange information in order to optimize the system. There is a common goal or mission for the organization and this cannot be achieved if each unit operates as its own island with its independent goals. In order to improve the system continuously, each unit must contribute by working hard to improve its work processes, reducing waste and supporting other units to achieve their common goal. The actions of each unit or process affect quality. If purchasing continues to award supply contracts on the basis of price tag alone, then production will not have any chance to improve quality because defect is built into the system. Purchasing must recognize the need to improve its process so that production can provide quality products. This point also emphasizes the need to minimize variance in the product or service. Although variation in products and services is inevitable, to achieve a stable or predictable process, it is important to minimize variation.

Institute training on the job

Training is an ongoing process and it is necessary to expose employees to new management styles and work tools. Employees need to be trained on how to use statistical control charts, the skills needed to improve their work processes and to understand their role in improving quality in the organization. Training is not a one-time effort. It is through training and education that employees can see the inadequacy of theory and appreciate the need for revision of theory. Through training they can take a critical look at their current work practices, query some of their activities, evaluate alternatives and perhaps develop new methods. Training increases innovation, improves performance and helps employees understand their jobs.

Overhaul leadership of management and production workers to help people and machines do a better job

Leadership must take charge of the workplace. Leaders must provide the tools necessary to do the work, understand the problems in the workplace and be able to identify problems as either common or special causes. A leader should be able to predict the future by working to create stable processes with low variation. Leaders should participate and support quality improvement, teamwork and reward innovation. They should cease from blaming employees for problems in the workplace and understand the limitations of the employee especially when the problem is systemic. Leaders must lead by example and should accept the risks associated with innovation.

Drive out fear to improve effectiveness

There are many angles to this point. The traditional Western management style was based on a hierarchy of authority with a vertical channel for transmission of information. For long, this organizational hierarchy has separated the different layers of management with operators being at the bottom of the hierarchy. However, with the advent of TQM, a call is being made to these operators traditionally at the bottom to openly express themselves, share information, report problems and even suggest solutions to problems. It is not easy to overcome the fear of retaliation and similar abuse of power that may occur when lower level employees identify the problems within the corporation. TQM can, however, survive only when management is able to drive out fear so every employee can participate actively in problem and solution identification without fear of reprisal. Employees need to know that the essence of such participation especially in teams is to be able to improve the system or process and is not finger pointing. Management must open itself to this new change in style, adapt to change for TQM to survive and, again, lead by example by encouraging mutual and honest exchanges between employees and management. A conducive environment for employees to probe their thoughts, generate new ideas and ask questions should be encouraged in order for the organization to improve its effectiveness. The key is to encourage innovation and there is no guarantee that innovation will always lead to desirable outcomes. Employees, therefore, cannot be punished or threatened when their goodwill efforts fail to produce desirable outcomes.

Break down barriers between departments and encourage teamwork

Organizational problems often stem from internal competition between different departments. This may create conflict as each department works to optimize its goals but ends up suboptimizing organizational goals. Another problem may be lack of coordination between the departments which may make it difficult to achieve synergy. For example, information may be departmentalized and access may be restricted to specific departments making it difficult to make sound decisions. Again, the organization as a system can only be optimized when these departments work for common goals and understand that their greater goal is to achieve the organizational goal.

Barriers between departments can be broken down by forming cross-functional or interdisciplinary teams. These teams can see the needs of the different departments and how they can be coordinated to achieve organizational goals. It is also important that training programs should be interdisciplinary. This makes it easier for employees to adopt a holistic view of organizational problems rather than seeing things from a micro perspective. An engineer should be able to design products based on the information gathered from marketing on the needs of customers. The Finance department needs to know the need for the production unit to update its processes to be able to compete and supply quality products. These departments cannot operate as separate islands with their own different views. They need to work together to achieve overall system objectives.

Eliminate slogans, exhortations and targets from the workforce

Deming believes that most slogans used in US businesses distract and insult workers and are often meaningless. For example, slogans such as 'Do it right the first time' or 'Increase revenue by 5 percent next year' are meaningless if employees are not given the tools to achieve such goals. For example, do employees have the training needed to produce quality work? Are suppliers selected on the basis of price tag alone? Is the process incapable of producing quality products? Some of these problems are inherent in the system and the worker has no control over the system. The worker cannot achieve these goals until management addresses the problems within the system. It may lead to emotional issues on the part of the powerless worker and may create other work-related problems.

Eliminate work standards, management by objectives and numerical goals

The use of numerical goals encourages quantity rather than quality. It can also be dysfunctional because those who meet the quota may not necessarily be the best workers because they produce a high proportion of defects and create more waste. Conversely, those that cannot meet the quota may be frustrated and feel threatened. Numerical goals are often arbitrary and fail to understand a system's capability. So, when the target is not met due to the system's incapability, the worker may be blamed. Numerical goals also discourage hard work as may be apparent from the use of management by objectives. Workers may work out with their supervisors an acceptable numerical goal and once that target is achieved, work is slowed down. There is potential too that system resources may be abused as an individual exploits them to meet his or her personal goals at the expense of the entire system (Gitlow *et al.,* 1995). Such goals may also pit workers against each other as everyone becomes selfish and acts to maximize personal utility rather than the system's goal. This leads to a lose-lose situation since organizational resources are suboptimized.

Remove barriers that rob the hourly worker, people in management and engineering their right to pride in workmanship

The term pride has been replaced with joy (Gitlow *et* aL, Ch. 1, 1995). There are many barriers to joy in workmanship and these barriers need to be broken down by management. Gitlow *et al.* identified some of these. They are listed below as:

- The mission of the organization is not properly communicated to employees so they do not know what is expected of them;
- Work is repetitive and does not encourage innovation;
- Systemic problems are blamed on employees;
- Products are not properly designed and tested;
- Poor supervision and training;
- Equipment, materials and methods are faulty;
- There is a focus on quick results and targets.

Deming also criticized the use of performance appraisal systems used widely for promotion and merit increases because they discourage teamwork since members work to maximize their own ratings.

Institute educational and self-improvement programs

The workforce must be abreast of changes in their work processes through education and retraining. Workers and management must continuously learn to improve themselves. They cannot optimize the system if they are not aware of new information, new tools and procedures and innovation. Workers are the most important assets of the organization. They invest their future in the organization, they care about the organization and for them to continue to work more effectively, the organization must invest in them by training and retraining them. It is through training that they can learn new theory, evaluate existing theory and apply the theory. As Deming noted, 'theory is a window into the world' (1986), without it, there will be no learning and without it, application cannot be improved upon.

Act to accomplish the transformation

Management must act to accomplish the transformation to this new management style. Top management must lead the quality movement. Its action sends out the message on the direction for the future. Management must commit the necessary resources and put in the effort necessary to make it work. Quality should get top-level attention since it influences the survival of the organization. When top management makes a commitment to quality, workers will notice and will adjust and adapt to this new style of management. In Deming's words, 'The transformation will lead to adoption of what we have learned to call a system and optimization of performance relative to the aim of the system. Individual components — teams, departments, divisions, plants — will not compete. Instead, each area will make choices directed at maximum benefit for the whole organization' (1986). It is the role of management to achieve this goal.

These 14 points of management outline some of Deming's work and the implementation of these points will lead us to other areas of his work such as the plan-do-check-act cycle, theory of variance and what he identified as the five deadly diseases and sins. These deadly diseases and sins are namely:

- Lack of constancy
- Concentration on short-term profits
- Over-reliance on performance appraisals
- Job hopping
- Overemphasis on visible figures.

While some of these deadly diseases may have been discussed above, you will encounter further discussions on others and more on Deming's work as you go through the book. We shall now look at the work of Dr Joseph M. Juran.

JURAN'S APPROACH TO TOTAL QUALITY MANAGEMENT

Dr Joseph M. Juran achieved almost the same acclamation as Deming in the total quality movement. Like Deming, he was influential in Japan in the early 1950s and was part of the team of lecturers that brought a new wave of quality management philosophies to Japan. Juran's contribution to the quality movement focuses on four areas, namely, cost of quality, quality habit, quality trilogy and universal breakthrough sequence. In this chapter, we shall discuss only the cost of quality and quality trilogy.

Cost of quality

Juran believed that in order to attract top management's interest in quality, they should be communicated to using the language they understand — money. Top management is interested in bottom lines and if that cannot be conveyed through quality, their interest will wane. To do this, he developed cost of quality (COQ). This identifies four categories of cost that are associated with quality. They are:

1. Internal failure costs — these costs relate to detection of defects prior to the shipment of the product to the end user. Such may include the cost of rework, scrap, salvage, inspection.
2. External failure costs — these costs are incurred after the product has reached the end user and defects are detected. This may include warranty costs, complaints from customers, loss of goodwill, returned materials, and repairs.
3. Appraisal costs — this involves the assessment cost for product quality levels. For example, incoming products are inspected for quality as well as outgoing products. Processes may be periodically inspected and maintained.
4. Prevention costs — this deals with the cost of trying to prevent defects such as training costs.

Quality trilogy

Juran blamed most quality problems on management. He argued that about 80% of quality defects can be controlled by management so management should correct them. He viewed quality management from a trilogy that consists of quality planning, quality control and quality improvement (1986).

1. Quality planning — he stressed the need to recognize and understand the customer group that the firm or business unit caters for. This customer group includes internal and external customers. Internal customers often arise when there is transaction or exchange between interdependent units or departments in the same organization. Their needs must be recognized in order to improve quality.

2. Break down the needs of the customer. This makes it clear to members of the organization and easier to develop a product design that will satisfy those needs. In a sense, this is a means of making customer needs operational.
3. Ensure that processes operate correctly and are capable of meeting product design specifications.

Quality control

He recommended the use of a statistical process control to monitor the process in order to detect variance and bring the process back to conformance. However, he recommended its use with caution since this may lead to a tool-driven approach.

Quality improvement

He encouraged changes in habit in order to reach the next frontier of quality. Quality control will only lead to maintaining a stable process. However, quality improvement may lead to breakthroughs which lead the organization to a higher level of quality performance.

CROSBY'S TOTAL QUALITY MANAGEMENT APPROACH

Crosby, unlike Deming and Juran, was more influential in the US quality movement. His influence was propelled by his book *Quality is Free* (1980). He advocated a more radical approach to managing quality. He insisted that managers must advocate zero defects and argued that quality is free because he believed that savings generated from quality improvement efforts will eventually outweigh the investment on quality. He rationalized quality as satisfying customers' needs. He was against the use of statistical control that will set acceptance levels since his goal was to achieve perfection (i.e., zero defects). Some of his views run contrary to some of the widely held views on quality management and, in some ways, contradict both Deming's and Juran's views of quality. For example, setting a goal to achieve zero defects is in direct conflict with Deming's points which we discussed above. Also, achieving 100% perfection contradicts the theory of variation expected from any normal process. Furthermore, Juran believed that there is no such thing as 'quality is free.' This has been illustrated by looking at the different costs of quality. However, all these quality leaders accepted that quality is a never-ending journey that will lead to continuous improvement. Crosby, however, has made some important contributions to the quality management field. His major contributions are outlined in his Management Maturity Grid that addresses management awareness for quality (1980). This five-stage process can help management to thoroughly assess and position its current status on quality and determine the future of the organization. These stages are briefly discussed.

Stage I: Uncertainty

Quality is not considered a strategic issue. Therefore, it is left as the responsibility of operators who rely mostly on inspection to improve quality. Problems are resolved as they occur without solving the more systemic problems. There is no knowledge of the cost of quality and the reasons for poor quality are not fully articulated.

Stage II: Awakening

Management accepts the importance of quality but is still unwilling to take the lead. Instead, quality management is delegated to a quality leader with limited functions. Emphasis is on appraisal of failures, operations management and engineering. Teams may be formed to deal with major problems in the short term. Quality improvement efforts are being driven by slogans.

Stage III: Enlightenment

Management is slowly getting into the mood and learning and supporting quality efforts. A quality department may be formed that reports to top management. An organized approach to resolve quality problems is developed with regular corrective action.

Stage IV: Wisdom

Management is more involved and actively participating in quality activities. It leads by example. Emphasis is shifted from appraisal to inspection in order to have an early detection of problems. A preventive approach to quality problems is adopted.

Stage V: Certainty

Management sees quality as part of the boardroom agenda. Quality is now necessary for corporate survival and growth. Quality leaders get visible positions in the organization. There is a continued emphasis on prevention with a target of zero defects. Efforts are made to eliminate problems from design. Quality improvement activities are ongoing. Crosby argued that once a firm has positioned itself in this Management Maturity Grid, it could then implement his 14 steps for quality improvement. These 14 steps are outlined in his book (1980).

KAORU ISHIKAWA'S QUALITY MANAGEMENT APPROACH

From Japan comes the late Dr Kaoru Ishikawa. A famous Japanese management professor who was very influential on Dr W. Edwards Deming's early beginning in Japan, Dr Ishikawa was strongly influenced by Deming's work. He was instrumental in the quality movement and developed the cause-and-effect diagram (also known as the Ishikawa diagram or the fishbone diagram, due to its fish like appearance) and quality circles.

Cause-and-effect diagram

This provides a structured approach to problem solving and can be used by workers to better manage the problems they encounter in the workplace. Problems are categorized in four ways namely: methods, manpower, materials and machines. The effect is normally the quality errors that may arise. Brainstorming is used to identify potential problems and categorize them. This may take several steps until the root causes of the problem are identified and effectively analyzed.

Quality circles

Quality circles were used widely by corporations to generate ideas from workers on how to improve products or processes. They are mostly loosely structured and informal. Their application can help improve worker motivation since they demonstrate that their ideas were valuable and that management cared for them. However, over the years, quality circles have either been replaced by teams or evolved into teams, the major reason being that teams are empowered while quality circles are, generally, restricted to making minor changes regarding their work. Quality circles may suffer from problems that groups normally face if not managed properly. Such problems such as 'groupthink' or a feeling of alienation may emerge.

GENICHI TAGUCHI'S QUALITY MANAGEMENT APPROACH

Taguchi made a significant contribution to quality management by revolutionizing the applications of statistics to quality and redefining quality. He argued that products should be robust enough to withstand variations that may result from environmental and production factors. His methods are based on the efficient use of experimental designs. His design approach enables one to determine the optimal combination of experimental factors that will give minimum cost with the highest uniformity of products. This is achieved by using his orthogonal array tables and linear graphs to focus on fewer combinations of process variables rather than the entire set of possible combinations of process variables. Although Taguchi's orthogonal array tables are similar to the use of standard fractional factorial designs in statistics, they are more practical and the use of linear graphs makes it easier to visualize (1980).

Taguchi's other important contribution was his definition of quality loss function (QLF) as a loss to the society for producing inferior products. QLF is a way of measuring the cost of quality by looking at variations from the target value of specification. In Taguchi's view, to the customer, there is no difference between a product that is just close to the lower or upper limits of acceptance specification levels or slightly outside that range. He argues that there is a cost to society any time there is a variation from the target. The cost to society as a result of deviation from the target value is estimated to be quadratic or follow a parabola.

Although there are many contributors to the total quality management movement, we have discussed some of the leaders the business community has come to know as quality gurus. The works of these quality leaders continue to make an impact on the way quality is practiced today.

TYPES OF VARIATION

Variation is inherent in any process and process performance varies from time to time. There is always some variation in the natural process. For instance, weather conditions change daily and there is always variance no matter how small. Because of this type of random variation, it is difficult to set up specifications that are strictly based on point estimates. Imagine for example, when you buy a box of cereal and the box is marked 13 ounces. Do you really expect that the box if measured will be exactly 13 ounces? In fact, if a simple random sample of 13 ounces boxes of cereal of the same brand and manufacturer is taken, it will be found that there are variations in the weights of these boxes. Some may be a little below 13 ounces and some may be a little above and some may even be exact. The 13 ounces is the target and once variations from it can be considered to be within the acceptable norm, then any box of cereal that weighs in within that range will be acceptable. Deming's theory of management emphasizes a lot on the theory of variation and the need for management to understand it. To understand this theory requires knowledge of the two types of variation in quality management namely common and special variation or what are commonly referred to as common and special causes.

In fact, these two types of variation were originally identified by Dr William Shewhart who referred to them as chance (natural) and assignable causes of variation. Dr W. Edwards Deming (1993) later referred to them as common and special causes of variation. There is no better explanation to these causes of variation than the one given by Deming himself in his message to the ceremonies of the 10th Annual Award of the Deming Prize in Japan. Deming is quoted as follows:

When you find most of the special causes and eliminate them, you have left common causes of variability, which may be any or several of various types — poor light, humidity, vibration, poor food in the cafeteria, absence of a real quality program, poor supervision, poor or spotty ray material, etc. Common causes are more difficult to identify than special causes are. Moreover, the removal of common causes calls for action by administration at a high level. Workers and foremen cannot change the lighting, nor write new contracts for raw materials, nor institute a quality program, yet these are examples of common causes of variation and of poor quality. Such action can be taken only by administration on a high level.

Statistical techniques thus turn the spotlight on the responsibilities for action in various levels and positions. They direct substantive knowledge to the problems where it can be most effective. If one understands something about the power of statistical method and understands where it will work, why it will work and where it won't work, he has a good start. The rest is up to the individual student to educate himself from then on (Kilian, 1992).

It is clear from this where the responsibility lies. Top management must deal with common causes while workers and operators must find and eliminate special causes of variation.

CONTINUOUS IMPROVEMENT VERSUS RE-ENGINEERING

In order to deliver quality products and services, products and processes need to be continuously improved and workers need to continuously improve themselves through education and training to sharpen their skills. Management also needs to continuously improve and update its knowledge. Quality improvement can be significantly enhanced if processes and people are continuously improved. Sometimes, continuous improvement may not be adequate. For example, a new process technology may be more productive, flexible and deliver speed and quality. In such cases, process modernization is needed rather than continuous improvement. A radical action is taken to replace the process. This leads to two important management philosophies for quality improvement, namely continuous improvement and re-engineering.

Continuous improvement is a management philosophy that emphasizes a never-ending process of improving machinery, labor, products and processes. Although it is now widely adopted in the US, this concept originated from Japan and is known as Kaizen (Imai, 1986). It emphasizes small-scale improvements in activities with the mission that any process can be continuously and forever improved. In other words, there is no end in sight when continuous-improvement philosophy is adopted. Continuous improvement forms a major premise of total quality management. There is a tendency to think that continuous improvement discourages innovation. Recently, Hammer and Champy (1993) introduced re-engineering and argued that it is "the fundamental rethinking and radical redesign of business processes to achieve dramatic improvements in critical, contemporary measures of performance, such as cost, quality, service, and speed"

(1993, p. 32). Some have referred to re-engineering as breakthrough thinking. Obviously, this philosophy of management encourages radical redesigning of business processes to achieve dramatic improvements in organizational measures of performance. Both continuous improvement and re-engineering can play critical roles in improving organizational performance. They can coexist and do not have to be treated as contradictory concepts.

TRANSFORMATION TO QUALITY ORGANIZATION

We know now that quality is an organization-wide effort. Members of the organization must embrace the quality culture and know that in today's competitive environment, the survival of their organization depends on its ability to satisfy customers' needs. That is, they have to deliver quality. Building a quality organization requires devotion and commitment. Resources need to be committed to quality; attitudes need to change; management style needs to change and everyone has to participate and contribute.

Management must take initiative in order to achieve quality. As we have shown from the approaches of Deming, Juran and Crosby, management has a leading role in achieving quality. It must be involved. It cannot relegate this important function to lower level employees in the organization. It is management who will deal with common causes, and you cannot achieve quality if common causes are not eliminated from the system. Management makes the decision to replace inefficient processes, replace suppliers of poor quality raw materials, train employees and commit resources to quality. If management fails to take such actions, systemic quality problems cannot be eliminated and no amount of effort to improve quality can save the organization.

The key to achieving quality transformation is to accept its importance in corporate survival and competitiveness. As Crosby showed in his Management Maturity Grid, when top management is enlightened about quality, it understands its importance and makes efforts to improve it. Similarly, Juran outlined the cost of quality and Deming identified the common causes that lead to quality problems. All these concepts help illustrate top management's role in improving quality and the implications of ignoring this role. It is not surprising that Deming's seminars in the early 1950s in Japan targeted high-level managers because they are the ones that can take the lead in solving their quality problems.

CONCLUSION

In this chapter, we have tried to expose the reader to basic concepts about total quality management. We have also presented some common definitions of quality and the views of popular quality leaders. However, the review cited here is by no means exhaustive. There are many quality issues we did not address or even mention in this chapter. The book will shed additional light on other quality issues, and their relationship to environmental management.

REFERENCES

1. Crosby, PB. (1980) *Quality is Free,* New York: Penguin Books.
2. Deming, W.E. (1986) *Out of the Crisis,* Cambridge, Mass: MIT, Center for Advanced Engineering Study
3. Deming, W.E. (1993) *The New Economics for Industry, Government, Education,* Cambridge, Mass: MIT.
4. Garvin, D.A. (1988) *Managing Quality: The Strategic and Competitive Edge,* New York: The Free Press.
5. Gitlow, H., Oppenheim, A. and Oppenheim, R. (1995) *Quality Management: Tools and Methods for Improvement,* 2nd ed., Burr Ridge, IL: Irwin.
6. Hammer, M. and Champy, J. (1993) *Reengineering the Corporation: A Manifesto for Business Revolution,* New York: Harper Business.
7. Imai, M. (1986) *Kaizen: The Keys to Japan's Competitive Success,* New York: Random House.
8. Juran, J.M. (1986) *The Quality Trilogy: A Universal Approach to Managing for Quality,* Quality Progress, Vol.19, No.8, pp.19-24.
9. Juran, J.M. (1988) *Juran on Planning for Quality.* New York: The Free Press.
10. Juran, J.M. (1989) *Juran on Leadership for Quality: An Executive Handbook,* New York: The Free Press.
11. Juran, J.M. (1992) *Juran on Quality by Design　The New Steps for Planning Quality into Goods and Services*, New York: The Free Press.
12. Juran, J.M. and F.M. Gryna, Jr (1980) *Quality Planning and Analysis,* New York: McGraw Hill Book Company.

13. Kilian, C.S (1992) *The World of W Edwards Deming,* 2nd ed., Knoxville, Tenn.: SPC Press.
14. Madu, C.N. and Kuei, C-H. (1995) *Strategic Total Quality Management,* Westport, CT: Quorum Books.
15. Nersesian, R. (1993) "A Comparative Analysis of Japanese and American Production Management Practices," in *Management of New Technologies for Global Competitiveness* (ed. C.N. Madu) Westport, CT: Quorum Books.
16. Scherkenbach, *W* (1991) *Deming's Road to Continual Improvement,* Knoxville, Tenn.: SPC Press.
17. Taguchi, G. and Wu, Y. (1980) *Introduction to Off-Line Quality Control,* Nagoya, Japan: Central Japan Quality Control Association

CHAPTER 2

HISTORY AND DEFINITION OF QUALITY FUNCTION DEPLOYMENT (QFD)

The American Supplier Institute defines Quality Function Deployment (QFD), 1989 as "a system for translating consumer requirements into appropriate company requirements at each stage from research and development to engineering and manufacturing to marketing/sales and distribution." Simply, QFD involves listening to the "voice of the customer" and systematically, translating the customer's requirements through each phase of the product development stage as requirements that the product must meet. It shifts away emphasis from meeting management and engineering demands in product development to that of meeting customers' demands. Customer requirements are translated into requirements that must be met to deliver quality products and services to the customer. Listening to the "voice of the customer" starts from the product development stage and it is deployed throughout the firm. The focus of QFD is to maximize resources and minimize waste. QFD is therefore, a planning tool for developing new products and improving existing product [Vonderembse and Van Fossen, 1998]. Other definitions of QFD are offered as follows: Akao [1990] defined QFD as "a method for developing a design quality aimed at satisfying the consumer and then translating the consumer's demand into design targets and major quality assurance points to be used throughout the production phase." Thus, QFD assures that quality is designed into the product. By doing this, a considerable reduction in product development time is achieved. Sullivan [1986] defined QFD as "The main objective of any manufacturing company to bring new (and carryover) products to market sooner than the competition with lower cost and improved quality." He went on to emphasize that this concept involves the translation of customer requirements to appropriate technical requirements for each stage of the product development and production. This process involves the marketing strategies, planning, product design and engineering, prototype evaluation, production process development, production and sales. Apparent from this definition is the fact that QFD applies also to existing products and services. Furthermore, QFD involves the entire product life cycle as well as the entire functional units of a business process. It leads to designing quality into the product by designing customer requirements into the product. More importantly, it significantly leads to a reduction in product development and introduction to the market place. Another objective of QFD is the optimal utilization of resources by ensuring that the product demanded by customers is produced correctly the first time and ensuring its introduction on a timely fashion.

QFD offers new challenges to businesses. It involves the entire "value supply chain" of the organization. It is important to evaluate each product development stage to see how it aligns with customer's requirements and the resources of the firm. This will therefore, lead to new set of standards and targets not only for engineers involved with product design but also to production workers at the floor level and suppliers. Thus, the entire supply chain is influenced by the "voice of the customer."

Clearly, listening to the "voice of the customer" and translating customer requirements into achievable targets to improve product quality is not easy. There will be some conflicting requirements. The customer may identify requirements that are not attainable at the same level, for example, the need to manufacture the best copy paper and also, protect the environment. These two are contradictory since the "best quality copy paper" will rely on 100 % virgin pulp which may conflict with the desire to protect the forestry. However, a copy paper that uses a mixture of virgin pulp and recycled pulp could be produced to balance this tradeoff. QFD attempts to resolve such conflicts by focusing on the most important requirements. Furthermore, customer needs have to be balanced with design requirements and specifications. Some of the customer needs may not be attainable or feasible due to limitations in technology or available resources. Thus, customer needs, which are often referred to, as "whats" should be balanced with design requirements, referred to as "hows." The translation of "whats" into "hows" could be difficult and complex, as these can be interdependent and therefore, negatively correlated to each other. This may present another source of conflict that will also need to be resolved.

We have focused on meeting customer requirements through QFD. There are many ways to solicit customer requirements. Notably, these requirements could be gathered through various market research methods such as customer survey questionnaires, interviews, focus groups, telephone surveys. A list of customer requirements is generated through this process and is referred to as "spoken" quality demands and performance expectations. However, there may be some product attributes that are assumed by the customer or the customer may not be aware of but may add to the value of the product. Such attributes should also be included and are referred to as "unspoken" attributes. Thus, the aim is not just to meet the requirements as specified or identified by the customer but also to go beyond and add as much features as possible and feasible to make the product the best in its class.

Brief history of QFD

The origins of QFD can be traced to Mitsubishi's Heavy Industries Kobe shipyard in Japan in late 1960s where QFD was used to facilitate cross-functional product development process [Eseteghalian, Verma, Foutz and Thompson, 1998]. A 1986 survey by the Japanese Union of Scientists and Engineers (JUSE) showed that more than half of the companies surveyed were using QFD. The application of QFD is pervasive in many of the manufacturing and service sectors in Japan. Toyota Motor Company and its suppliers are also among the major companies that have applied QFD in Japan. It is reported that Toyota auto body achieved a 60 % reduction in start-up costs for its new car model launch as a result of QFD application. Although pre-production cost went up slightly, other major costs were slashed by about 80 %. US manufacturers were however, slow in applying QFD. Its first major applications were in the automotive and electronic industries.

QFD is known by several names. The original name for QFD in Japan is *hin shitsu, ki nou, ten kai* [Emmanuel and Kroll, 1998]. There are several translations for these words including "features mechanization evolution, qualities function diffusion, or quality function deployment." The problem here is in the direct translation of the original Japanese words to English language. Other popular names used for QFD include Policy Deployment, Voice of the Customer, House of Quality, Customer-Driven Engineering, and Matrix Product Planning.

Motivation for QFD

Undoubtedly, the increased competition in both the US and global markets helped to focus the attention of US businesses on the application of QFD. As Emmanuel and Kroll [1998] note, the QFD as a planning tool, reached the US during the quality revolution of the 1980s. Japanese companies were gradually taking over many businesses once dominated by US manufacturers. As such, there was a significant interest by top management to understand Japanese management practices especially as they relate to product quality. Major companies in the US embarked on studying the new quality philosophies that were coming out from Japan. Furthermore, they understood that in order to compete effectively, they must realign their strategies and develop plans similar to their Japanese counterparts which focus on achieving customer satisfaction. QFD became one of the important tools that could help them understand the customer and integrate the customer's requirements into the design and production of goods and services. By doing so, they will be able to regain lost markets and compete effectively. The incentive for survival in today's business was therefore, a motivating force in the adoption of these new practices by American businesses.

Hales and David [1995] note that product failures could be devastating to a company and may drain both the human and financial resources. They point out that some companies that maintain volumes of information pertaining to the customer and state-of-the art design and manufacturing tools have witnessed high-profile flops. Examples include products such as, "new Coke", "dry beer", and "smokeless cigarettes". Therefore, the emphasis with QFD is not merely to collect volumes of information on customer requirements but to develop a structured and systematic approach when analyzing information and translate its results to the design and manufacture of customer-driven products. They note that sometimes, products or services that customers do not want manifest themselves in terms of "functionality, practicality, quality, cost, timing" etc. They advocate the use of QFD with target costing to get a company to be customer-focused. QFD emphasizes the fact that the product can be designed and produced to meet the customer requirements. However, cost should be a consideration in determining what the market can bear.

Benefits of QFD

QFD has many demonstrable benefits especially for firms interested in achieving competitiveness, increasing market share, improving productivity and improving the bottom line. Those companies that have adopted QFD have reported significant cost reductions. How these gains are achieved is outlined below:

- Reduction in cycle time is achieved. The product is introduced to the market faster. Start-up costs are lower. Quality is improved. There is a reduction in number of engineering changes that may be required.
- Products are produced at a lower cost due to the reduction in operational cost.
- QFD is normally applied in a cross-functional team context. For example, members from the different functional areas of the firm organize to develop new product concepts. Members of the cross-functional team have diverse backgrounds and are able to share common information and understand each other's views. This process of sharing information and listening to each other helps resolve potential conflicts and assures that organizational goals are not suboptimized. Members begin to develop a more holistic picture of the problem. Information gathered from the different functional teams can also be shared. For example, marketing, sales and distribution departments often have more contact with customers. They are able to relay information obtained through this process to those in engineering that will have to incorporate such considerations during product design and development.
- Information gathering is an ongoing process in the use of QFD. It is important to maintain a database of customer requirements that may be gathered from different sources. This information could be used repeatedly to design new product or improve existing products.
- Design and production efficiency is achieved through QFD. Members of the cross-functional teams develop a critical analysis of their functions and ensure that customer requirements are integrated at every phase of product development. This will ensure that the products are designed

and produced right the first time. Thus, reducing the cost of production, minimizing waste, and maximizing efficiency.

- Organizational harmony may foster through formation of cross-functional teams. The functional units will no longer be competing against each other rather; they will be working towards a common goal. Such teams foster increased openness and sharing of information with the ultimate goal of designing and producing products that will lead to high customer satisfaction.

- Problems are easier to identify by listening to the "voice of the customer." These problems can be corrected to achieve successful introduction of the product in the market place. Also, a decision making process may include significant customer groups in the team to help ensure that the products are designed and produced with the customer in mind.

- Market information gained through QFD can be used to determine product price, quality, and functionality.

- Product development is customer-driven and supports value-engineering analysis in order to cut cost and add value to the product.

- Bottom line is improved through the application of QFD. Some of the reported influence on bottom line are as follows:

- High market acceptance of the product

- Reduction in design cycle time

- Increased competitiveness

- Reduction in design changes

- Reduction in production cost

- Improved efficiency.

- Improved worker morale.

VOICE OF THE CUSTOMER

Quality function deployment (QFD) is a process of listening to the "voice of the customer," identifying the customer's needs, and incorporating those needs in the design and production of goods and services. We noted that this process involves the entire supply chain with the goal of producing the goods or services that the customer actually wants and adding value to those goods and services. Listening to the "voice of the customer" ensures the manufacturer or service provider that features the customer wants are included in the product or service. The key fact however, is listening to the "voice of the customer" and identifying customer requirements as articulated by the customer. The aim of this part is to specifically outline how manufacturers can make effective use of this learning process.

There are three levels in listening to the "voice of the customer." The first level involves an understanding of the basic wants and needs of the customer. This involves the use of experimental techniques to identify customer requirements. Experimental approaches to be taken here include the use of field surveys, focus groups, questionnaires, to identify a list of requirements that are "important" to the customer. These requirements must be translated into measurable operational forms. For example, a homeowner's requirement to a builder that the house be well built is vague and does not identify what features will make the house well built. Therefore, the request needs to be broken down to specific points such as: the foundation should be supported by adequate pillars, the electric outlets work, the trims are in place, the doors close properly, the walls are smooth, the ceilings are high, etc. In other words, vague statements by customers must be broken down to operational forms. These as we stated earlier are the "spoken" quality attributes that must be present in the home. However, there are other "unspoken" attributes that the builder must include. For example, what effect will extreme weather conditions have on the house? Is the house accident proof? Thus, both the "spoken" and "unspoken" customer requirements must be present if the "voice of the customer" is to be heard.

The second phase involves the extension of the product design beyond these "spoken" and "unspoken" customer requirements. There are some customers' requirements that are not apparent from the first phase that designers should be aware of. Designers need to scrutinize how and why customers use their product [Vonderembse and Van Fossen, 1998]. Alternative ways should be offered to cover this range of applications and usage by customers. For example, consider a college in a metropolitan area that attracts adult students. These students may be primarily interested in a quality education but may also be interested in the convenience of obtaining higher education. There is a variety of ways that the college could provide this service to its student population. One way may be to offer evening programs. Another way may be to offer weekend classes. Other more technologically advanced forms may be to offer lectures through video-conferencing or the Internet. By doing this, QFD drives the company by forcing the design team to identify hidden customer requirements and offering ways to satisfy such requirements.

Third, there are many features of the product that the customer may be unaware of. However, the cross-functional team that works on the QFD can identify these features and point them out to the customer. Customers are often unaware of advances in technology and research that could help improve the quality of the product. For example, with the growing focus on sustainable development, a manufacturer may identify new ways to minimize waste or use less energy in product design and production. This may increase customer satisfaction and help the manufacturer expand its market share. The manufacturer can increase customer satisfaction by trying to understand the customer beyond the horizon of the product and determining what is important to the customer. It is important to understand the customer's behavior and how that may affect some of his actions. For example, a customer interested in buying a new car may identify operational features such as aesthetics, dependability, and availability of service as features of interest to her. However, the same customer may be interested in cars that burn cleaner and consume less gas. Safety issues may also be important and the customer may prefer cars that offer a combination of product features.

Formation of Cross-Functional Teams

Cross-functional teams are used in most QFD projects. The team will comprise of representatives from the different functional departments or units that are either directly or indirectly affected by the project. In a business organization, this team could include representatives from engineering, marketing, production, and finance. The objective or the goal of the team will be to find an efficient method to address customer needs or requirements in the design, production and delivery of products and services. Thus, this team must address the feasibility of using the organization's resources to satisfy customer requirements. The use of cross-functional teams also has other important benefits to the organization as follows:

- It ensures that all the related functional units are committed to the project. When members of these teams participate in the project, they are committed to the successful completion of the project.
- Organizations use their resources more efficiently if the various functional units work towards a common goal. The

use of cross-functional teams exposes members of the team to the need for achieving organizational goals and helps reduce internal competition. Therefore, marketing will not see its goals as different from that of engineering. The different units will come to understand the purpose of the organization as that of satisfying customer requirements in a more efficient way. And, once that is achieved, customer satisfaction will also be attained and the business will thrive.

- The use of teams enables information sharing. For example, product designers come to learn from marketing how the customer perceives certain aspects of the product. Designers come to learn from finance about the financial viability or feasibility of certain projects. Through teams, information flows laterally and can be used timely for effective decision-making.
- Customers are the major beneficiaries of cross-functional team activities. The different functional groups have different worldviews, which helps broaden each participant's scope and view. These different perspectives could be instrumental in designing products that appeal to a wider range of consumer groups.
- Members in cross-functional teams are empowered. They feel the responsibility to make decisions and take corrective actions. This will help increase their organizational commitment and also, helps reduce organizational waste. Morale and motivation may also improve.
- Through cross-functional teams, brainstorming sessions can be held to generate ideas for product improvement and development.

Although cross-functional teams are heralded as useful in designing and producing high quality products, however, such teams could become counter-productive if not well implemented. Some of the problems that may arise are as follows:

- Group-think mentality can often emerge from any team. This happens when members perceive domination of the team by one or few individuals. So, rather than team members actively participating and contributing their ideas, they become subjected to accept the view of one or more dominant members of the group. This has to be avoided if customer requirements are to be satisfied.

- Feeling of alienation may emerge. This again, is related to the group-think mentality. This happens when members feel that they have no role to play other than to rubber stamp pre-conceived ideas.

- Conflicts may often arise. However, it is important to productively resolve any conflicts and avoid formation of interest groups within the cross-functional groups. Formation of conflicting sub-groups will invariably lead to sub-optimization.

- It is important for members of cross-functional teams to have an open mind about the problem to be solved and work towards a common goal – that of the organization's success by improving customer satisfaction. This can be achieved by focusing on what is important to the customer and how the organization can satisfy the customer using its resources.

Identifying Customer Requirements

The entire premise of QFD rests on identifying and satisfying customer requirements. Although many studies on QFD have presented examples of customer requirements and how they match design requirements, few have discussed in detail how customer requirements are identified. Granted, many have mentioned techniques such as the use of focus groups, marketing information, etc., it is important to have a systematic way to identify customer requirements. Customer requirement forms the foundation of QFD. If the wrong requirements are identified, the product designed to meet such requirements will lose its appeal and will therefore, fail. The "identification of customer requirements" is the most critical step in developing a QFD. We shall examine two popular methods to identify customer requirements. These methods focus mostly on identifying the "spoken requirements" of the customer. Hayes [1992] refers to the first method as "quality dimension development approach." The second method was developed by Flanagan [1954] and it is known as the "critical incident approach".

Quality Dimension Development

The use of the term "quality dimension" is synonymous to the term "customer requirements." Customer requirements specifically represent the attributes or features of a product or service that the customer deems important in order to achieve satisfaction. Clearly, a customer can perceive several attributes and these attributes may differ depending on the product and service. However, certain industries have universal attributes. For example, in the auto industry, attributes such as safety are always important to the customer. In the service sector for example, Kennedy and Young [1989] identified four common attributes or quality dimension as availability, responsiveness, convenience, and timeliness. Authors of SERVQUAL model present five dimensions of service quality as tangibles, reliability, responsiveness, assurance, and empathy [Parasuraman, Zeithmal and Berry, 1988]. These quality dimensions are however, specific to service organizations. Through extensive literature reviews, members of the cross-functional teams for QFD can identify specific quality dimensions for their particular industries. However, such dimensions of quality may not cover all the important attributes or customer requirements for a specific product. It is therefore, important to go beyond the "generic industry attributes" to identify specifically the attributes of the product that the customer needs. Thus, there is a need for the cross-functional team to conduct a detailed study of the product or service to identify other hidden attributes. Such studies employ knowledgeable experts and focus customer groups who understand the product and are able to offer insights on the customer's expectations of the product. Through this, a list of quality attributes can be identified. It is important also, to conduct benchmarking analysis to identify other attributes present in competitor's products. The attributes identified have to be clearly stated to avoid ambiguities. For example, important consumer research publications that do a comparative analysis of products could be an important source of information since such publications often compare similar products by looking at quality attributes that are important to customers.

The quality dimension approach relies heavily on the cross-functional teams as experts who know and understand the product's purpose or function. Such teams could therefore, breakdown the product into its functional components and study and analyze it to see how the needs of the customer are satisfied. Suppose we take an auto manufacturer as an example, a sample of customer requirement issues may include the following:

- *Operational*: The ease of opening the car door; the length of time or mileage between scheduled services.
- *Aesthetics*: The size or shape of the car.

- *Availability of Support*: The availability of mechanical services.
- *Responsiveness*: The time it takes to perform scheduled service.

These attributes can be grouped into keywords or dimensions of quality and each evaluated to eliminate redundancies. The cross-functional team can now work with specific quality dimensions that cover a range of customer requirement issues. In addition to these attributes which we have referred to as the "spoken requirements," there are "unspoken requirements" that the members of the cross-functional teams must also identify and ensure that they are present in the product. For example, certain levels of safety should be guaranteed; the car should meet emission standards; the car must have an aesthetic appeal; the price should be reasonable; etc. Thus, both "spoken" and "unspoken" requirements should be present.

When a long list of attributes is generated, it is possible that some of the attributes may not be important or may add little or no value to the product. Rather than the team wasting valuable resources to tackle insignificant problems, it is important that some method be devised to assign priorities to the customer requirements that have been identified. The focus should be on solving the critical and important problems. It is more important to resolve the major customer requirements in a satisfying manner than to marginally consider every conceivable factor. We shall now discuss the critical incident approach.

Critical Incident Approach

Flanagan [1954] developed this approach. It could be used to develop customer satisfaction questionnaires to understand customer requirements. This method views organizational performance from the perspective of the customer. The customer views organizational performance from the aspects of the organization it is directly in contact with. With respect to manufacturing, the customer is in direct contact with the product. And, with respect to service, the customer is in direct contact with the staff. The customer looks at the product or service attribute on how the attribute may positively or negatively affect organizational performance. An attribute that will have a negative effect would impact on the customer's positive perception of the organization thereby, negatively affecting organizational performance. However, an attribute that has a positive impact will be more desirable to the customer. Critical incidents are therefore, the "quality attributes" of the organization that the customer is directly in contact with. These critical incidents could be obtained either through individual or group interviewing. This process is conducted by dealing directly with people who have used the product or service and are in a position to offer specific judgments on the different attributes of the product or service. It is recommended that about 10 to 20 customers be interviewed and each customer should be asked to describe 5 to 10 positive and negative instances for the product or service respectively [Hayes, 1992]. In addition, the questions should be specific and avoid the use of general terms. This should help the customer to focus on specifics. The use of a large number of customers helps to reduce the possibility of obtaining incomplete information. For example, information not obtained from one interviewee can be compensated from subsequent interviews with other customers. From the interviewing process, a list of critical incidents could be developed which can be grouped again into specific "quality attributes."

Analysis of Quality Attributes

It is important to solve the critical problem. A major problem that may arise from using these techniques to solicit customer requirements is that a long list may be generated that may be unmanageable. Our recommendation will be to identify both the "spoken" and "unspoken" product and service attributes through these methods. Organize the attributes into quality dimensions and develop a "customer satisfaction survey" to relate quality attributes to the specific product or service. The aim should be to identify from a more typical group which customer requirements are important. The survey should be administered to a random sample of existing and potential customers. The survey should be analyzed statistically to identify which quality attributes are significant or important in achieving customer satisfaction. This will help to narrow down the list of "critical incidents" to quality attributes that a typical group of the customer base views as important. The cross-functional team can then focus its effort in satisfying those significant requirements. This approach will help the cross-functional team address the most important customer requirement issues, save time, and optimize the use of limited resources.

HOUSE OF QUALITY

In this section, we will discuss how to build the 'House of Quality.' In the previous section, we discussed how product or service characteristics that are important to the customer could be identified. However, these product characteristics must be integrated into the design of the product. Charts are important in building the 'House of Quality.' By using charts or diagrams, information obtained by listening to the 'voice of the customer' can be summarized and compared to design requirements. The 'House of Quality' is therefore, a blueprint for product development. We shall breakdown in a stepwise form, how the 'House of Quality' can be built.

Step 1: In the previous section, we identified customer requirements. We also noted that this could be an extensive list and it is important to identify the significant requirements and eliminate any redundancies that may exist. A list of the important customer requirements should be constructed and should include product or service attributes as identified by customers. This list is often referred to as 'whats' to signify what the customer actually wants to see in a product or service. However, care must be taken to ensure that these 'whats' can be made operational. For example, consider the subscription to Internet Online servers. It is not enough for a customer to state that he or she needs a 'reliable or good online service.' The term 'reliable or good' is broad and should be broken down to attributes that could be used to define such an adjective. For example, a good online server may have the following attributes: local access numbers, broadband capability, support for a wide range of modems, accessible online and telephone help, easy access to Internet, ease of access to the server, etc. Thus, the 'whats' of a customer has to be broken down to primary, secondary, and tertiary levels of information. It is apparent that the primary objective in this example is to have a good or reliable online server. However, the attributes used to qualify the adjective "good" are secondary and must be present to achieve the primary objective. These secondary objectives can be further broken down to tertiary levels of information. For example, 'ease of access to the server' may include offering several local access numbers that the user can dial up if one is busy. The list of 'whats' as identified by the customer should be clearly defined.

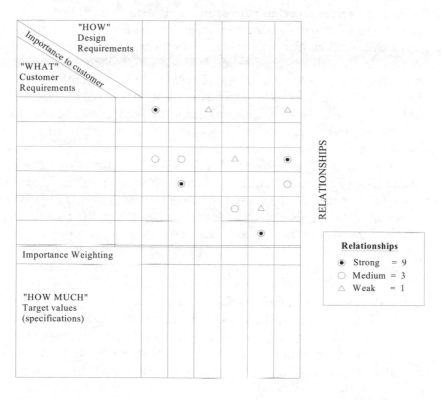

Figure 2.1: QFD Relationship Matrix

Step 2: Once this list of 'whats' is clarified, a list of the design requirements known as the 'hows' should be developed. This list of 'hows' shows how design requirements can influence the attainment of 'whats' as identified by the customer. The design characteristics are often under the control of the manufacturer or the producer and are at times, referred to as 'engineering characteristics.' They could be expressed in technical terms within the organization and are measurable. For example, what is the maximum transfer rate of information that the online server provides (i.e., 56kbs). This could partly measure the ease of access to the Internet or World Wide Web. This step involves the translation of customer requirements to design requirements. This process is compounded by the fact that there may exist interdependent relationships between customer requirements and design requirements. In other words, some of the customer requirements may conflict with design requirements or rather, the 'whats' and 'hows' may negatively influence one another. However, this is to be expected because there are multiple goals identified in the 'whats' and in trying to achieve all these goals, there will be some tradeoffs. If such conflicts do not exist, it is possible that an error has been made. A well-designed product or service is likely to involve tradeoffs (American Supplier Institute, 1989). Potential conflicts that are identified must be resolved effectively. With the use of QFD, such conflicts can be effectively resolved during the product design stage thereby, reducing the need for significant engineering changes downstream.

Step 3: Steps 1 and 2 form the basis for the first QFD chart (Figure 2-1). Figure 2-1 has several components. First, this figure must contain the list of significant customer requirements (whats) shown on the right side of the matrix as rows and a list of design requirements (hows) listed in columns near the top. A definition is given on the top left side of the relationship symbols used to show the relationship between a customer requirement and a design requirement. For example, a Δ symbol shown at an intersection point between customer requirement and design requirement means the weakest design requirement to satisfy that customer requirement. This figure also contains a column titled 'importance to customer.' This column denotes the relative importance of the customer requirement attributes to the customer. This will help designers focus more attention on achieving those attributes that are of utmost importance to the customer. The figure also has at the bottom, the 'target values or specifications or how much,' and a row that contains the importance weighting. The importance weighting at the bottom is similar to the 'importance to customer' column. This denotes the importance for the different design requirements. The target values are the specifications that could be achieved through engineering design. For example, suppose that one customer requirement in a new car is the "ease to close the car door." A design requirement may be to investigate the "energy requirement to close the door," and the target specification may be to reduce energy level to 7.5ft/lb (Hauser and Clausing 1988). Thus, the target values deal with the 'how much' or specifics. The QFD cross-functional team generates these values, as they believe them to satisfy customer requirements. Design requirements must be compared to measurable targets that are under the control of the designer.

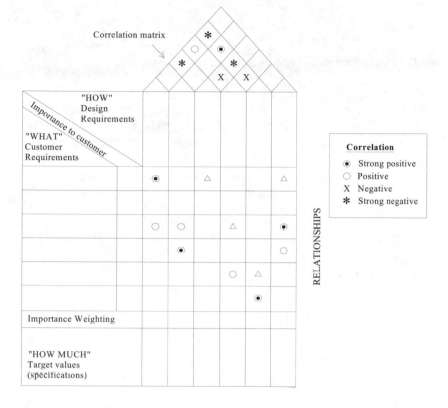

Figure 2.2: QFD Relationship and Correlation Matrix

Step 4: Figure 2-2 is used to illustrate this step. This involves the addition of the correlation matrix to actually form a 'house' or rather, the house of quality. This correlation matrix shows the correlation between the different design requirements. On the right side of figure 2-2 is the definition of the symbols used for the correlation. For example, the use of the symbol * denotes strong negative correlation between two design requirements and *X* denotes negative correlation. Of utmost importance is the negative and strong negative correlation observed between the design requirements. Such relationships imply that there is a conflict in trying to achieve both requirements jointly. Thus as one is being achieved, the other is being compromised. This conflict needs to be resolved or a trade-off decision has to be made. Such decision could involve retaining the design requirement that has the higher importance weighting.

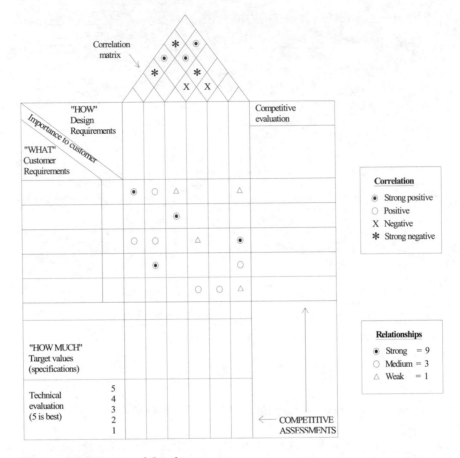

Figure 2.3: House of Quality

Step 5: Figure 2-3 is a modification of figure 2-2 to include two new components namely "competitive evaluation" and "technical evaluation." These two offer a benchmarking of the manufacturer's product or service to that of competitors in several ways. For example, with the competitive evaluation, the manufacturer is compared to its competitors on each of the customer requirements identified by the customer. Similarly, for the technical evaluation, the manufacturer is compared against its competitors based on the design requirements to satisfy customer requirements. One thing not shown yet in this diagram is that the manufacturer is positioned in a scale against its competitors. Ideally, the manufacturer will like to out perform its competitors. Thus, the manufacturer has to make the effort to be the best in class. To put all these in perspective, we shall illustrate with an example. Figure 2.4 is adapted from the case presented by Hauser and Clausing [1988].

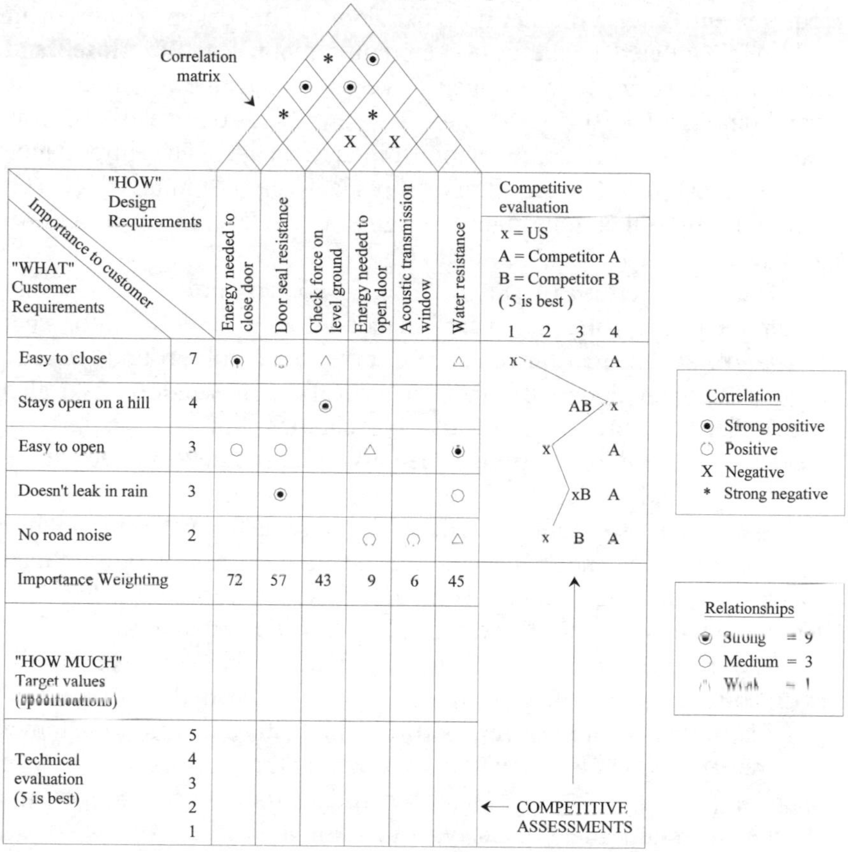

Figure 2.4: QFD Example

A Case Example

We shall adapt the example presented by Hauser and Clausing. In that example, they showed that for a particular product, series of sub-charts could be created. For example, they considered developing the QFD for the door of an automobile. This alone will require its own QFD chart, which eventually could be tied in with the other QFDs that may be needed to build a quality automobile. Customer attributes for a car door are developed and grouped as primary, secondary and tertiary. Thus, the example we present below will focus on designing and building a quality car door to satisfy customer requirements.

Using this figure, we can determine the importance weighting for the design requirements. For example, consider the design requirement "energy needed to close door." This design requirement is strongly related to the customer requirement "easy to close" and medium related to "easy to open." We can determine its importance weighting as $(7 \times 9) + (3 \times 3) = 72$ where the strong relationship is rated as 9 and the moderate relationship is rated as 3. The 'importance to customer' weights are 7 and 3 respectively. Similarly, we can determine the other importance weights as 72, 57, 43, 9, 6, and 45 respectively.

Thus, in terms of importance, we can order the design requirements as follows: energy needed to close door, door seal resistance, water resistance, check force on level ground, energy needed to open door, and acoustic transmission window. We also notice that there are some negative correlations. For example, energy needed to close door is strongly negatively correlated to check force on level ground. Thus, this conflict has to be resolved or a trade-off has to be made. In terms of trade-off, it is seen from the importance weighting that the energy needed to close door is more important than check force on level ground. Similarly, this example shows that door seal resistance is positively correlated with water resistance.

The other important information that is gained here is the competitive assessment information. As seen from the information provided, this manufacturer is the worst in the first 'customer requirement' which is "easy to close door" and also worst on "easy to open" and "no road noise." However, it appears to be the best on the "customer requirement" "stays open on a hill." The Xs are all connected to help position the manufacturer against its competitors. We can also derive similar interpretations for the technical evaluation.

The steps outlined so far are useful for documentation purposes. They present the requirements the product should have to satisfy customer requirements but the House of Quality as shown here, does not represent product design. This process could be taken further to link it to other QFD activities within the organization. For example, engineering or design requirements could be further broken down to parts characteristics which may be broken down to key process operations down to production requirements [Vonderembse and Van Fossen, 1998]. It is important to note that the deployment of information is not unidirectional but iterative. For example, modifications on the QFD obtained at the early stage may be necessitated by the information acquired at a later stage. The stepwise approach to link the different QFD charts helps to trace information backward to the original customer demands.

CONCLUSION

In summary, QFD is a planning tool that can help businesses plan product design and production with increased efficiency. Its aim is to ensure that customer requirements are integrated in the design and production of the product. By so doing, a product that meets high quality standards as defined by the customer can be produced. This ensures that the product is not offered to the customer as seen by the design engineer but rather as seen by the customer itself. If the customer's requirements are effectively considered, then it is likely that the customer will accept the final product. This will help improve the competitiveness of the manufacturer, ensure customer loyalty, reduce waste, and improve the bottom line.

The formation of cross-functional teams to identify customer requirements for a product or service is necessary to achieve the needs of the customer. The two most important methods to identifying customer requirements are quality dimension development and critical incident approach. The use of questionnaire surveys administered to a random sample of customers to identify significant customer issues, could help the cross-functional QFD team to focus on the most important customer requirement issues, better utilize its resources, and timely design and produce the product and service needed by its customers.

Once customer requirements are identified, there is a need to build the House of Quality. This is done graphically by developing charts to organize "customer requirements" and "engineering or design requirements" needed to satisfy the customer. An example on how to interpret the information from the QFD chart is presented in this chapter. However, we must caution that this example is for illustrative purposes only. Different organizations may modify the QFD chart to suit their needs. QFD is an iterative process that requires linking each phase. The procedures are similar however; every stage may involve its own QFD chart. For example, there may be a need for a QFD chart for design requirements as they may be met by "parts characteristics" and "parts characteristics" as they may be satisfied by "key process operations" and so on. By linking all of these different QFD charts, it becomes easier to trace information back to their original sources. Although the final QFD charts may look complicated, they are not difficult to generate once the relevant information is available.

REFERENCES

1. Akao, Y., Quality Function Deployment, Cambridge, MA: Productivity Press, 1990.
2. American Supplier Institute (1989) Quality Function Deployment Implementation Manual, American Supplier Institute, Dearborn, MI.
3. Day, R. G., Quality Function Deployment – Linking a Company with its Customers, Milwaukee, WI: ASQC Quality Press, 1993.
4. Emmanuel, J.T., and Kroll, D.E., "Concurrent Engineering," in Handbook of Total Quality Management, Boston, MA: Kluwer Academic Publishers, 1998 (ed., Madu, C.N.)
5. Eseteghalian, A., Verma, B., Foutz, T., and Thompson, S., "Customer focused approach to design: new methodologies consider environmental impact on product development," *Engineering & Technology for a Sustainable World*, 06-01-98, pp 7(2).
6. Evans, J.R., and Lindsay, W.M., The Management & Control of Quality, 4th edition, Cincinnati, OH: South-Western Publishing, 1999.
7. Gale, B. T., and Wood, R.C., Managing Customer Value-Creating Quality and Service that Customers Can See, NY: The Free Press, 1994.
8. Hales, R., and Staley, D., "Mix target costing, QFD for successful new products," *Marketing News*, Jan. 2, 1995, 22(1), pp. 18-20.
9. Mears, P., Quality Improvement Tools & Techniques, NY: McGraw Hill Inc., 1995.
10. Sullivan, L. P., "Quality Function Deployment," *Quality Progress*, June 1986.
11. Vonderembse,M.A., and Van Fossen, T., "Quality Function Deployment," in Handbook of Total Quality Management, Boston, MA: Kluwer Academic Publishers, 1998 (ed., Madu, C.N.).
12. Flanagan, M., "The critical incident technique," Psychological Bulletin 51: 327-358, 1954.
13. Hayes, B.E., Measuring customer satisfaction: Development and use of questionnaires, Milwaukee, Wis.: ASQC Quality Press, 1992.

14. Kennedy, D.A., and Young, B.J., "Managing quality in staff areas," Quality Progress 22 (10), 87-91.
15. Parasuraman, A., Zeithaml, V.A., and Berry, L.L., "SERVQUAL: A multiple-item scale for measuring customer perceptions of service quality," Journal of Retailing 64: 12-40, 1988.
16. American Supplier Institute (1989) Quality Function Deployment Implementation Manual, American Supplier Institute, Dearborn, MI.
17. Hauser, J.R., and Clausing, D., "The House of Quality," Harvard Business Review, May-June 1988, pp. 62-73.

CHAPTER 3

●─────────────────────●

INTRODUCTION TO ISO AND ISO QUALITY STANTARDS

In this chapter, we shall review a list of quality standards that have been introduced by the International Organization for Standardization (ISO) based in Geneva, Switzerland. These quality standards are almost universally accepted. We shall review the origins of ISO and why its quality standards (ISO 9000 and ISO 14000 series) have gained such international recognition. We also discuss these quality standards as to their intents and how they can help organizations become more competitive. The discussions here are introductory and fundamentally basic. The aim is to expose the reader to perhaps the most influential quality standards. There are several books written on these standards and additional information may be obtained from these sources.

HISTORY AND THE ORIGINS OF ISO

The International Organization for Standardization (ISO) was formed in 1947 as a non-governmental organization with the purpose of promoting, the development of standards to facilitate the international exchange of goods and services. It also will seek international co-operation in scientific, technological and economic activities. ISO consists of about 100 countries as members although its number keeps growing and these member nations are mostly represented in ISO by their national standards organizations. ISO is used as the short form for the International Organization for Standardization rather than IOS. The term ISO is derived from the Greek word 'isos' which means 'equal,' thus the use of equal standards to guide the international exchange of goods and service.

As defined by the Central Secretariat of ISO, the aim of international standardization of facilitating trade exchange and technology transfer can be achieved through:

- Enhanced product quality and reliability at a reasonable price;
- Improved health, safety and environmental protection and reduction of waste;
- Greater compatibility and interoperability of goods and services;
- Simplification for improved usability;
- Reduction in the number of models and thus reduction in costs;
- Increased distribution efficiency and ease of maintenance ('Introduction to ISO' from *ISO Online*).

International standards serve a critical function in today's global markets. They remove significantly, as ISO notes, 'technical barriers to trade.' Such barriers could be expected when there is no uniformity in standards among similar industries and technologies around the world. Increasingly, nations in the same regions are aligning themselves to protect their market turf and without standardization of industrial practices, it will be extremely difficult to compete outside one's regions. International standardization is expected to continue to grow in its popularity worldwide. We adapt the reasons provided by the Central Secretariat of ISO as follows.

Worldwide progress in trade liberalization

Trade liberalization has led to opening of markets worldwide, thereby expanding the sources of supply and markets. The expansion of markets has led to increased competition since regional and national companies now have to compete with foreign companies even in their own local markets. To achieve fairness, it is important that industry-wide standards be established that are internationally recognized and accepted by trading partners.

Interpenetration of sectors

Industrial sectors are inter-dependent. Being a world-class company requires knowledge of industrial standards from inter-dependent technologies and ensuring that these standards are maintained through the supply chain. Quality is after all holistic and can only be suboptimized if stages through the supply chain fail to follow industry standards.

Worldwide communication systems

Certain fast growing industries need to be 'quickly and progressively' standardized at a global level. The secretariat uses the computer industry as an example and already has the Open Systems Interconnection (OSI) series to ensure full compatibility among such systems. This will help to foster healthy competition, encourage innovation and improve productivity.

Global standards needs for emerging technologies

With emerging technologies, it is more difficult to set standards because there may not be adequate information and functional prototypes may not exist. Standardization could help to accumulate information and define terminologies.

Developing countries

Standardization can help to guide economic policies worldwide and especially in newly industrializing and developing countries. This will help to achieve sustainable development, provide guidance for indigenous manufacturers and producers on international industry standards that can help make their products competitive and marketable in international markets. Understanding the need to achieve these standards will help to improve productivity, safeguard countries that are mainly import-oriented and expose export-oriented countries to the market demands abroad. We see that standardization is healthy for businesses since it fosters healthy competition, encourages innovation and most importantly, brings world markets and needs to uniformity and, in the long run, will help to attain sustainable development. Now that we know the makeup and purpose of ISO, we shall review some of its most profound quality standards. ISO 9000 is perhaps one of the most widely recognized quality standards. We shall now discuss the origins and the intents of ISO 9000 series.

ORIGINS OF ISO 9000

The UK member of ISO and TEC (International Electrotechnical Commission) a close associate of ISO and the British Standards Institute (BSI) submitted a proposal in 1979 to ISO requesting that a technical committee be formed to develop international standards on quality assurance techniques and practices. ISO's technical committees consist of qualified experts from industry, research institutes, government agencies, consumer agencies and international organizations from around the world whose main task is to resolve global standardization problems. In response to this proposal, a technical committee was approved and titled Quality Assurance with a reference number ISO/TC 176. Original members of this committee came from 20 member countries with several others serving as observers. The goal of this technical committee was to develop 'generic' quality management standards that will be universally applicable. Thus, these standards were not to be industry-specific. ISO / TC 176 work was however facilitated by the existence of national standards on quality management practice especially from Britain and Canada. In the UK, the BS-5750 was already broadly applied and similarly in Canada, CSA-Z299 was widely used.

This committee's work indirectly benefited from the military standards established by the United States Department of Defense. In 1979, the British Standards Institution adopted the US Dept. of Defense quality standards MIL-Q9858 but expanded it to include the entire business process. Thus, BS-5750 has its roots in MIL-Q9858. The committee improved the standards established in both BS-5750 and CSA-Z299 to achieve an international appeal. By 1986, the first editions of ISO 9000 standards that include ISO 9000, 9001, 9002, 9003 and 9004 were completed. In the early part of 1987, these standards were published and were adopted by the International Organization for Standardization (ISO). These series of standards establishes guidelines and principles to assess quality in business processes. These standards are embodied in five major parts now known as ISO 9000 series.

EVOLUTION OF ISO 9000 SERIES

Since the inception of ISO 9000 series, they have been adopted by more than 100 countries as the international standards for quality and tens of thousands of companies have complied with these standards and are duly certified. In his speech at the Quality Expo TIME-International conference Linking Standards to Practices, held April 28—30, 1992 at the O'Hare Expo Center, Chicago, Dr Lawrence D. Eicher, secretary-general for Standardization at ISO, the International Organization for Standardization (Geneva, Switzerland), characterized the ISO 9000 phenomenon as follows:

- At least 51 countries have adopted ISO 9000 without change. The list of countries adopting these standards include the 12 member countries of the EC (France, Germany, UK, Italy, Spain, Ireland, Denmark, Portugal, Greece, The Netherlands, Belgium, Luxembourg) and EFTA (Finland, Norway, Sweden, Iceland, Austria, Switzerland) countries. Japan and USA have also adopted ISO 9000.
- Increasing numbers of companies are seeking registration through third-party assessment and such services exist in more than 32 countries.
- ISO 9000 standards are viewed as the basic building block for the development and operation of the European Organization for Testing and Certification (EOTC). There is an increased interest in ISO 9000 as a precursor to doing business in the integrated European markets.
- ISO 9000 is viewed by several national and internationally acclaimed product certification systems as a first-phase requirement for achieving its product approval.
- Multinational corporations with worldwide operations are developing programs to implement ISO 9000 standards at their operation sites.
- Several government agencies in several countries, i.e. the United Kingdom, Singapore and the United States are requiring that large suppliers have ISO 9000 registration.

Clearly, there is a growing interest in ISO 9000 and with the worldwide acceptance of these standards; these interests will continue to grow.

COMPONENTS OF ISO 9000

There are five parts to ISO 9000 standards. ISO 9001 is considered to be the highest level and it is the most stringent. It is most comprehensive and therefore, more demanding in terms of documentation and auditing. ISO 9001 is the model for quality assurance when there is need to conform to specified requirements in the five stages of production namely design, procurement, production, installation and servicing (Chase and Aquilano, 1995). ISO 9002 has a lesser requirement than ISO 9001 and requires conformance to specified requirements only when the interest is in the stages of procurement to production to installation. ISO 9003 is the least stringent and deals only with conformance to specified requirements in the production process. ISO 9000 and 9004 deal with guidelines for use.

ELEMENTS OF ISO 9000

ISO 9000 offers guidance to firms that wish to be certified. It offers a framework for self-assessment and positioning of oneself to assess future performance and direction. It makes a firm aware of its quality strategy and how such strategies can be continuously improved. There are 20 specific elements to enhance a quality program that a firm can adopt from ISO 9000. Once these standards are adopted, a firm must pass a rigorous auditing by a third party to achieve certification. These 20 elements are contained in section 4 of ISO 9000 Guidelines. As we have discussed above, the three standards ISO 9001, ISO 9002 and ISO 9003 vary in terms of application while ISO 9001 focuses on total process conformance, ISO 9002 and ISO 9003 are much narrower in their applications. Likewise, the application of these elements varies from standard to standard with, again, ISO 9001 being the most demanding and the most comprehensive. These 20 elements were well articulated in an article published in *Quality Progress.* They are listed below:
1. Management responsibility
   - The quality policy shall be defined, documented, understood, implemented and   maintained.
   - Responsibilities and authorities for all personnel specifying, achieving and monitoring quality shall be defined. In-house verification resources shall be defined, trained, and funded.

A designated management person sees that the Q91 program is implemented and maintained.

2. Quality system
   - Procedures shall be prepared.
   - Procedures shall be implemented.

3. Contract review
   - Incoming contracts (and purchase orders) shall be reviewed to see whether the requirements are adequately defined, agree with the bid and can be implemented.

4. Design control
   - The design project shall be planned.
   - Design input parameters shall be defined.
   - Design output, including crucial product characteristics, shall be documented.
   - Design output shall be verified to meet input requirements.

5. Document control
   - Generation of documents shall be controlled.
   - Distribution of documents shall be controlled.
   - Changes to documents shall be controlled.

6. Purchasing
   - Potential subcontractors and sub suppliers shall be evaluated for their ability to provide stated requirements.
   - Requirements shall be clearly defined in contracting data.
   - Effectiveness of the subcontractor's quality assurance system shall be assessed

7. Customer-supplied material
   - Any customer-supplied material shall be protected against loss or damage.

8. Product identification and trace ability
   - The product shall be identified and traceable by item, batch, or lot during all stages of production, delivery and installation.

9. Process control
   - Production (and installation) processes shall be defined and planned.
   - Production shall be carried out under controlled conditions: documented instructions, in-process controls, approval of processes and equipment and criteria for workmanship.
   - Special processes that cannot be verified after the fact shall be monitored and
   - Controlled throughout the processes.

10. Inspection and testing
   - Incoming materials shall be inspected or verified before use.
   - In-process inspection and testing shall be performed.
   - Final inspection and testing shall be performed prior to release of finished product.
   - Records of inspection and test shall be kept.
11. Inspection, measuring and test equipment
   - Equipment used to demonstrate conformance shall be controlled, calibrated and maintained:
     - ➢ Identify measurements to be made.
     - ➢ Identify affected instruments.
     - ➢ Calibrate instruments (procedures and status indications).
     - ➢ Periodically check calibration.
     - ➢ Assess measurement validity if found out of calibration.
     - ➢ Control environmental conditions in metrology lab.
   - Measurement uncertainty and equipment capability shall be known.
   - Where test hardware or software is used, it shall be checked before use and rechecked during use.
12. Inspection and test status
   - Status of inspections and tests shall be maintained for items as they progress   through various processing steps.
   - Records shall show who released conforming product.
13. Control of non-conforming product
   - Non-conforming product shall be controlled to prevent inadvertent use or installation.
   - Review and disposition of non-conforming product shall be accomplished in a formal manner.
14. Corrective action
   - Problem causes shall be identified.
   - Specific problems and their causes shall be corrected.
   - Effectiveness of corrective actions shall be assessed.
15. Handling, storage, packaging and delivery
   - Procedures for handling, storage, packaging and delivery shall be developed and maintained.
   - Handling controls shall prevent damage and deterioration.
   - Secure storage shall be provided. Product in stock shall be checked for deterioration.

- Packing, preservation, and marking processes shall be controlled.
- Quality of the product after final inspection shall be maintained. This might include delivery controls.

16. Quality records
    - Quality records shall be identified, collected, indexed, filed, stored, maintained and dispositioned.

17. Internal quality audits
    - Audits shall be planned and performed.
    - Results of audits shall be communicated to management.
    - Any deficiencies found shall be corrected.

18. Training
    - Training needs shall be identified.
    - Training shall be provided.
    - Selected tasks might require qualified individuals.
    - Records of training shall be maintained.

19. Servicing
    - Servicing activities shall be performed to written procedures.
    - Servicing activities shall meet requirements.

20. Statistical techniques
    - Statistical techniques shall be identified.
    - Statistical techniques shall be used to verify acceptability of process capability and product characteristics.

(Source: Dennis R. Arter, 'Demystifying the ISO 9000/290 Series Standards,' Quality Progress, Nov., 1992, p. 66, ASQC. Reprinted with permission.)

Some of these elements may not be applicable to some standards. In Table 3.1, we list the elements that are inapplicable to either ISO 9002 or ISO 9003. Notice that all these elements are applicable to ISO 9001 since it is the most comprehensive and most stringent standard. The requirement for the application of certain elements varies depending on the quality standard that is adopted. Again, ISO 9001 is the most stringent followed by ISO 9002 and then ISO 9003. To show the strengths of these applications for those elements, we use Table 3.2. We have also adopted a scheme that involves using codes of 1, 2 and 3 with 1 implying the most stringent, 2 the next stringent and 3 the least stringent. Table 3.2 shows the relationship between these three standards in terms of application of these elements.

Using our code, when a code of 1 is assigned to both ISO 9001 and ISO 9002, that means the requirements for the particular element are the same. All 20 elements were considered in developing Table

3.2. Again, the Table shows clearly that the requirements for the quality system standards increase as a firm moves from ISO 9003 to ISO 9002 to ISO 9001.

Elements	ISO 9002	ISO 9003
Contract review		X
Design control	X	X
Purchasing		X
Customer-supplied material		X
Process control		X
Corrective action		X
International quality audits		X
Servicing	X	X

Table 3.1: Elements not applicable to ISO 9002 and ISO 9003

Elements	ISO 9001	ISO 9002	ISO 9003
Management responsibility	1	2	3
Quality system	1	1	3
Contract review	1	1	
Design control	1		
Document control	1	1	3
Purchasing	1	1	
Customer-supplied material	1	1	
Product identification	1	1	3
Process control	1	1	
Inspection and testing	1	1	3
Inspection, measuring and test equipment	1	1	3
Inspection and test status	1	1	3
Control of non-conforming products	1	1	3
Corrective action	1	1	
Handling, storage, packaging and delivery	1	1	3
Quality records	1	1	3
Internal quality audits	1	2	
Training	1	2	3
Servicing	1		
Statistical techniques	1	1	3

Table 3.2: Scope of application of quality elements for ISO 9000 quality system

ACHIEVING ISO CERTIFICATION

The value of ISO certification cannot be underestimated. For the reasons stated below, more firms are seeking ISO 9000 certification.

- ISO 9000 certification is a tool for competitiveness in international markets. Unlike regional or national quality awards such as the Deming Prize and Malcolm Baldrige National Quality Award, ISO 9000 series are viewed to have a wider scope since the standards are accepted by member nations. It is increasingly more important to be recognized as ISO certified for market purposes since it has more international recognition than many national or regional quality awards. While many firms continue to seek regional and national awards, they may view ISO 9000 certification as the key to penetrate into global markets.

- The increasing formation of Free Trade Zones such as EC, EFTA, NAFTA and others, and the acceptance of ISO 9000 standards by member nations of these free trade zones suggest that in order to be competitive in those regions, ISO 9000 certification should be acquired.

- Certification in some regions implies a legal status especially in Europe. Meeting the ISO standards can help a firm avoid liability suits stemming from the use of their product.

- Developing and emerging markets use ISO 9000 certification as a basis of selecting partners, vendors and suppliers. Especially in the context of technology transfers, these standards may help to select partners who have demonstrated high quality through the certification.

- Adoption of ISO 9000 by member nations and applications of its standards by other countries may make it difficult to compete for government contracts without ISO 9000 certification.

There are three forms of ISO 9000 certification. These are:

1. First party: the firm audits itself using the ISO 9000 standards.
2. Second party: a supplier is audited by its customer.
3. Third party: the firm is audited by a 'qualified' national or international standards or certifying agency. Third party auditing, while more rigorous, is the best. Once a firm passes through third party auditing, it is certified and can now be

registered and recorded in a registry of certified companies as having achieved the ISO 9001 status.

ISO 9000 standards are not static. In fact, they are to be revisited every five years to determine whether to affirm, revise, or modify them.

Major firms are now ISO 9000 certified. The list of companies includes Dow Corning, AT&T, Pall Corporation, Pitney Bowes and several others. Les Schnoll, ISO Program and Quality Auditing Manager, outlined 10 benefits to Dow Corning's from ISO 9000 registration (Profile of ISO 9000). We summarize his points as follows:

1. Customer/supplier partnering relationship — ISO 9001 standard has helped to improve competitiveness as customers have become moo receptive to form customer/supplier partnering with the company.

2. Prevention pays — ISO 9001 standards have helped to cut quality cost as more emphasis is now placed on prevention.

3. Documentation — documentation of quality program can serve as evidence to customers of the firm's quality progress. It shows positive quality attitudes and management commitment.

4. Training — employees are gaining better knowledge of the jobs and the quality system through training in the quality system and quality principles.

5. Customer focus — there is increased focus on the needs of customers.

6. Competitiveness — competitiveness has been enhanced and ISO 9001 registration is helping in countries where there are trade barriers.

7. Reduction in customer-audits — there has been a reduction in the number of costly and time-consuming customer audits.

8. Objective evidence of compliance — the use of third party auditing ensures compliance to quality programs based on a set of non-biased criteria. This ensures customers that an effective quality program is in place.

9. Reduction in inspection — time and money are saved as the number of incoming inspections conducted by customers is reduced.

10. Enhanced marketability — the use of ISO recognized logo/mark and certificate number in Dow Corning's

communications with the exception of its use in products, has enhanced marketability.

IMPLEMENTING ISO 9000

Implementation of ISO 9000 standards will be easier in organizations or firms that have already adopted most of the total quality management principles. In fact, the goals of TQM and ISO 9000 are similar since the aim of both is to assure that the quality of products or processes meet some specified standards that customers expect. However, there are some differences especially in terms of the documentation and auditing required by the ISO 9000 standards. We shall suggest ways to implement ISO 9000 and our implementation process borrows from a basic strategic planning framework.

Like in the implementation of total quality management, top management must give the go ahead for ISO 9000 implementation, be fully supportive and committed to ISO 9000 standards. For example, if the plan is to institute ISO 9001, the entire business process including the supply chain will be affected and must conform to ISO 9000 standards. Only top management has the authority to get the commitment of the several business units that may be involved.

Our framework for implementing ISO 9000 starts with the planning phase. The planning phase constitutes four different tasks that must be performed. These tasks are briefly discussed:

SWOT analysis

The firm must first understand and accept its strengths, weaknesses, opportunities and threats and how these can affect or harness the implementation of ISO 9000 standards. We have already listed some of the opportunities a firm gains by being ISO 9000 certified. These opportunities also demonstrate the threats that are present without the certification. There is a threat of losing businesses in markets where ISO certification is required or used as the yardstick for quality assurance. Such loss may affect the ability of the firm to compete. It is also important to understand strengths and weaknesses. Current strengths may arise from the existence of TQM programs that may have helped to develop an organizational culture that is supportive of quality and continuous improvement. In such an environment, the implementation of ISO 9000 standards will not be a completely new thing since there are some overlaps as we compare some of the elements of ISO 9000 to total quality management. Also, in such an environment, certain weaknesses may have been identified that will need to be improved. All these efforts, will also work positively toward the implementation of ISO 9000 standards.

Self-assessment

It is always important for a firm to know where it is, where it wants to be, and when it wants to get there. All of these depend on the resources available to the firm and its ability to effectively market its products and services. Self-assessment will help a firm develop a time frame or schedule for achieving ISO 9000 certification and most importantly, it will help the firm articulate its needs and decide what level of ISO 9000 certification it wishes to be registered in.

Once this analysis is complete, the next step will be to formulate strategies on how ISO 9000 certification can be accomplished. This will contain guidelines, schedules, cost analysis, resource allocation and expected benefits from the certification. Approval of these strategies by management will necessitate an implementation process.

Implementation

The implementation will involve a cascading approach whereby these broad strategies are broken into phases to make them more operational. Formation of teams or steering committees will be necessary to guide different phases of the implementation process. These teams should be interdisciplinary to ensure that total organization views are considered at each phase of the implementation process. The teams will decide on the schedules, training requirements, resource allocation and development of action plans for each phase of the implementation. The teams will routinely organize self-assessment and gap analysis to ensure that the goals and objectives of each phase are being satisfied. Most importantly, there must be documentation of all the actions implemented. Every step must be completely documented. Documentation is very important for ISO 9000 certification.

Data collection

After implementation of the action plan, it is important to collect data on process performance and behavior. The data has to be carefully analyzed to identify deficiencies and limitations so that corrective actions will be taken. Through data collection, gaps that may still exist between the firms performance and ISO 9000 standards can be further analyzed and corrected. It is also important that internal auditors are trained using the ISO 9000 standards. These auditors will conduct internal auditing of the firm and make recommendations on where corrective actions should be taken. The aim should be to improve the process on a continuous basis. When internal auditing identifies such deficiencies, corrective actions should be taken and further auditing conducted to ensure that the problem has been corrected in a satisfactory manner.

The next stage is to submit an application for certification. A decision has to be made on whether the firm is ready or not. If not ready, it may be the time to revisit the entire process starting from the planning to see what may have gone wrong. If ready, internal auditing may be conducted again for the last time to identify any loopholes to correct and then, a third party registration assessment should be sought.

Once registration is achieved, it is important to continue to maintain registration. This can be achieved through a continuous improvement process, use of internal and external auditors, organizing team review sessions and taking corrective actions when necessary. We shall now look at another set of new standards also introduced by ISO namely ISO 14000 Series.

ISO 14000 SERIES

By 1996, the evolution of quality management focus on environmental quality issues prompted the adoption of new sets of standards. These new standards, like the ISO 9000 series, deal with the guidelines and principles of environmental management systems to make businesses aware and concerned about the growing need of environmental protection. These new standards are known as ISO 14000 series.

HISTORICAL BACKGROUND

The origins of ISO 14000 can be traced to the organization of 50 business executives interested in sustainable development. This organization is known as the Business Charter for Sustainable Development (BCSD). In 1992, the growing concern about the pollution of the natural environment led to the United Nations conference on Environment and Development in Rio de Janeiro, Brazil. The International Organization for Standards (ISO) in response to these growing interests formed the Strategic Advisory Group on the Environment (SAGE) which was charged with the evaluation of the international standard on environmental management systems. SAGE recommendations in 1993 led to ISO 14000. A technical committee (TC) 207 subsequently replaced SAGE and the role of TC 207 was to develop standards for global environmental management systems and tools. This committee was to focus in the following areas:

- Environmental management systems (EMS);
- Environmental auditing;
- Environmental labeling;
- Environmental performance evaluation (EPE);
- Life cycle assessment (LCA);
- Terms and definitions;
- Environmental aspects in product standards (EAPS).

The work of this committee was completed in the third quarter of 1996 and led to the publication of a series of standards to help firms manage and evaluate the environmental aspects of their operations. These standards are presented in Table 3.3.

Standard number	Title
ISO 14000	Environmental management systems — general guidelines on principles, systems and supporting techniques
ISO 14001	Environmental management systems — specifications with guidance for use
ISO 14004	Environmental management systems — general guidelines on principles, systems and supporting techniques
ISO 14010	Guidelines for environmental auditing — general principles of environmental auditing
ISO 14011	Guidelines for environmental auditing — audit procedures — part 1: auditing of environmental management systems
ISO 14012	Guidelines for environmental auditing — qualification criteria for environmental auditors

ISO 14020	General principles for all environmental labels and declarations
ISO 14021	Environmental labels and declarations — self-declaration environmental claims — terms and definitions
ISO 14022	Environmental labels and declarations — self-declaration environmental claims — symbols
ISO 14023	Environmental labels and declarations — self-declaration environmental claims — testing and verification
ISO 14024	Environmental labels and declarations — self-declaration environmental claims — type I guiding principles and procedures
ISO 14031	Environmental management — environmental performance evaluation guideline
ISO 14040	Life cycle assessment — principles and framework
ISO 14041	Life cycle assessment — inventory analysis
ISO 14042	Life cycle assessment — impact assessment
ISO 14043	Life cycle assessment — interpretation
ISO 14050	Terms and definitions
ISO 14060	Guide for the inclusion of environmental aspects in product standards

Table 3.3 ISO 14000 series standards

Although we have listed all the standards for ISO 14000 series, they are all at different stages of development. Before a committee's draft is accepted as a standard, it must be approved following a consensus process. Briefly, the following steps are taken:

- A working draft (WD) is developed by a work group (WG) and WG members may share the WD within their own countries.
- Comments received from participating WG members are used to revise the WD which can again be shared within each WG member's country. This procedure is followed until a consensus is reached by the WG members on the WD.
- The WD is then presented to the subcommittee (SC) to be accepted as a committee draft (CD). Subcommittees are responsible for developing the standards within a defined area.

- The CD is distributed to all SC members as a CD for ballot on four options as follows: Approve as is as a draft international standard (DIS); approve as a DIS with comments; disapprove the CD as a DIS; and abstain.
- If two-thirds of the returned ballots approve the CD as a DIS as is and/or with comments, it is elevated to a DIS.
- The DIS is forwarded to technical committee members after necessary revisions have been made and the members may approve or disapprove it as an ISO standard.
- If approved, all necessary editorial changes are done and a final ballot is taken on the revised DIS now refereed to as final or FDIS. Passage of this final ballot results in an ISO standard.

In Table 3.4, we present the status of these standards as of January 1997.

Standard number	Status
ISO 14001	International Standards
ISO 14004	International Standards
ISO 14010	International Standards
ISO 14011	International Standards
ISO 14012	International Standards
ISO 14021	Draft International Standards
ISO 14040	Draft International Standards
ISO 14020	Committee Draft International Standards
ISO 14024	Committee Draft International Standards
ISO 14041	Committee Draft International Standards
ISO 14060	Committee Draft International Standards
ISO 14031	Working Draft
ISO 14013	New Work Item
ISO 14014	New Work Item
ISO 14015	New Work Item
ISO 14022	Preliminary
ISO 14023	Preliminary
ISO 14042	Preliminary
ISO 14043	Preliminary

Table 3.4 ISO 14000 series working drafts

ISO 14001 is considered the core standard because it is the only standard with specified requirements that firms must meet in order to achieve certification. A firm can therefore be audited on ISO 14001 standards. All the other standards listed in Table 3.4 are guidelines to help implement ISO 14001. These standards are not required for certification and a firm may not be audited on their basis. We shall briefly discuss the core areas covered by the ISO 14000 standards.

Environmental Management Systems (EMS)

The core elements of an environmental management system (EMS) are presented in ISO 14001. The core consists of requirements that a firm can be audited on for certification. It deals only with environmental management standards and does not consider performance issues. To help implement EMS, ISO 14004 offers general guidelines on principles, systems and supporting techniques.

The involvement of top management is necessary when developing an environmental policy. The environmental policy must consider the environmental impacts of the activities, products or services of the firm. Management must be committed to continuous improvement efforts, and develop and implement plans for pollution prevention. It is important for management to ensure compliance to environmental legislation and regulations, and also to other regulations that the firm may already be committed to. This may involve establishing communication links with various interest groups. There must be an established framework to review environmental objectives and targets and the environmental goals of the firm must be documented and effectively communicated to all employees. The public should also be made aware of the environmental policy of the firm. Thus, top management has the responsibility of making the public aware of its environmental policy.

Planning

A firm must develop a plan to help it achieve its environmental policy. Components of the plan are environmental aspects; legal and other requirements; environmental objectives and targets; and environmental management programs. Environmental aspects deal with procedures that the firm maintains to identify the environmental aspects of its activities, products or services. The firm makes an assessment of these impacts and determines its control over them and their expected impacts on the natural environment. The significant impacts must be considered in setting up environmental objectives. This information should be updated over time. It is a dynamic process that requires the firm to continuously monitor its environmental influence and impacts on the natural environment and update the available information as needed.

With regards to legal and other requirements, it is the responsibility of the firm to be aware of the legal requirements it must comply with. It should maintain procedures to enable it to assess such requirements that are applicable to the environmental aspects of its activities, products or services.

The firm must have environmental objectives and targets. These must be consistent with the environmental policy and commitment to pollution prevention. It is important that documentation is maintained at each relevant function and level within the organization. The objectives and targets should be cognizant of the legal and other requirements that the firm subscribes to, its significant environmental aspect, its technological options, financial, operational and business requirements as well as the views of other environmental interest groups. The targets should be measurable and specific and may be used to achieve the environmental objectives within a specified time-frame. Environmental management programs are the operational procedures to achieve environmental objectives and targets. They involve a breakdown of responsibilities for achieving objectives and targets; actions to be taken; resource allocation; and time-frame.

Implementation and operation

To effectively implement the environmental management program, the firm must develop the necessary capabilities and support mechanisms. This involves a well-structured organizational process where job responsibilities and authorities are well defined, documented and communicated. Resources needed to implement the program must be provided and management must be involved to ensure system viability and assess the performance of the program. A major aspect of implementation and operation of the environmental program is training, awareness, and competence. Competence may be developed through education and training.

It is important that trainees are aware of the requirements of the system. Thus, appropriate training should be made available. Communication is also an important aspect of implementation. The firm should have procedures for responding to relevant communications from external interested parties; and procedures for both internal and external communications. Like in many of the ISO standards, documentation is very important and could be either in paper or in an electronic form. However, there must be full document control procedure. Implementation must also deal with operational control of activities that are done under specified conditions. Suppliers and contractors should also be made aware of the procedures of the firm. The firm should have procedures to respond to emergency situations. This will involve a plan to respond to emergencies and procedures for accident prevention. These plans should be revised when an incident occurs and should be periodically tested.

Checking and corrective actions

This step requires the firm to be able to measure, monitor and evaluate its environmental activities. This requires the firm to be able to monitor and measure key measures of performance, track operational performance, operational controls and objectives and targets. The monitoring process is only effective if the program complies with laws and regulations. Corrective and preventive actions may also be necessary when there is non-conformance. Auditing is conducted to assess conformance and proper implementation of procedures. A report is made available to management for review.

Management review

This requires the firm to review and continually improve its environmental management system in order to improve the overall environmental performance. Periodic review by management will ensure suitability, adequacy and effectiveness; address the need for policy changes or any other changes of the environmental management system; and documentation of the review.

We shall now focus on the other aspects of the ISO 14000 series.

ENVIRONMENTAL AUDITING

This provides the standards that may be used for environmental auditing of the firm. ISO 14010 offers the general principles for environmental auditing. This standard deals mainly with the objectives and scope of the auditing, professionalism of the auditor, procedures, criteria, reliability and reporting.

It is the firm that commissions the auditing and states the scope and objectives of the auditing. Auditors however, are expected to be fair and avoid conflict of interest. They must also have the required professional skills and experience to enable them to fulfill these important responsibilities. Information obtained from auditing and the resulting report should be kept confidential unless the firm approves disclosure. Auditors must also follow documented and well-defined methodologies to carry out their auditing of a firm's environmental program. There must be consistency of auditing reports. In other words, other competent environmental auditors should be able to independently, reach the same conclusions. Auditors should also recognize that they are working with sample information and must therefore include some levels of uncertainty in their audits. All auditing findings should be communicated in a written form to the firm.

ENVIRONMENTAL LABELING

The aim of environmental labeling is to reduce the environmental impact that may be associated with the consumption of goods and services. This serves several purposes:

1. Labels are used to provide information on the environmental impact of a product or service and the consumer is made aware of that.
2. The information content of the label may affect the purchasing behavior of the consumer.
3. When purchasing behavior is influenced by the information content of the label, market shares may subsequently be affected.
4. This will affect the attitude of manufacturers or firms who will respond to consumers' needs if they intend to remain competitive and increase their market share.
5. There will be less burden associated with the product or service.

ENVIRONMENTAL PERFORMANCE EVALUATION (EPE)

This deals with a measure of performance. The ISO Sub Committee (5C4) defines it as a process to measure, analyze, assess, report, and communicate an organization's environmental performance. It is intended as a tool that assists company management in understanding environmental performance; determining necessary actions to achieve environmental policies, objectives, and targets; and communicating with interested parties.' (Block 1997, p. 17). EPE focuses on three major areas: management systems, operational system and the environment. The management systems aspect deals with peoples' management. People within the organization take actions that may have an impact on the environment. There is a need for procedures and practice guidelines that relate to the management of the organization's environmental aspect. Operational system deals with process management. Here, the emphasis is on the transformation process to produce goods and services. Attention is given to the process itself in terms of equipment and physical structures and the materials and energy that are used to produce goods and services. The environment emphasis is to focus organizational attention on its potential impact on all aspects of the natural environment. The organization is to assess the influence of its management and operational system performance on the environment.

LIFE CYCLE ASSESSMENT

The emphasis here is to evaluate manufacturing efficiency. Inventory analysis is employed to compile relevant inputs and outputs of a production system.

Terms and definitions

The aim is to co-ordinate the terms and definitions used by the various sub-committees and their work groups.

Competing through Environmental Management Systems

Clearly, businesses are paying attention to ISO 14000 series of standards. Adherence to these standards can help an organization to be more competitive and increase its market share in a market environment that is increasingly focusing on 'green' products. The Standards Council of Canada (1997) in its publication provides a list of reasons why many companies are interested in adopting an internal environmental management system. These reasons are:

- Reduction of liability/risk;
- Improvements of a company's image in the area of environmental performance and compliance with regulatory requirements;
- Pollution prevention and energy/resource savings;
- Insurance companies' unwillingness to issue coverage for pollution incidents unless the firm requesting coverage has a proven environmental system in place;
- Better resale value of a company's property assets;
- Desire to profit in the market for 'green' products;
- Improved internal management methods; and
- Interest in attracting a high-quality work force.

These reasons serve as a motivating force for companies to adopt the standards. We must also add that increased consumer awareness and the activity of environmental interest groups have greatly influenced attention on the environment. Consumers are now concerned about the environmental quality of the product and purchase decisions are influenced by environmental issues. It is a business and marketing strategy for organizations to achieve certification in environmental management system to show their responsiveness to environmental management.

IMPLEMENTING ISO 14001

As we mentioned above, ISO 14001 is the core standard and it is the only standard that a firm can be audited on for certification. We also listed and briefly discussed the four core elements of ISO 14001 as environmental policy, implementation and operation, checking and corrective action and management review. In order to implement ISO 14001, an organization must go through these elements in a step-by-step procedure. These core elements are actually motivated by the Shewhart Cycle popularized by Dr W. Edwards Deming and now widely known as the PDCA (plan-do-check-act) cycle. The PDCA cycle is commonly used in implementing quality management programs. We shall use this cycle to show how these core elements of ISO 14001 can be implemented.

Plan — the planning stage requires the organization to develop an environmental policy. The environmental policy is akin to developing a mission statement that will detail the organization's roles, objectives, goals, and vision with regards to environmental performance. The objectives and targets specified in this statement must be realistic and achievable with the resources dedicated to attaining the environmental policy. Environmental policy is the motivating force of the organization's environmental management system. The organization however can only plan when it has relevant information. It needs to know its history, the nature of its business, and the mode of its interaction with the natural environment through its organizational activities. Thus, there is a need to have information and knowledge on 'environmental aspects.' The environmental impact of the organization's activities on the natural environment should be estimated, considered and used in setting environmental objectives and goals. The business or organization must also know the legal and regulatory requirements that guide its operations and how it is expected to comply to them. With this knowledge base and top management commitment, achievable objectives and targets can be developed and appropriate resources devoted to their attainment.

Do — after the plan stage comes the do stage or what has been dubbed the execution step. This involves implementation and operation. Once the environmental policy is known, it is broken down into actions to be taken and responsibilities duly assigned to members of the organization. Necessary training is offered to sensitize and make members of the organization aware of the environmental policy, and to develop the needed competence on environmental management issues. They are also trained and made aware of the need to document their procedures. Emphasis is also placed on operational control and emergency preparedness and response.

Check—Act — the check stage involves monitoring the entire procedure and obtaining feedback. In the EMS document, it is referred to as checking and corrective action. The essence of this step is to evaluate outcomes of key performance measures and see if they meet expected standards or targets. The monitoring is done on a regular basis so that deviations from expected targets can be detected early. The targets or standards may be based on compliance required by existing legal and regulatory requirements. When the system is detected as not meeting these standards, corrective actions can be taken promptly. The compliance requirements are part of the environmental policy so there is a target to aim for. The act stage is included in this step because actions are taken as the situation may warrant solving impending problems such as system's deviation from expected norm.

The fourth core element of ISO 14001 is management review. This requires top management to be involved as an active participant of environmental management system. This is necessary, because certain actions or decisions can be taken at the top management level. Top management is required to review the EMS to ensure its continuing suitability and effectiveness. This review may lead to changes in environmental policy. For example, the original policy may not be adequate given some organizational transformation or process changes that may have taken place or it may not have been effective. Management will then require a revision of the environmental policy or development of new environmental policy that will align with corporate objectives and goals. The environmental policy drives the EMS and the organization's overall environmental performance so it is important that top management takes charge of this step. Once this step is concluded, the process continues.

The implementation process offered here is generic and does not relate to any specific industry. It is a stepwise procedure that has to be taken irrespective of the industry.

CONCLUSION

In this chapter, we have discussed the ISO as an organization and its quality standards. We focused mainly on ISO 9000 series which have profound effects on product quality and the ISO 14000 series which are now emerging as the environmental management system standards for organizations. ISO 9000 and ISO 14000 series formats are similar in that they both require the development of frameworks to either manage product quality or the environment; they focus on continuous improvement and documentation procedures; and they rely on training and top management involvement. They, however, differ in content. ISO 9000 series focus much on customers and their needs but ISO 14000 series focus on 'environmental stakeholders' rather than customers. The organization must pay attention to the needs of this larger group that may not necessarily be its customers but have a stake in the natural environment. The need to attain sustainable development and protect our natural environment from degradation and pollution is a universal problem that is now transcending beyond business operations. So corporations of the future must pay attention to the need for sustainable development.

The increased number of environmental disasters such as the explosion of the Union Carbide's pesticide production plant in Bhopal, India, in 1984 and the Exxon Valdez oil spill in Prince William Sound, Alaska, have brought much focus on corporate responsibility. Madu [1996] points to the emergence of new environmental laws meant to regulate the operations of businesses and protect the natural habitat. With the avalanche of local, regional and national laws that corporations are expected to comply with, the cost of doing business in an environmental-sensitive society is increasingly high. It is important and cost effective to have international standards on the environment that can guide businesses and help them meet their corporate and social responsibility functions to the society at reasonable costs. ISO 14000 series of standards can achieve such a goal if they are widely accepted and adopted by member nations. Certification of corporations as meeting such standards can help reduce tensions and suspicions that often exist between communities and corporations. This will effectively enhance the image of corporations.

REFERENCES

1. Affisco, JR 'TQEM — Methods for continuous improvement,' in *Handbook of TQM* (ed., Christian N. Madu), Chapman & Hall, London, 1988.
2. Allyn and Bacon (1992) *Profiles of ISO 9000,* Needham Heights, Mass
3. Arter, DR. Demystifying the ISO 9000/290 Series Standards, *Quality Progress.*
4. Block, M.R. (1997) *Implementing ISO 14001,* ASQC Quality Press, Milwaukee, Wis.
5. Chase, R.B. and Aquilano, N.J. (1995) *Production and Operations Management Manufacturing and Services,* Seventh Edition, Irwin, Chicago, IL.
6. Introduction to ISO', ISO Online, retrieved 12/15/96 from http://www.iso.chi infoe/guide.html.
7. Madu, C.N. (1996) *Managing Green Technologies for Global Competitiveness,* Quorum Books, Westport, CT.
8. Standards Council of Canada (1997) 'What will be the ISO 14000 series of international standards — ISO 14000,' January.

CHAPTER 4

●————————————————————●

STATISTICAL QUALITY CONTROL

In this chapter, we shall discuss the statistical tools for managing quality. This discussion will be broken up into two major sections namely acceptance sampling and statistical process control. The section on acceptance sampling will focus on the testing of the quality of incoming products such as raw materials or outgoing products such as finished products. The section on statistical process control will focus on how to test the quality of products while the work is in progress, for example, the quality testing of products along the assembly line. Statistical quality control (SQC) embodies these two aspects of statistical quality management. The term 'control' is used to denote that the actual performance of the product is being prepared to an established standard to observe if there is deviation from the standard and to take corrective action to remedy the problem. The uniformity in the quality of products and the stability of the process itself is improved if corrective actions are timely. Before our discussions on these two sections, we shall first introduce the types of measurement we are going to use.

TYPES OF MEASUREMENT

There are two types of measurements in quality control: measurement by attributes and measurement by variables.

Measurement by Attributes

Measurement by attributes is used when the characteristic of the product we want to measure the quality of is in a discrete form or can be expressed categorically. For example, when we make purchase decisions, we often examine or inspect identical products before selecting one or more for purchase. Our decision on which product to select is influenced by some quality attributes we expect from the product. For example, in buying a gallon of homogenized milk, the purchaser may look at the expiration date and make a decision on the expiration date; the purchaser may also look at the appearance of the container to answer questions such as, is the container clean? The response to such questions will be either Yes or No. There are only these two possibilities. If the decision is yes, purchase decision is favorable; otherwise the purchaser will lean towards not purchasing the product. These categorical decisions that lead to yes or no, good or bad, 0 or 1, reject or do not reject, win or lose, are based on measuring the quality of the product by attributes. These categorical decisions are in fact, discrete. There are other cases that fall into attribute measurement that are somewhat different from our example. Consider situations where we may have to count the number of errors in a book, the number of defects in a lot, the number of accidents in a ten-mile span of a road, etc. In these cases, we are involving the use of counts. But, notice that there are similarities to our categorical example. There is an attribute of quality we are looking for and that attribute is either present or not present. Thus, each product or item we sample may either have or not have that particular attribute. Thus, when we can categorize the quality attribute of a product, the type of measurement we use is known as measurement by attribute or we can say that we are conducting sampling by attributes.

Measurement by Variables

Quality attributes are not always discrete. Suppose we consider a manufacturer of a popular brand of breakfast cereal. This manufacturer expresses the content of a box of cereal by weight and determines the price of the box of cereal by its weight. Say the manufacturer bags 13 oz boxes. It is difficult for the manufacturer to guarantee that every box coming out from its production line will weigh exactly 13 ounces. This is because it is not easy to get an exact weight. Some boxes may be slightly above, below or exact. It will be too expensive and time consuming to ensure that each weight is exactly 13 ounces. Rather, the manufacturer may specify an acceptable weight range that each box should comply with. The manufacturer may for example, specify that the weights should be 13 ± 0.05 oz. Thus, rather than the measurement being discrete, it is expressed in a continuous form. When the quality characteristic that is being measured is expressed in a continuous form, the type of measurement we are using is known as measurement by variable. There are some dimensions of measurement that can only be expressed in a continuous scale. Such include weights, time, temperature, height, length, etc. These measures contain more information than attributes and are therefore more powerful. We shall now discuss acceptance sampling procedures.

ACCEPTANCE SAMPLING

As we mentioned in the discussion above, acceptance sampling is a statistical procedure that is used to inspect if an incoming or outgoing product conforms to a specified quality attribute. Consider again the manufacturer of a popular brand of breakfast cereal. Lots that are coming from the assembly line are inspected for quality. The manufacturer has set the standard that a box should weigh 13 ± .05 oz. If more than three boxes are found to weigh outside this range, the lot is rejected. Otherwise, it is accepted. Notice that the decision being made is to either reject or accept the lot. Thus, this decision is based on acceptance sampling. We have been using the term 'sampling' without explaining it. Indeed, a simple random sample of three boxes is taken from each lot and inspected for the quality characteristic hence the term sampling. Decisions made about the three boxes will affect the acceptance or rejection of the lot. The decision to either reject or accept a lot is known as lot sentencing. The use of simple random sample in lot sentencing has some merits. It is very efficient and information derived from it may form the basis for carrying out 100% inspection on the lot. For example, when a lot is rejected, it is further scrutinized by inspecting every box to identify the non-conforming boxes and then adjusting them to meet the weight requirement. However, if from the sample, a decision is made to accept the lot, only the non-conforming items in the sample are adjusted. The entire lot is concluded as meeting the specified standard. One may wonder why we do not carry out a 100% inspection of the lot since that would seem to guarantee the quality level of the product rather than the acceptance sampling. In the next section we shall contrast these two strategies.

Acceptance Sampling vs. 100% Inspection

Obviously, if our objective is to eliminate defects as it is in quality management, one would expect that this could be better accomplished through 100% inspection of all products. The use of acceptance sampling does not guarantee zero defects. In fact, there is an ongoing debate on the use of acceptance sampling since it will potentially allow some defects to get through in an accepted lot. However, 100% inspection also cannot guarantee zero defects especially when very large numbers of products are being inspected for quality There is no way to guarantee zero defects. However, efforts are being made to significantly diminish the number of defects that may be present in an accepted lot. One of the better known standards is the six-sigma established by Motorola. Although this standard does not guarantee zero defects, it states that no more than 3.4 defects in a million parts are acceptable. Some of the reasons why acceptance sampling may be preferred to 100% inspection are listed below:

- Cost is an important factor to consider in managing quality. In many high volume operations like mass production systems, it is impractical and ineffective to inspect every item. If 100% inspection is instituted, that will lead to exorbitant costs due to the intensive labor and machinery requirements for the inspection process.

- As we mentioned above, 100% inspection does not guarantee zero defects. There are several reasons that may contribute to that. One is human error which may result from fatigue and monotonous inspection operations. A second is equipment malfunction which may not be detected on time and as a result, the testing equipment may not operate to standards. A third reason may be that wrong standards are established. All these make it difficult to achieve zero defects.

- Not all products are amenable to 100% inspection. For some products, inspection may be detrimental. For example, to assess the quality of bombs, they have to be detonated. If the bomb explodes as it is expected, then it meets its quality standards but on the other hand, the bomb is destroyed. For marketing purposes, the producer will not have any bombs to sell if 100% inspection is carried out. 100% inspection could also be disastrous to items such as light bulbs. Similarly, if a light bulb is designed with life time of 750 hours, inspecting to ensure that each bulb meets this design criterion may ultimately lead to burning out the light bulb and therefore not being able to sell it.

- Time is of the essence. In mass production systems, it will be time consuming to carry out 100% inspection. Also, when quick introduction of the product into the market is needed to be competitive, 100% inspection may lead to a considerable loss of time.

Designing acceptance sampling

The sequential procedure for acceptance sampling is given in Figure 4.1. These steps are outlined as follows:

1. Incoming or outgoing lot is received.
2. A sample of size n is taken from the lot.
3. The sample is inspected to determine the number of defects or nonconforming items.
4. The number of non-conforming items is compared to a pre-established quality standard (i.e. $c \leq 2$ where c is the number of defects and 2 is the most number of defects expected in a lot). This established criterion is known as the acceptance criterion and it shows the maximum allowable defects in a sample for the lot to be accepted as meeting the quality standard.
5. After accepting the lot, it moves to the next stage of the production process or it is shipped out to customers. If the lot is rejected, corrective actions may be taken. Such actions may include (a) returning the lot to the supplier and (b) conducting 100% inspection on the lot and reworking potential defects that may be found.

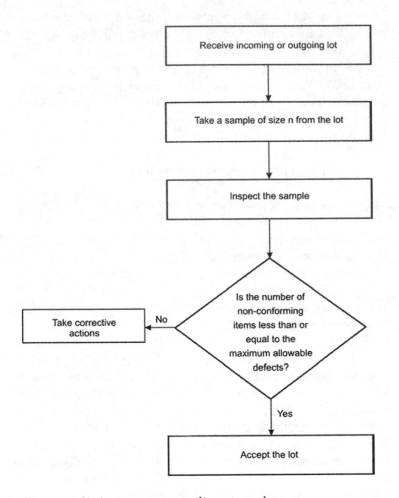

Figure 4.1: Acceptance sampling procedure

Producer and Consumer Risks

From the procedure for acceptance sampling, it is apparent that we can make some errors when we use the sample to determine whether to accept or reject a lot.

Some of the decisions we make through acceptance sampling can be itemized as follows:

1. The lot from which the sample is taken is of acceptable quality and based on the sample information; we decided to

accept the lot. Thus, we have made the correct decision by accepting a lot that is of acceptable quality.

2. The lot is of acceptable quality but from our sample information we have decided to reject the lot. An error is committed here because a lot that should have been accepted is being rejected. This occurs because we took a 'bad' sample or a sample that does not typically represent the lot.

3. The lot is not of acceptable quality and based on our sample, we decided to reject the lot. Like in the case of (1), we made a correct decision by rejecting a lot that truly has a large number of nonconforming items.

4. The lot is not of acceptable quality but based on our sample, we have decided to accept the lot. Again, like in the case of (2), we have committed an error by using an atypical sample to accept a lot that should have been rejected.

The errors we commit in cases (2) and (4) have potential consequences. In (2) for example, by rejecting a lot that should have been accepted, we may end up sending the lot to the supplier who will conduct 100% inspection to try and rectify the problem. But the supplier will find out after all the corrective measures have been taken, that there is actually no problem with the lot. Due to the error committed by rejecting the lot, the supplier or the producer incurs some cost by trying to solve a nonexistent problem. Thus there is some risk involved. The risk to the producer that a good quality lot is rejected is known as the producer's risk, or in probabilities, the probability of the Type I error. This risk is measured using α.

The consumer also faces a risk that a non-conforming lot may pass inspection and then be shipped out to the consumer. The consumer ultimately, will incur the inconvenience of receiving poor quality items and returning them back to the producer. This risk to the consumer is on the other hand, known as the consumer's risk and in probabilities, the probability of the Type II error. This risk is measured using β.

In designing a sampling plan therefore, n, which is the sample size, and c, which is the maximum allowable non-confirming items in the lot, must be specified. From a producer's viewpoint, a good sampling plan should have a high probability of accepting a good lot or a low probability of rejecting good lots. The consumers on the other hand, would like a low probability of accepting bad lots.

Advances in technology and increased use of automated facilities have made 100% inspections widely available and economical for some product lines. The use of acceptance sampling remains, however, effective and the only way out for some products. We shall now discuss different methods for acceptance sampling or what are known as sampling plans.

Single sampling plan

Figure 4.2 is used to describe the single sampling plan. It is defined by two numbers n and c. The steps for this plan are as follows:

1. Specify n and c.
2. Take a sample of size n from the lot.
3. Identify the number of defects in the sample of size n.
4. If the number of defects is less than or equal to the acceptance number c, accept the lot as meeting the quality standard. Otherwise, reject the lot.

Note that the sample size n taken from the lot could fall in the range $1 \leq n \leq N$ where N is the lot size.

Double sampling plan

Figure 4.3 is used to describe this two-stage sampling process hence the name double sampling plan.

1. Specify sampling plan n_1, c_1, n_2, c_2, c_3.
2. If the number of defects $x_1 < c_1$, accept the lot. Otherwise, go to step 3.
3. If $x_1 \geq c_2$ is a second acceptance criterion, the lot is rejected. Otherwise go to step 4.
4. If $c_1 < x_1 < c_2$, a second sample of size n_2 is taken.
5. Identify the number of defectives in the second sample (x_2).
6. If the sum of the number of defectives in both samples $(x_1 + x_2)$ is less than or equal to a third acceptance criterion (c_3), that is $x_1 + x_2 \leq c_3$ accept the lot. Otherwise, reject the lot. In many instances, $c_3 = c_2$.

Sequential sampling plan

The sampling plan can be extended beyond the double sampling to include a triple sampling plan and even more. However, as you can see from the double sampling plan, when we extend the sampling plan, the procedure becomes more complex. A preferred plan is therefore a sequential sampling plan. This plan involves sampling items individually and recording the defects observed at each stage of the process. These defects are added up and used to decide whether to reject or accept a lot, or even to continue with the sampling. Irrespective of the sampling plan that is adopted, we must always ensure that both the producer's and consumer's risks are satisfied.

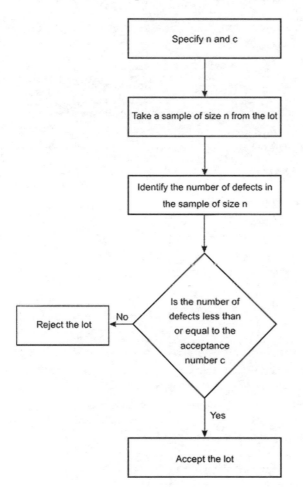

Figure 4.2: Single sampling plan.

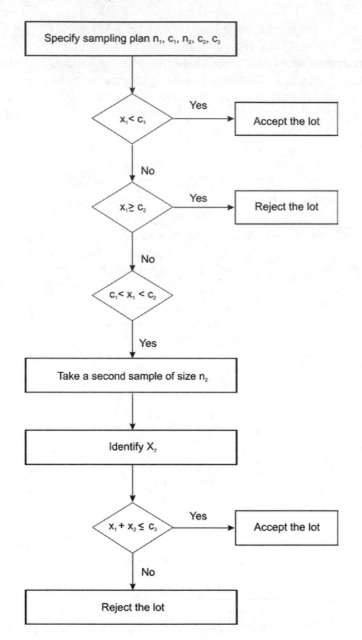

Figure 4.3: Double sampling plan

Operating characteristic curve (OC curve)

In designing an acceptance sampling plan; it is important to know *n* and *c*. However, a good sampling plan should have a high probability of accepting good lots and a low probability of accepting non-conforming lots. Lots that meet the specified acceptance criterion as defined by *c* are said to have acceptable quality level (AQL). Producers will generally like to see a sampling plan that will minimize the producer's risk. However, as we mentioned already, producers are not the only ones that incur risks. Customers also do incur risk. They would like a sampling plan that will have high probability of rejecting defective lots. Thus, lots with defectives higher than the specified acceptance criterion should be rejected. The percentage defective that exceeds the specified acceptance level is known as lot tolerance percent defective (LTPD). These two risks are measured using α and β where α is the probability of rejecting a good lot (producer's risk) and, β is the probability of accepting a bad lot (consumer's risk). Therefore, to determine an acceptance sampling plan *(n, c)*, we must specify α, β, AQL and LTPD. An acceptance sampling plan should meet both the needs of the producers and consumers by considering the levels of quality that are acceptable to them and their associated risks.

The different sampling plans are represented using the operating characteristic curves. Each sampling plan will have a unique OC curve. These curves show the probabilities of accepting lots for different percent defectives. The OC curve is therefore useful in showing the discriminating power of a sampling plan. We can, for example, see how well a sampling plan discriminates between good and bad lots.

Let us illustrate with an example, how to develop an OC curve. As we mentioned above, the OC curve shows the probability of accepting a lot for the different percentages of defects in the lot for a given sampling plan. We shall look at the following plans: (n = 10, *c* = 0); *(n= 10, c= 1); (n = 15, c= 0)* and *(n = 15, c = 1)*. We shall compute the probabilities of accepting a lot using the binomial probability distribution. The binomial is used here because it will simplify the calculation. Also, the assumptions that lead to the Bernoulli process are satisfied, namely:

- There are two mutually exclusive outcomes, i.e. reject or accept;

- The probability of defect is constant;
- The samples are independent.

The binomial table for selected probabilities when $n = 10$ and $n = 15$ are presented in Table 4.1.

From this table, we are able to generate Table 4.2, which gives the probability of accepting a lot for the different sampling plans.

N	c	0.1	0.2	0.3	0.4	0.5
10	0	0.3487	0.1074	0.0282	0.006	0.001
	1	0.7361	0.3758	0.1493	0.0464	0.0107
	2	0.9298	0.6778	0.3828	0.1673	0.0547
	3	0.9872	0.8791	0.6496	0.3823	0.1719
	4	0.9984	0.9672	0.8497	0.6331	0.377
	5	0.9999	0.9936	0.9527	0.8338	0.623
	6	1	0.9991	0.9894	0.9452	0.8281
	7	1	0.9999	0.9984	0.9877	0.9453
	8	1	1	0.9999	0.9983	0.9893
	9	1	1	1	0.9999	0.999
15	0	0.2059	0.0352	0.0047	0.0005	0
	1	0.549	0.1671	0.0353	0.0052	0.0005
	2	0.8159	0.398	0.1268	0.0271	0.0037
	3	0.9444	0.6482	0.2969	0.0905	0.0176
	4	0.9873	0.8358	0.5155	0.2173	0.0592
	5	0.9978	0.9389	0.7216	0.4032	0.1509
	6	0.9997	0.9819	0.8689	0.6098	0.3036
	7	1	0.9958	0.95	0.7869	0.5
	8	1	0.9992	0.9848	0.905	0.6964
	9	1	0.9999	0.9963	0.9962	0.8491
	10	1	1	0.9993	0.9907	0.9408
	11	1	1	0.9999	0.9981	0.9824
	12	1	1	1	0.9997	0.9963
	13	1	1	1	1	0.9995
	14	1	1	1	1	1

Table 4.1: Selected values for the binomial cumulative distribution function

% Defective	(n=10,c=0) Probability of acceptance	(n=10,c=1) Probability of acceptance	(n=15,c=0) Probability of acceptance	(n=15,c=1) Probability of acceptance
1	0.9044	0.9866	0.8601	0.9904
1	0.8171	0.9672	0.7386	0.9647
1	0.7374	0.9427	0.6333	0.9271
1	0.6648	0.9141	0.5421	0.8809
1	0.5987	0.8823	0.4633	0.8291
10	0.3487	0.6974	0.2059	0.5491
15	0.1969	0.5096	0.0874	0.3186
20	0.1073	0.3489	0.0352	0.1671
25	0.0573	0.2252	0.0134	0.0802
30	0.0282	0.1372	0.0047	0.0352

Table 4.2: Probabilities of acceptance for different sampling plan

Figure 4.4 shows the OC curves for these four sampling plans. However, to select a sampling plan, the values of AQL and LTPD must be specified as well as the risks (α and β) associated with them. AQL will be used to control for the producer's risk while LTPD will be used to control for the consumer's risk. Suppose for example, that AQL = 5%, LTPD = 12%, α = 0.15 and β = 0.3. The two points we need to find from the OC curve are (AQL, 1 - α) and (LTPD, β) which we have now as (5%, 0.85) and (13%, 0.3). We notice that the sampling plan n = 15, c = 1, will have a producer's risk of about 12% when AQL is 5% and when LTPD is 12%, the consumers risk is 3%. The producer's risk observed is better than the specified and yet consumer's risk is controlled. Thus, the better sampling plan is n = 15, c = 1, for this problem. If either the producer's or consumer's risk is found to be higher, then the sampling plan will be inappropriate and we will need to look for other sampling plans. Perhaps, the sampling plan may not even be contained in our figure. Figure 4.5 shows this sampling plan.

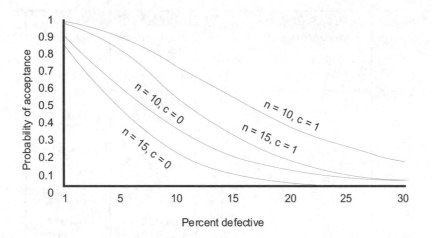

Figure 4.4: Operating characteristics curves

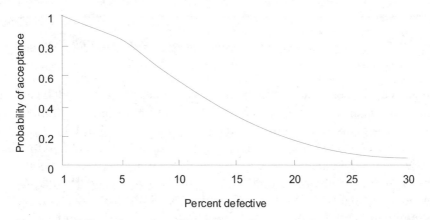

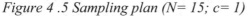

Figure 4 .5 Sampling plan (N= 15; c= 1)

It is tedious and often difficult to use the OC curves to find the sampling plan. Their use requires having several OC curves with the different producer's and consumer's risks to find a sampling plan. The US Department of Defense has published tables for attribute sampling that are widely in use. These tables are known as MIL-STD-105D, Sampling Procedures and Tables for Inspection by Attributes. The use of these tables significantly simplifies the calculation and finding of sampling plans.

Acceptance sampling for variables

When the quality characteristic of interest in a product is expressed in a continuous rather than discrete form, we use measurement by variables. For example, a farmer may specify that the weight of a steer before it is sold should be between 250 ± 10 pounds. We know that weight is measured in a continuous scale and it will be very difficult to aim for exactly 250 pounds since random variation in the weights of these animals can be expected. Rather than aim for an exact weight, a range is specified and all that fall within that range will be acceptable as meeting the weight criterion. Notice that this is different from the measurement by attributes where our interest was in the presence or absence of an attribute. There are many situations where measurement by variable will be more appropriate. For example, there are many products where weight is also considered as an attribute of quality. Such products include breakfast cereal, baby food, fertilizer and others.

When we use measurement by variables, the form of analysis to find the operating characteristic curve will be different. In the case of measurement by attributes, we used the binomial probability distribution because we can classify our outcomes and there were only two mutually exclusive outcomes. With variables, we are dealing with a continuous scale that is expressed in ranges rather than discrete points. Many of these variables can be analyzed using the normal probability distribution. We shall show this with an example.

Shawn Cereal Retail Inc. is a major retailer of a popular breakfast cereal. It orders lots of cereal that are delivered by the manufacturer in batches of 1000 15-ounce boxes. Shawn Cereal Retail Inc. has worked out a contract with the manufacturer to inspect 50 boxes from each lot to ensure that they satisfy the weight requirement. Based on records kept by Shawn Inc. over a period of time, its management has determined that the weights of these boxes of cereal are not always exact but have a standard deviation of 0.45 ounces. Due to this random variation, management is concerned that it cannot fully guarantee customers that the boxes will be 15 oz. Instead, it has decided that it would like a 95% probability that the manufacturer is supplying lots of cereal with a mean of at least 15 oz. Thus, a producer's risk α is being set at 0.05 or (1-0.95). Based on this producer's risk, management would like to know the minimum sample mean of the 50 boxes of cereal it inspects that will be considered as meeting the requirement that on the average, the boxes of cereal will be 15 oz.

What we are trying to do is to set up a standard or an acceptance criterion that will be used for inspecting the lots. We want to set a criterion that will state that if $\overline{x} \geq c$, accept the lot. Otherwise, reject it as not meeting the weight criterion. Notice that several random samples are taken and their sample means are computed. These sample means are random variables. In other words, the values they take are due to chance occurrence. One of the important theorems in probability and statistics is the Central Limit Theorem. This theorem states as follows: if a simple random sample of size n is selected from a population, the sampling distribution of the sample mean can be approximated by a normal probability distribution as the sample size gets larger and larger. This law applies to sampling from both normal and non-normal populations. Note that in using the normal distribution, you must know the mean and standard deviation. Using the Central Limit Theorem, we can therefore outline the steps for computing the OC curve for measurement by variables as follows:

- Compute the standard error of the mean, which is given as $\sigma_{\overline{x}} = \sigma / \sqrt{n}$, where σ is the population standard deviation.

  Often times, the population standard deviation will be unknown so we can use the sample standard deviation to approximate it. Thus, the sample standard error of the mean will be expressed as

$$s_{\overline{x}} = \frac{s}{\sqrt{n}} \tag{4.1}$$

where s is the sample standard deviation.

- Compute the z-score from the standard normal distribution table.
- Using the equation for the z-score given as

$$z = \frac{\overline{x} - \mu}{\sigma_{\overline{x}}} \tag{4.2}$$

- Compute $\overline{x} = \mu + z\sigma_{\overline{x}}$
- Set the acceptance criterion.

We shall illustrate these steps using the example we presented above.

- First, we find the standard error of the mean

$$\sigma_{\bar{x}} = \frac{\sigma}{\sqrt{n}} = \frac{0.45}{\sqrt{50}} = 0.0636 \qquad (4.3)$$

- Second, from the normal distribution table and using the producer's risk of $\alpha = 0.05$, we find that $z = -1.645$. Thus, $\bar{x} = \mu + z\sigma_{\bar{x}} = 15 - 1.645(0.0636) = 14.90$.

- Third, the acceptance criterion is set as $\bar{x} \geq 14.90$.

If we go back to the second step, we notice that the z value is negative because we are interested in the left side of the normal distribution curve shown as Figure 4.6. This shows that there is only 5% chance of rejecting a lot with a mean weight of 15 oz or more. As we discussed in the case of measurement by attributes, we are also concerned about the consumer's risk or what we have referred to as β. From the acceptance criterion it is clear that any sample mean that is observed to be less than the critical value c will lead to a rejection of the lot. Management may be interested in knowing the probability that a sample mean taken from the lot will be greater than or equal to the acceptance criterion thus leading to erroneously accepting the lot. This can be expressed in a probability form as $P(\bar{x} \geq c)$ and can be computed by finding the z value and looking it up in the normal distribution table to find the probability. This is shown using Figure 4.7.

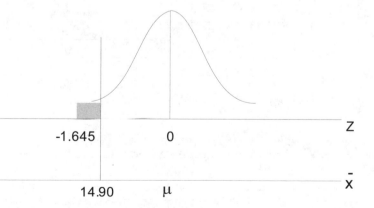

Figure 4.6: Probability under the left side of the normal curve.

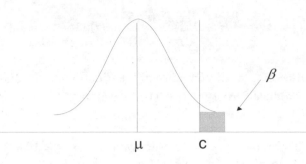

Figure 4.7: Probability under the right side of the normal curve.

This probability is the consumer's risk. Simply, the OC curve in this case will give the probability of accepting lots with different true means μ given the acceptance criterion that has been established for the problem. Table 4.3 shows the probabilities of accepting the lots with different true means.

Lot mean (μ)	z	Probability of acceptance
14.70	3.14	0.0000
14.75	2.34	0.0096
14.80	1.57	0.0582
14.85	0.77	0.2206
14.90	0.00	0.5000
14.95	-0.79	0.7852
15.00	-1.57	0.9418
15.05	-2.34	0.9904
15.10	-3.14	1.0000
15.15	-3.93	1.0000

Table 4.3: Probabilities of acceptance for measurement by variables

These probabilities are used to construct the OC curve shown in Figure 4.8. We express the z in general form for these cases as

$$z = \frac{14.9 - \mu}{0.0636}$$

AVERAGE OUTGOING QUALITY

In the acceptance sampling for attributes, we are confronted with the decisions to either accept or reject a lot based on sample information. For example, with a sampling plan of *(n* = 15, c 1), a lot is accepted if there are at most one defect in the sample. Otherwise, the lot is rejected. When we accept a lot, we base our judgment on the sample we have inspected. However, it is possible that the *(N — n)* items that have not been inspected may contain some defects. Obviously, if a defect or defects are found in the sample taken from the lot, the defects are either reworked or replaced with items that meet the quality standards. When a lot is rejected based on the sample information, the entire lot undergoes 100% inspection and all non-conforming items are replaced. By replacing defective items so they can conform to our quality standards, we are on the average improving the quality of the items in the lot. Thus before the lot is shipped out, its quality level is enhanced through this procedure. The quality of the lot after this has been accomplished is known as the average outgoing quality (AOQ). There are in fact, two scenarios that are involved in using the AOQ. These scenarios are:

- AOQ includes all the accepted lots with non-conforming items in the sample replaced or reworked.
- AOQ includes all the rejected lots that have undergone 100% inspection and all the non-conforming items replaced or worked.

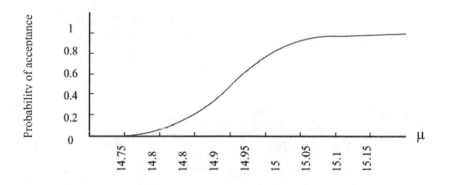

Figure 4.8: OC Curve for measurement by variables

Notice that AOQ cannot guarantee zero defects because even if in the second scenario we may be able to attain a zero defect goal, the first scenario contains *(N — n)* items that were not inspected. Consider a situation where there are 5% defects in the incoming lot and the probability of accepting the lot is 95%. What is the average outgoing quality? Suppose we refer to P_a as the probability of accepting a lot and P_d as the probability of defect in an incoming lot or the proportion of nonconforming items in an incoming lot. Then, the first scenario will lead to $P_a P_d$, which represents the acceptance of a lot with a proportion of nonconforming items, and the second scenario will lead to $(1 — P_a)(0)$ which is the rejection of a lot and subsequent rectification to remove all defects. Thus, we can express the average outgoing quality (AOQ) as follows:

$$AOQ = P_a P_d = (0.95)(0.05) + (0.05)(0) \; 0.0475$$

Thus, the AOQ is 4.75%. Notice that due to the procedure taken to rectify potential defects, we have managed to reduce the original proportion of defects in the lot from 5% to 4.75%. You can also observe that if the probability of accepting a lot is lower, then more of the lots will be rejected and will have to undergo 100% inspection. As a result, the AOQ is lower. For example, suppose that the probability of accepting a lot is 85%, then $AOQ = (0.85)(0.05) + (0.15)(0) = 0.0425$. Thus, the AOQ has improved from 5% to 4.25%.

Average outgoing quality limit

Suppose we revisit the acceptance sampling plan we developed for the case where *(n = 15, c = 1)*; we can find the AOQ for the different probabilities of defective items as shown in Table 4.4 below.

% Defective	(n = 15, c = 1) Probability of acceptance	Average Outgoing Quality (AOQ)
1	0.9904	0.0099
2	0.9647	0.0193
3	0.9271	0.0278
4	0.8809	0.0352
5	0.8291	0.0415
10	0.5491	0.0549
15	0.3186	0.0478
20	0.1671	0.0334
25	0.0802	0.0201
30	0.0352	0.0106

Table 4.4: Average outgoing quality for (n = 15, c = 1)

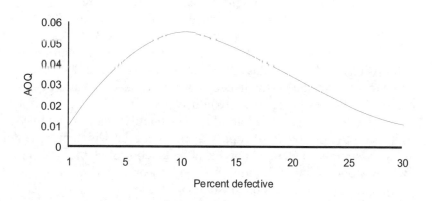

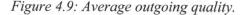

Figure 4.9: Average outgoing quality.

Figure 4.9 shows the plot of the average outgoing quality over the proportion of defects in incoming lots. This figure is concave and it shows that the AOQ reached its peak when the proportion of defects in the incoming lot is 10% and then it gradually drops to zero. This point is known as the average outgoing quality limit (AOQL) and it is equal to 0.0549. This shows that the maximum average outgoing quality that will be achieved in the long run cannot exceed 0.0549.

In computing the AOQ, we assumed that the sample (n) is small relative to *N (N ≥ 50n)*. When this is not the case, AOQ can be computed as

$$AOQ = P_a P_d - \frac{n}{N} \qquad (4.5)$$

STATISTICAL PROCESS CONTROL

Statistical process control (SPC) is a statistical procedure that uses graphical displays or rather, control charts to detect shift in the process from design specifications. SPC is widely used for work in progress or work in process and when shifts from design specifications are identified, actions are taken quickly to remedy the problem. Possible corrective actions that bring the process back to conformance may include improving operators' training, changing suppliers, replacing or oiling worn parts in machinery, retooling. The aim of SPC is to improve the entire production process. The use of SPC is based on the assumption that variation is present in any process. This concept was introduced in the 1920s by Dr Walter Shewhart at Bell Laboratories. Dr Shewhart identified two causes of variation in a process namely common (natural) and special (assign-able) causes of variations. The common or natural causes of variations are attributed to chance occurrences and may not be easily controlled. For example, the strength of material may be influenced by temperature, pressure or humidity. The quality of a product may be influenced by the source of supply of raw material which an operator at the assembly line may not be able to control. Other examples include poor lighting conditions, poor work environment, poor process design, etc. Although some of these are controllable, the operator does not have the authority to control them. Top management has this authority. The operator works with the tool and the environment he/she is presented with which may affect the quality of the work. Conversely, special and assignable causes of variation are controllable by the operator. Such may include developing the skills to do the job, obtaining the required training, identifying and correcting operator's error, removing a defective item from the production line. These are actions that the operator can take to improve work performance. Clearly, when common causes of variation arise, top management intervention is often needed to correct the problem. For example, it is top management who has to make a decision to replace a supplier that consistently supplies poor quality items. It is top management who has to make a decision to replace procedures that generate waste; and top management has to provide a conducive environment for productive work. The operator lacks the authority to make such critical decisions.

Statistical process control is used to identify only assignable causes of variation so that operators can take corrective actions. When the only type of variation in a process is common cause of variation, the process is said to be stable. When the process is stable, then it is operating as expected. That process is also said to be predictable because its future performance can be assessed and it will be able to meet customers' expectations. A stable process is operating within statistical control and statistical control charts are used to detect when the process is out of control.

Control Charts

Control charts are graphical displays that are used to detect shifts from design specifications due to special or assignable causes of variation. When such shifts are detected, operators take corrective actions to bring the process within conformance. Figure 4.10 is a typical example of a control chart.

There are three horizontal lines to denote the lower control limit (LCL), the centerline which is normally the process mean and the upper control limit (UCL). Measurements are then taken from the process and its points are plotted as shown with the dots. Points falling within the LCL and the UCL may indicate conformance with design specification. Points outside may indicate the need for corrective action to bring the process to conformance.

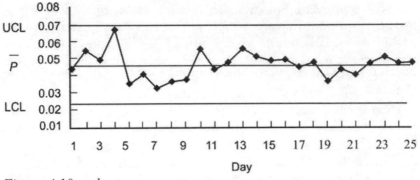

Figure 4.10 p-chart

The construction of the LCL and UCL is based on statistical principles. An assumption is made that the natural variability observed in a process can be described by the normal probability distribution. It is therefore important to maintain a high probability that samples taken from the process will fall within the control limits. The standard practice is to establish control limits with ±3 standard deviations of the mean. This indicates that 99.7% of the process output is expected to fall within the control limits while 0.3% of the process output is expected to fall outside the control limit when the process is stable. We shall present two different types of control charts to deal with measurement by attributes and measurement by variables.

STATISTICAL PROCESS CONTROL CHARTS FOR ATTRIBUTES

We shall discuss four popular control charts for attributes namely the p-chart, c-chart, np-chart and u-chart.

p-chart

The p-chart is useful when the interest is on the proportion or fraction of non-conforming items. There may be an interest for example, in the proportion of errors in a page of a book, the proportion of defects in a sample and so on. We define the proportion (p) as follows:

$$\overline{p} = \frac{Total\ number\ of\ non-conformig\ items}{total\ number\ of\ items\ inpected} \qquad (4.6)$$

which is also the centerline. The limits are established as follows:

Upper control limit for,

$$p = \overline{p} + 3\sqrt{\overline{p}(1-\overline{p})/n} \qquad (4.7)$$

Lower control limit for,

$$p = \overline{p} - 3\sqrt{\overline{p}(1-\overline{p})/n} \qquad (4.8)$$

We shall illustrate with an example.

For a period of 25 days, Avion Electronics has obtained information on the fraction of defective microcomputer chips that it manufactures. Use this information to construct a p-chart and interpret the chart. The data is presented in Table 4.5.

The upper and lower control limits for p are therefore obtained as:

$$\overline{p} \pm 3\sqrt{\frac{\overline{p}(1-\overline{p})}{\overline{n}}} = 0.046 \pm 3\sqrt{\frac{0.046-(1-0.046)}{766.12}} = 0.046 \pm 0.0227 \qquad (4.9)$$

The control limits are therefore, 0.0233 for the LCL and 0.0687 for the UCL. From Figure 4.10, we observe that the process is stable since all the observations seem to fall within the control limit. In computing the control limits, it is possible to compute a LCL that is less than zero or negative. When that happens, the LCL should be set equal to zero. Notice also that the average sample size of 766.12 was used here. If the sample size taken each day is the same, then we can simply use that value of n since the average will be the same. When a point falls outside the control limit, we try to identify the causes of the problem and such causes are corrected to bring the process to conformance.

Day Number	Number of chips inspected	Number of non-conforming chips	Proportion of non-conforming chips (p)
1	800	35	0.044
2	746	40	0.054
3	775	38	0.049
4	825	55	0.067
5	720	25	0.035
6	745	30	0.040
7	680	22	0.032
8	700	25	0.036
9	750	28	0.037
10	820	45	0.055
11	790	34	0.043
12	760	36	0.047
13	695	38	0.055
14	780	40	0.051
15	765	37	0.048
16	810	40	0.049
17	795	35	0.044
18	805	38	0.047
19	810	29	0.036
20	738	32	0.043
21	745	30	0.040
22	776	36	0.046
23	805	40	0.050
24	798	37	0.046
25	720	34	0.047
Totals	19153	879	
Averages	766.12	35.12	0.046

Table 4.5 Proportion of non-conforming chips made by Avion Electronics

np-chart

We shall extend this example to consider an *np*-chart. This chart deals with the number of non-conforming items in a subgroup. You may recall from your knowledge of probabilities that *np* is the mean of the binomial distribution. The use of *np*-chart is similar to that of a p-chart except that here the size of the sample inspected for each subgroup must be the same. Using the problem above for the p-chart, we note that the mean or expected number of defectives is 35.12. That is equivalent to np since after all np is a mean value. We can therefore express the control limits for the np-chart as follows:

$$\text{Centerline} = n\overline{p} = 35.12$$
$$\text{UCL and LCL} = n\overline{p} \pm 3\sqrt{n\overline{p}(1-\overline{p})} \qquad (4.10)$$
$$= 35.12 \pm 3\sqrt{35.12(1-0.046)}$$
$$= 35.12 \pm 17.36$$

Thus, the lower control limit is 17.76 and the upper control limit is 52.48. The np control chart is similar to the p-chart and the same out-of-control points will be found. Our problem did not perfectly fit into the use of np-chart since the sample sizes for the subgroups vary. However, these variations are small so the np-chart offers a reasonable approximation and is adequate here for illustration purposes. Since the outcomes of the p-chart and the np-charts are similar, we therefore do not intend to repeat a similar control chart diagram. However, we should mention that the vertical line (i.e. y axis) in the chart will assume the np values for the centerline and the control limits rather than the p values used for the p-chart. We shall now look at the u-chart.

u-chart

The u-chart is useful when the interest is on the number of defects or the number of non-conformities over a given area of interest. For example, we may be interested in the number of potholes in different areas of a highway. Alternatively, we may be interested in the number of accidents observed in different spans of a road or the number of errors observed in different sizes of a paper. The key here is that the areas of interest may all be different. For example, in the case of the potholes observed in a given highway, the sections of the highway inspected for potholes may have different dimensions and therefore, different areas. If the number of nonconformities observed is denoted as c_i and the area of interest is given as a_i, then the ratio $u_i = c_i / a_i$ is the number of non-conformities per area of interest. It is important that the occurrence of these non-conformities in the different areas of interest is independent. These areas of interest can be viewed as lots that are inspected and the number of non-conformities or defects counted. Consider for example, a long stretch of a highway that is being inspected because of travelers' complaints about the increased number of potholes in the road. The road has been broken down into 25 segments to be examined for potholes. Due to the terrain of the road, it is not possible to break it up into equal segments. Furthermore, the occurrences of these potholes are independent. Table 4.6 shows the number of potholes observed for the different segments of the road.

We can now compute the average number of potholes per 1000 square feet which is also the centerline as

$$\bar{u} = \frac{\sum c_i}{\sum a_i} = \frac{\sum u_i}{n} \qquad (4.11)$$

where $i = 1, 2, \ldots, n$. Thus, using the same convention as in both the p and the np-charts, the control limits can be computed as:

$$\text{LCL and UCL} = \bar{u} \pm 3\sqrt{\frac{\bar{u}}{a_i}} \qquad (4.12)$$

Inspection lot i	Area of interest (in 1000 square feet) (a_i)	Number of potholes in lot (c_i)	Defects per 1000 square feet (u_i)
1	2.5	2	0.80
2	1.7	5	0.59
3	1.0	1	1.00
4	2.0	2	1.00
5	0.8	2	2.50
6	2.8	8	2.86
7	1.75	12	6.86
8	1.5	10	6.67
9	2.1	6	2.86
10	2.4	8	3.33
11	2.2	8	3.64
12	1.6	5	3.13
13	1.8	7	3.89
14	1.9	3	1.58
15	1.4	2	1.43
16	0.9	0	0
17	1.1	0	0
18	0.75	1	1.33
19	0.67	4	5.97
20	1.10	3	2.73
21	2.24	2	0.89
22	1.13	4	3.54
23	2.46	2	0.81
24	0.78	3	3.85
25	0.96	2	2.08
Total	$\sum a_i = 39.40$	$\sum c_i = 102$	

Table 4.6: Number of potholes per 1000 square feet of a road

If the lower control limit is observed to be negative, its value should be set to zero. Notice that the control limits will be different for each lot so the control limits must be computed for each of the 25 subgroups we are considering. We can now calculate the centerline

$\bar{u} = (102/39.4) = 2.59$ and the control limits for each case as shown in Table 4.7.

Inspection lot i	Area of interest (in 1000 square feet) a_i	LCL	UCL
1	2.5	0	5.64
2	1.7	0	6.29
3	1.0	0	7.42
4	2.0	0	6.00
5	0.8	0	7.99
6	2.8	0	5.48
7	1.75	0	6.24
8	1.5	0	6.53
9	2.1	0	5.92
10	2.4	0	5.71
11	2.2	0	5.85
12	1.6	0	6.41
13	1.8	0	6.19
14	1.9	0	6.09
15	1.4	0	6.67
16	0.9	0	7.68
17	1.1	0	7.19
18	0.75	0	8.16
19	0.67	0	8.49
20	1.10	0	7.19
21	2.24	0	5.82
22	1.13	0	7.13
23	2.46	0	5.67
24	0.78	0	8.06
25	0.96	0	7.52

Table 4.7: Control limits for the number of potholes per 1000 square feet of a road

Figure 4.11 shows the u control chart for this problem. Notice that when the LCL is negative, its value is set to zero. From this figure, we observe that Lots 7 and 8 are out of the control limits so there may be presence of assignable or special causes. The sources of such variation should be identified, evaluated and eliminated from the process if necessary.

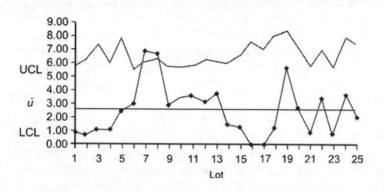

Figure 4.11: u-chart

As we have seen, the u-chart has variable control limits. The computational effort can become tedious and the process itself can be confusing especially when done manually. It requires the collection of large amounts of data and yet future control limits cannot be predicted from the past even when the process may appear to be stable. As a result, it is incapable of tracing out-of-control points on time. In fact, these out-of-control points become apparent after they have occurred. This makes it costly to implement corrective actions on time. One of the ways to deal with some of these problems is to calculate approximate control limits. This assumption will be reasonable provided that the areas of interest do not vary by more than ± 25%. Thus using that assumption, we can approximate the control limits for the u-chart as:

$$LCL \text{ and } UCL = \bar{u} \pm 3\sqrt{\frac{\bar{u}}{a}} = 2.59 \pm 3\sqrt{\frac{2.59}{1.56}}$$

$$= 2.59 \pm 3.87 \text{ where } \bar{a} = \frac{\sum a_i}{n}$$

(4.13)

This calculation gives the LCL as -1.28 and the UCL as 6.46. Because the LCL is less than zero, it is set to equal zero. Once these limits are found, they are used like the regular control charts with constant limits. If any points fall out of the control limits, such points should be further investigated to take corrective actions. On the other hand, if the points fall within the control limits, then the process is stable. However, when points fall too close to the control limits, their actual UCL and LCL should be compared to observe any possible presence of assignable causes. Figure 4.11 shows the u-chart for the pothole problem assuming constant limits. Notice also that there are points outside the control limits. There is therefore a need to take corrective actions.

c-chart

The c-chart is equivalent to the u-chart. With the u-chart, we noted that the areas of interest may vary and as such, the computation of the control limits is tedious. When we use the c-chart, we assume a constant area of interest for each lot considered. For example, we have a constant number of defects per area of interest. We can therefore express the centerline as a constant rate and use it to construct the control limits. For example, we can find the number of potholes per 1000 square feet and that will serve as the centerline. Thus, if the centerline is defined as 5, then the control limits can be expressed as follows:

$$LCL = \bar{c} \pm 3\sqrt{\bar{c}} \qquad (4.14)$$

We shall illustrate this with an example. Using our example for the number of potholes in 1000 square feet of a road, if the lot size is a constant rather than a variable as in the previous illustrations, we can express the u-chart as follows:

$$LCL \text{ and } UCL = \bar{u} \pm 3\sqrt{\frac{\bar{u}}{n}} \qquad (4.15)$$

where n is a constant sample size taken from each lot. Notice that if n = 1, the u-chart becomes exactly the same as the c-chart. Suppose we consider a different kind of example. For a period of 20 days, record has been kept on the number of accidents in a ten-mile stretch of a popular highway. The record reveals the information presented in Table 4.8. Construct a c-chart for this problem.

Day number	Number of accidents
1	2
2	0
3	1
4	4
5	0
6	2
7	1
8	4
9	6
10	2
11	3
12	2
13	0
14	0
15	1
16	0
17	0
18	1
19	2
20	5
Total	36

Table 4.8 Daily number of accidents

Thus, c = (36/20) = 1.8 accidents/day and the control limits are determined using the formula as 1.8 ± 4.02 where the LCL is -2.22 and the UCL is 5.82. Since the LCL is less than zero, it is again set equal to zero. Notice from Figure 4.12 that on day 9, there were six accidents and it is outside the control limit. We need to find an explanation for this unusually high accident rate. We shall now shift our focus to designing control charts for measurement by variables.

STATISTICAL PROCESS CONTROL CHARTS FOR VARIABLES

We shall look at two types of control charts here. One deals with control charts for individual observations and the other deals with control charts when the mean and standard deviation of the process are known or can be estimated using samples.

Average charts (X and R)

These are control charts that are based on the sample means and ranges of the subgroups to detect process precision and accuracy. The sample mean is used to measure accuracy to the process's location while the range measures the precision or process variability. The range rather than the standard deviation is used to measure the process variability because of its ease of use and ability to provide timely information in the field. The subgroup sizes are normally less than five. However, if it arises that the subgroup size is large *(n > 10)*, the standard deviation rather than the range should be used for computing the 3σ control limits.

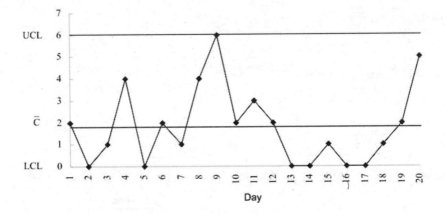

Figure 4.12: c-chart

The centerline is the grand mean of subgroup's sample means. Thus we can compute the limits as:

$$LCL \text{ and } UCL \text{ for } \overline{X} = \overline{\overline{X}} \pm A_2 \overline{R} \qquad (4.16)$$

and for the range chart, we obtain the following.

$$UCL \text{ for } R = D_4 \overline{R}$$
$$LCL \text{ for } R = D_3 \overline{R}$$

When $n > 10$ for the subgroups, the control limits are computed using the standard deviation as follows:

$$LCL \ and \ UCL \ for \ \overline{X} = \overline{X} \pm A_1 \overline{s} \qquad (4.17)$$

The control limits for the s chart rather than the R chart are then computed as follows:

$$UCL \ for \ s = B_4 \overline{s}$$
$$UCL \ for \ s = B_3 \overline{s}$$

An example is presented here only for the ($\overline{X}$ and R) charts.

The procedure to construct the ($\overline{X}$ and R) charts is as follows:

- Compute the sample means of each subgroup;
- Compute the range of each subgroup;
- Compute the mean of all the subgroups. That mean is the grand mean and it is the centerline for the $\overline{X}$ chart;
- Compute the mean of all the subgroups range. That overall mean is the centerline for the R chart;
- Compute the control limits for R and plot them with the centerline;
- Plot the subgroup's individual R values on the same chart with the centerline and the control limits;
- If no out-of-control points are present in the R chart, then process precision is stable. Otherwise, identify the reasons for variation and take corrective actions;
- When process precision is stable, construct the $\overline{X}$ chart using the centerline and control limits found above;
- Plot the subgroup's respective means on the $\overline{X}$ chart and check if the process is stable or whether corrective action should be taken.

Tables for B_3, B_4, D_3, D_4, E_2 and the normal distribution are presented in the appendix.

We shall discuss further how to interpret control charts. The information presented on that topic should be used in deciding whether a process is stable or operating in an out-of-control state. But first, we shall present an example. The $\overline{X}$ chart and R chart are based on the 3σ control limits. Using the models presented above, we shall now present an example.

Tropical Blend is a major manufacturer of 12 oz bottles of coffee. It maintains a 24-hour operation. However, only 20 hours are used for production since the machinery has to undergo extensive maintenance operation to continue supporting its heavy manufacturing load. Tropical Blend assures its customers high quality and has decided that it must effectively control the weight of coffee in each bottle so that it is not significantly lesser or higher than the targeted 12 oz weight. It therefore decides that every hour, a sample of four bottles should be taken from the process and inspected to see if the target is being reasonably satisfied. Table 4.9 presents the 20 samples collected for each of the 20 hours that the process is in production. Using this information, construct the $\overline{X}$ chart and R chart.

Using the models for the ($\overline{X}$ and R) charts we calculate the control limits as follows:

$$UCL \text{ for } R = D_4 \overline{R} = 2.28 \ (0.05) = 0.0114$$
$$LCL \text{ for } R = D_3 \overline{R} = 0(0.05) = 0$$

From the plot of the R chart shown as Figure 4.13, we observe that all of the ranges for the 20 subgroups fall within the control limits. Therefore, the process precision is stable. We now need to evaluate the process accuracy in targeting the 12 oz weight by constructing the X chart. This we obtain as:

$$LCL \ \text{ and } \ UCL \ \text{ for } \ X = X \pm A_2 R = 12 \pm 0.73(0.05)$$

Thus, the LCL is 11.96 and the UCL is 12.04. Figure 4.14 shows the control chart for this problem. As shown in this figure, all the subgroup means fall within the control limit. So, the process is stable.

Sample number	1	2	3	4	Average $\overline{X}$	Range R
1	11.97	12.01	11.98	12.00	11.99	0.04
2	12.02	12.03	11.99	12.01	12.01	0.04
3	11.99	11.98	12.02	12.01	12.00	0.04
4	12.02	12.01	11.99	11.97	12.00	0.05
5	12.01	12.00	12.00	11.98	12.00	0.03
6	11.97	11.98	12.02	12.00	11.99	0.05
7	12.01	12.00	12.01	11.96	12.00	0.05
8	11.98	12.03	11.97	11.98	11.99	0.06
9	12.00	12.00	12.02	12.00	12.01	0.02
10	12.01	12.03	11.98	11.97	12.00	0.06
11	12.02	12.00	12.01	12.00	12.01	0.02
12	11.96	12.01	12.02	11.98	11.99	0.06
13	12.03	12.00	12.00	11.96	12.00	0.07
14	11.97	11.98	12.00	12.01	11.99	0.04
15	12.02	11.96	11.99	11.98	11.99	0.06
16	12.00	12.01	12.04	11.94	12.00	0.10
17	12.02	12.03	12.05	11.96	12.02	0.09
18	12.03	12.04	11.97	11.95	12.00	0.09
19	12.01	11.98	11.97	11.98	11.99	0.04
20	12.02	12.04	11.96	12.01	12.01	0.08
Average					12.00	0.05

Table 4.9 Samples of 12 oz bottles of coffee for Tropic Blend

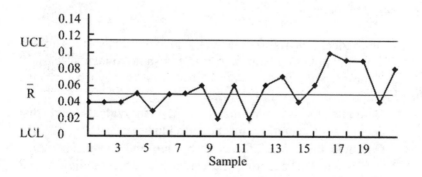

Figure 4.13: R - chart

Individuals charts for X and Range R

Individuals control charts for X and range *R* involves taking only one observation per lot or batch for inspection and then plotting the individual points over the control limits created using the sample mean and range of all the observations. These control charts are useful in instances where inspection may be destructive to the product as in the case of bombs; where inspection cost is very high it may not be possible to inspect several products; or where a relatively long interval of time must elapse before a product becomes available for inspection. Due to the sampling of single observations for inspection rather than the use of averages, individual charts are not as sensitive as the $\overline{X}$ chart. The control limits for individuals charts can be compared directly to tolerance limits.

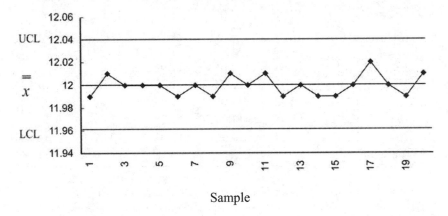

Figure 4.14: x-chart

The individuals charts assume that the individuals are sampled from a normal population. However, it is advisable to take at least 30 individual observations in subgroups of at least two when possible. The procedure is developed as follows:
- Compute the sample mean of the individuals and that becomes the centerline for the individuals X chart;
- Compute the range of each subgroup and the mean of the ranges and that becomes the centerline for the individuals *R* chart;
- Compute the 3σ control limits using the models presented below;

- Compute the 2σ control limits as two-thirds of the 3u band using the models presented below.

Note that this step is done since the individuals chart is not sensitive. As a result, 2σ control limits are commonly used. The models are therefore, presented as follows:

$$LCL \text{ and } UCL \text{ for } X = \overline{X} \pm E_2 \overline{R}$$

$$UCL \text{ for } R = D_4 \overline{R}$$

$$LCL \text{ for } R = D_3 \overline{R}$$

Applying the 2σ control limits, we modify the control limits as follows:

$$LCL \text{ and } UCL \text{ for } X = \overline{X} \pm 2/3 \; E_2 \overline{R}$$

The values of E_2 and D factors are obtained from the Appendix for the different subgroups of size n.

We shall now present an example and a control chart for this case. Consider a manufacturing process where batches of items arrive every eight hours and only one item is inspected from the batch. This facility operates on a 24-hour schedule thus three batches are received on a given day. For a period of 12 days, 36 batches are received and the measurement of interest is the weight of the item expressed in pounds. Construct an individual chart for this problem.

Subgroup	X1	X2	X3	Range
1	120	121	119.6	1.4
2	127.8	126	132	6
3	128	125.9	132	6.1
4	127	127.9	133.1	6.1
5	121	119.8	124	4.2
6	128	125	125	3
7	127.8	130	130.5	2.7
8	129	32.8	133	4
9	128.9	130	131.2	2.3
10	132	135	136	4
11	133	134.5	136	3
12	138	136	137	2
Totals			4646.8	44.8
Average			129.08	3.73

Table 4.10: Subgroup information for individuals chart

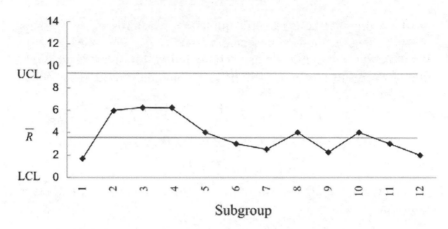

Figure 4.15: Individual R-chart

In plotting the control charts, we should always start with the R chart. If the R chart is out-of-control, then the X chart will also be out-of-control and there will be no need for the computation until the source of variation in the R chart can be explained. Thus, using the models presented above, we compute the R chart as:

$$\text{UCL for } R = D_4\overline{R} = 2.57\ (3.73) = 9.59$$
$$\text{LCL for R} = D_3R = 0$$

From Figure 4.15, we notice that the R chart appears to show a stable process. Thus we proceed to compute the control limits for X.

$$\text{LCL and UCL for X} = \overline{X} \pm E_2\overline{R}$$
$$= 129.08 \pm 1.772\ (9.59) = 129.08 \pm 16.99$$

We observe a LCL of 112.09 and an upper control limit of 146.07. However, as we mentioned above, we prefer to use the 2u control limits. Thus, the lower and upper control limits are computed as LCL and UCL for

$$X = \overline{X} \pm 2/3\ E_2\overline{R} = 129.08 \pm (0.667)\ (16.99) = 129.08 \pm 11.33$$

Thus, the lower and upper control limits are 117.75 and 140.41 respectively. Figure 4.16 shows the control chart for the X chart. Clearly, all the individual observations fall within the control limits. Therefore, the process is stable or operating under statistical control.

INTERPRETATION OF CONTROL CHARTS

We have shown that when a process is stable, the sample points will tend to fall within the control limits. However, when the process is unstable or out-of-control, the sample points will fall outside the control limits. When a process is observed to be out-of-control, corrective action must be taken to bring the process to conformance. There are several explanations for out-of-control points. Some explanations may deal with errors relating to the performance on the job such as malfunctioning processes, wrong reading of measurement instruments, operator's error, or even errors in computing and plotting the control limits. So, before a determination is made on the cause of the error, we must carefully evaluate our calculations. When the source of error is unexplainable, it is possible that the process mean has shifted and the current control limits are no longer adequate for tracking process variability. New control charts will then be plotted with new control limits.

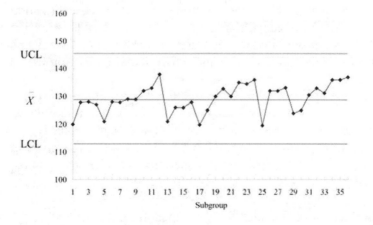

Figure 4.16: Individual $\overline{X}$ -chart

Sometimes, a process may appear to be stable when in fact it is unstable. This happens when a control chart tends to show that all the sample points fall within the control limits. Thus, when we observe that all points are within the control limits, we should not rush to conclusions on the stability of the process. We must look for the following indicators of out-of-control process:

1. Are successive sample points below or above the centerline for say six or more samples? This may result when there are problems such as equipment malfunctioning, changes in work schedules or materials or operators. It is important to investigate the source of this variation.

2. Is there evidence of a trend when the sample points are plotted? Such pattern may indicate an out-of-control process even when it appears that the process is stable.

PROCESS CAPABILITY

Through our discussion in this chapter, it has become apparent that variations are inherent in any process. As a result, when a target such as a mean weight of 12 oz is specified, it is often associated with some deviation. For example, Tropical Blend cannot target to achieve 12 oz weight for each bottle of coffee because the risk of being wrong is very high — as much as 50%. It could therefore state for example that bottles of coffee weighing 12 ± 0.03 oz will be acceptable. Thus, any bottle that weighs between 11.97 oz and 12.03 oz will be considered acceptable. This range is however a design specification and may differ from actual observation in practice. This design specification established by the manufacturer is known as the process capability. It simply reflects the range where natural variation of the process will occur.

Our interest however is to determine the proportion of the process output that will fall within this design specification. It is important to know that the design specification is feasible and achievable. If it is set too tight, it becomes unachievable and a lot of waste is created in trying to achieve an unrealistic design specification. We shall use the Tropical Blend problem to illustrate this concept. The steps are as follows:

- Collect reasonable number of samples from the process;
- Calculate the sample mean and sample standard deviation;
- Construct a 99.7% confidence interval which is given as $\overline{X} \pm 3\,s$;

- Use the control limits of the target and assume that the process output is normally distributed with mean and standard deviation equal to that computed from the sample and compute the percentage of process output that will fall within the design specification;
- Make decision on the process capability.

Illustrating with the Tropical Blend problem, we have that $\overline{X} = 12$ oz and s = 0.0241. Thus, the 99.7% confidence interval is 12 $\pm$ 3(0.0241). Thus, the LSL is 11.9278 and the USL is 12.0722 where LSL and USL are lower and upper specification limits respectively. They are also known as lower and upper tolerance limits respectively. The process capability appears to be poor given that the design specification is 12 $\pm$ 0.03 oz. This target is therefore, not being accomplished in practice. Using the normal distribution assumption, we observe that the proportion of process output that meets the design specification is obtained as:

$$z_{USL} = \frac{USL - \overline{\overline{X}}}{\sigma} \quad and \quad z_{LSL} = \frac{LSL - \overline{\overline{X}}}{\sigma} \tag{4.18}$$

Therefore,

$$z_{USL} = \frac{12.03 - 12}{0.0241} = 1.25 \tag{4.19}$$

$$z_{USL} = \frac{12.03 - 12}{0.0241} = 1.25 \tag{4.20}$$

Thus, *P (-1.25 < z < 1.25)* = 0.788. Thus, only 78.8% of the process output will meet the specified target and 21.20% will be off target. Figure 4.17 is used to show this probability information.

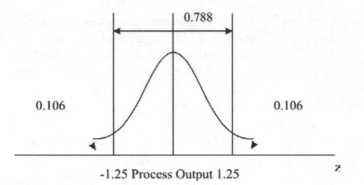

Figure 4.17: Process output

Notice that since we are establishing our control limits with the 3σ, if any of these z values is more than 3, then the process will produce almost no nonconforming items. The process capability index can be used to detect the direction of shift in the process mean. It shows the ability of the process to meet acceptable tolerance as specified by design specifications. We shall compute the process capability index C_P as follows:

$$C_P = \min\left[\frac{\overline{\overline{X}} - LSL}{3\sigma} \ or \ \frac{USL - \overline{\overline{X}}}{3\sigma}\right] \qquad (4.21)$$

Let us illustrate how this could be used. We have already assumed that the process mean is 12 oz with a standard deviation of 0.0241. Suppose we assume further that the process mean is exactly at the center of the normal distribution curve thus implying that $Z=0$ as shown in Figure 4.18.

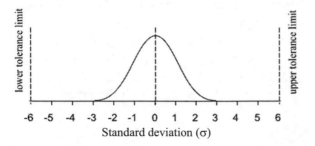

Figure 4.18: Process capability

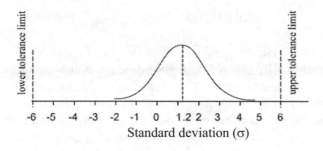

Figure 4.19: Process capability with a shift in the process mean

Since the mean is at the center, we obtain the process capability as min [0.41, 0.41] = 0.41. Notice that these two values are the same since the process mean occurs at the center. Suppose now that there is a shift in the mean to $+1.2\sigma$, then the process mean becomes 12 + 1.2 (.0241) = 12.02892. The new process capability is computed as

$$C_P = \min\left[\frac{12.0282 - 11.97}{3(0.0241)} \quad or \quad \frac{12.03 - 12.0282}{3(0.0241)}\right] \quad (4.22)$$

$$= \min\left[0.81, 0.02\right] = 0.02$$

This shows that the new process average is 0.81 standard deviations above the lower specification limit and 0.02 standard deviations below the upper specification limits. Thus there is a higher likelihood of producing 12 oz bottles of coffee that conform to the weight standards. As we see from Figure 4.19, this shift in the process has resulted in a slight movement of the process mean to the right as the mean shifts by 0.02 standard deviations so a slight number of the process output may be found to fall above the upper specification limit.

Although we showed how to compute process capability index of measurement by variable, this concept is also applicable to measurement by attributes.

CONCLUSION

In this chapter, we have managed to introduce the fundamental concepts of statistical quality control. Our discussion was broken up into two major components: acceptance sampling and statistical process control. We noted that acceptance sampling is more applicable in inspecting incoming and outgoing products while statistical process control is useful for work in progress. In both cases, we classified the type of measurement, as measurement by variable and measurement by attributes. We have demonstrated by examples and provided procedures for applying these measurements in studying quality management problems. Statistical quality control is a major part of total quality management. Without knowledge of it, it will be almost impossible to effectively manage quality.

REFERENCES

1. Anderson, DR., Sweeney, D.J. and Williams, T.A. (1993) *Statistics for Business and Economics,* 5th ed., West Publishing Company, St Paul, MN.
2. Chase, RB. and Aquilano, N.J. (1995) *Production and Operations Management Manufacturing and Services,* 7th ed., Irwin, Chicago, IL.
3. Gitlow, H., Oppenheim, A. and Oppenheim, R. (1995) *Quality Management Tools and Methods for Improvement,* 2nd ed., Irwin, Burr Ridge, IL.
4. Shainin, D. and Shainin, RD. (1988) 'Statistical Process Control,' in *Juran's Quality Control Handbook* (ed. J.M. Juran and F.M. Gryna), 4th ed., McGraw-Hill Book Company, New York, NY.

CHAPTER 5

MANAGING QUALITY IN THE NEW ECONOMY

Much of today's businesses are conducted through the Internet. Such businesses are now commonly referred to as *e*Business or *e*Commerce when they involve online purchasing. Online businesses are generally classified as business-to-business (B2B) or business to consumer (B2C) and have been growing since 1998. According to Keenan Vision, online purchase revenue in B2C operations has jumped from $8 billion in 1998 to $45 billion in 2000. It is projected that online purchases in the B2C category will grow to $300 billion by the year 2003. Accordingly, revenues for US *e*Commerce goods have been growing rapidly. Forrester Research notes that revenues from B2C in 1999 were $8 billion and $43 billion for B2B. It is projected that by the year 2003, revenues for B2B will similarly climb to $1.3 trillion.

Unlike physical business operations, eCommerce provides a vast opportunity to businesses and breaks the geographical barriers that traditional businesses faced. Many countries are now trying to unravel the keys to successes in *e*Business since competitive forces are different in a virtual environment. In a recent study, Price Waterhouse Cooper identified some barriers to online purchasing. Such barriers include credit card security, disclosure of personal details, distrust of web retailers, complex order process, time consuming order processes and unfamiliarity with online Web storefronts. In a study published in *Decision Support Systems*, Shaw et al. [1997] noted that research opportunities abound in ecommerce since many of the traditional management principles may no longer apply.

The aim of this chapter is to identify the features or dimensions that customers use to assess the quality of a virtual service or operation. It will focus on identifying those characteristics that are perceived by customers as a necessity in achieving customer satisfaction in a virtual operation.

Introduction

In quality management, the focus is traditionally divided between product and service. With product, a physical item is involved such as goods and the features of quality are easily identifiable. With service, a human element is usually involved and the mode of interaction between the service provider and the customer influence the perception of quality. When a physical product is involved the notion of quality is objective and standardized. However, when the operation is purely service-oriented, it is more difficult to measure quality since customer's perceptions and expectations may widely differ. With eCommerce, a third dimension, which is virtual operation, is introduced. Virtual operation in this context can be said to involve, neither product nor human interaction. The present chapter will focus on e-Quality. The aim is to identify the features or dimensions that customers use to assess the quality of a virtual service. It will focus on identifying those characteristics that are perceived by customers as a necessity in achieving customer satisfaction in a virtual operation. We shall investigate quality management issues that affect the competitiveness of Web storefronts and their ability to deliver quality products and services to customers. Our goal will be to classify existing literature with the intention of creating dimensions of quality for virtual operations. This chapter will address issues such as the following:

- What features in a website will help increase repeat visitation by customers to the site?
- What factors may influence customers to actually make a purchase and not just browse through the site?
- What factors increase traffic flow to the site?
- What factors increase customer retention? In essence, what features do customers perceive as high quality in evaluating virtual operations?

Our aim in this chapter is to make virtual businesses listen to the "voice of the customer" by understanding the customer perspective and providing services that meet the needs and expectations of the customer. Although traditional businesses may have addressed some of these questions, however, virtual businesses are remarkably different and face stiff competition partly due to the relative ease of starting online business and the gradual shift of many businesses to the online trend as more and more people make Internet usage a daily routine.

This chapter will therefore, make an immense contribution to the literature by specifically addressing a key management problem currently afflicting online businesses by offering guidelines on how to improve the quality of services delivered to customers.

Background

The use of computer systems that rely on packaged software and are protected by network security measures to transact businesses such as buying and selling goods or services over the Internet is referred to as E-commerce. The use of E-commerce for business operations has been on a steady rise since the 1980s due to the advent of the Internet and the efficiencies that accrue from its usage. A new industry of dot-com companies was created as a result and operated their businesses with virtual dependence on the Internet. Even the established brick-and-mortar companies have found that e-commerce could help them become more efficient and save millions of dollars in their operations. Such major companies as IBM, Ford Motors Co. and General Motors have made significant shifts in their business models to create their e-commerce operations. For example, IBM has extended its ecommerce operation to e-procurement—a process of using user-friendly Internet-based purchasing system to process orders and improves administrative functions to buyers and suppliers in order to achieve operational efficiencies and reduce costs. In early 2000, Ford Motor Co. and GM created world's largest e-marketplace as a site where auto companies could buy and sell from their suppliers. Suppliers could also leverage the large manufacturers' buying power for items of their need. The list of successful eBusiness include the online bookstore giant Amazon.com and the auction site eBay. These are just few of the corporations that have embraced ecommerce. Ecommerce operation now spans all industry including banking and healthcare. The question is no longer whether to go the route of ecommerce but how to make it more efficient and create a competitive strategy through ecommerce.

Ecommerce is often referred to as eBusiness and it is generally classified into four types: business-to-business (B2B), business-to-consumer (B2C), consumer-to-consumer (C2C), and consumer-to-business (C2B). B2B refers to online transactions between business organizations as well as governments and nonprofit institutions. B2C refers to electronic business transactions between businesses and individual consumers who are buyers. C2C involves online transactions as in auction sites between consumers. C2B involves individuals selling their product or services online to businesses. According to Forrester Research, the B2B component comprises of 80% of all e-commerce operation and is expected to grow to $1.3 trillion dollars in the United States by the year 2003 (*epaynews.com, downloaded 12/20/00*).

Given the tremendous growth in ecommerce application and the greater dependence by both consumers and businesses on it as a major means for transactions and procurement, it is important to identify factors that could enable ebusinesses to achieve customer satisfaction and competitiveness. This will require understanding customer needs and designing those needs into the virtual services that are offered to customers. In other words, what attributes in an ebusiness will serve as impetus for attracting and retaining customers? This question is critical as more and more companies are transforming their operations to make them suitable for ebusiness operation. These companies are not only faced with the high cost of instituting an enterprise resource planning platform for their supply chain but also, with the fact that new entrants into online market place may significantly cut into their traditional market share and intensify the level of competition. New rules of the game need to be learned and reengineering of procurement and marketing operations may affect the organizational culture thereby threatening the existing organizational structure. To better understand this, we look at the dimensions of quality for both products and services.

Dimensions of Quality

The term "quality" is widely used as a measure of excellence. It is not a new concept and has been used since the beginning of times to measure the quality of products and houses that were built in the ancient times (Madu 1998). Garvin (1991) however, identified key attributes that a product or service must have to be considered of high quality. These attributes referred to as dimensions of quality are:

- Performance—this deals with the primary purpose of the product or service or how well the product or service is achieving its objective.
- Features—this deals with added touches, bells, and whistles or secondary characteristics that the product or service possesses or extra features present in the product or service.

- Reliability—this attribute measures the consistency of performance of the product or service over time.
- Durability—measures the useful life of the product or service.
- Serviceability—deals with the ease of servicing the product when necessary or resolving conflicts and complaints from customers. Many of the issues here deal with service after sales.
- Conformance—deals with how the product or service satisfies customer's expectations.
- Perceived quality—this is often referred to as reputation since it is the perceived reputation of the product or service based on past performance and other intangibles that may influence its perceived quality.
- Aesthetics—this deals with sensory characteristics and outward appearance of the product or service. Characteristics such as feels, looks, sounds, are important.

These dimensions have been very well applied in measuring the quality of products and to a lesser extent in measuring the quality of services. Unlike products, services are intangible and may vary from customer to customer. It is more difficult to standardize services and to use the same yardstick for products to measure the quality of services. The quality of service is more or less in the eye of the beholder. First attempt to measure the quality of services was developed by Berry and Parasuraman (1994). They identified five dimensions for measuring the quality of service. While some of the dimensions identified here are already covered in Garvin's eight dimensions of quality. However, Berry and Parasuraman added new dimensions to cover the human element in service quality. Garvin for example, covered the first three dimensions listed below while the last two are specifically designed for service quality. These dimensions for service quality are:

- Tangibles—deals with the appearance of physical facilities, equipment, personnel and communication materials.
- Reliability—deals with the dependability and accuracy of service.
- Responsiveness—deals with the ability to provide prompt services and support to customers.
- Assurance—deals with the trust and confidence on the service provider based primarily on the knowledge and courtesy of employees.

- Empathy—deals with the provision of caring and individualized attention to customers.

Although the two models presented here by Garvin, and Berry and Parasuraman are the popular ones, there are many other extensions notably by Chase and Stewart (1994) and Pisek (1987). These extensions however, have not dealt with the emerging area of e-commerce and the importance of developing dimensions to measure the quality of virtual operations. Our purpose is to synthesize different research papers on quality and ancillary information on e-commerce to arrive at a set of dimensions that could be used to assess the quality of virtual operations.

Dimensions of *e*-Quality

Our dimensions are based on the review of the literature and identifying both the positive and negative elements that affect the perceptions of customers of virtual operations. Customer is used as a generic term to refer to web users. As will be seen in our dimensions, it is a synthesis of both Garvin and Berry and Parasuraman models although we have added unique dimensions that virtual operations customers are concerned with. Further, even though some of the dimensions bear similar labels, their definitions in a virtual operation may vary. An important article by Abels, White and Hahn (1997) provides some of the definitions that will be adapted to our dimensions. The dimensions for e-quality are:

- Performance—the performance of a virtual operation is based on its ability to offer two key features. These key features as identified by Abels, White and Hahn are Use and Content. The Use feature deals with ease of use of the web site, ability to get an overview of the structure, and ease of navigation. Online users can easily be turned off when the website is not easy to navigate, difficult, and thereby time consuming. Further, it is important that the site is rich in Content. Content deals with a variety of factors including the accuracy of information presented, concise nature of the information, and the timeliness of the information. When the web site is not frequently updated, the information becomes outdated and therefore cannot deliver the expected performance. The information provided has to also have some uniqueness and be presented in a form that is readable and not ambiguous. One thing online users are conscious of is time. It is therefore important to ensure that information is presented in a concise and timely manner.

- Features—what other features are available through the site? Does the site anticipate and provide enough access to the questions that the user may have? Does the site provide the user with links to other sites that may better deal with some issues of interest to the user? These are things that customers often want to know in order to be satisfied with a virtual service operation. Other important features include the search capability of the site and the customer's ability to link to the web site from any search engine. It is also important to design with user control in mind. For example, the use of flash to control users may often be abused and lead to dissatisfied users [Flazoom.com 2000]. Users want to have control and this may be a key issue in establishing their trust of the web site.

- Structure—this deals with how information is presented on the web site. Are the information organized with the appropriate key words or sub-headings that the user can identify with? The structure will also deal with how hyperlinks are used within the pages and whether such links lead to sources of information or to dead ends. This in fact, requires a special skill on presentations and organizations. If the site is not well organized, it becomes difficult to find information that may actually be contained in the site. There will be no repeat users if the user is not able to locate key information. An overview of the entire web site should also be presented in a page so that from the onset, the user knows where to find information.

- Aesthetics—this attribute deals with the appearance of the web site namely its visual attractiveness. It has to do with the color combinations that are used, the type and size of fonts, the animation, the sound effects, the clarity and readability of texts.

- Reliability—How consistent is the performance mentioned above over time? For example, is the web site able to keep up with changes by updating material timely and providing accurate information to the customer? Another issue is the availability of the web site. How often is the website available for usage? The issues of accessibility, speed and ability to quickly download information come into play when measuring the reliability of the web site. Also, how reliable is the site in recording information and customer transactions.

- Storage capability—another major issue in using online services is the storage capability of the site. How easy is it for users to retrieve information when needed? For example, online bank users may want access to download their transaction information for a period of a year. Does the site have the capability to store the information and make it easily available to its customer?
- Serviceability—this deals with how well conflicts and complaints from customers are resolved. The effectiveness of online usage also depends on the user's knowledge and ability to click the right responses. There is bound to be some mistakes with amateur users and that may trigger complaints that may have to be resolved to make them satisfied. How able the web site is in resolving complaints and creating a happy customer will influence customer perception of the site.
- Security and System Integrity—Price Waterhouse Coopers [epaynews.com downloaded 12/20/00] reports that credit card security is a major barrier to online purchasing with 79 percent of their respondents citing it. Likewise, users are worried about providing personal information online since it could potentially get into the wrong hands or be abused. The quality of an online site is intertwined with the site's ability to safeguard and protect information that is provided to it.
- Trust—Trust is closely associated with security and system integrity. Trust affects the willingness of users to disclose personal information or make purchases online. Users are often concerned about dealing with virtual organizations that may not have a physical location where they could be tracked. It is therefore imperative that a virtual operation build trust by being highly reliable and dependable in the manner it responds to customer inquiries and complaints.
- Responsiveness—online stores also have to worry about courtesy. How courteous is the customer service in responding to customer needs through email? And how flexible is it about its policies? Even when usage agreements may be appended in the websites, the customers are not often privileged by time to go through all the fine prints. How will

the store respond to the concern of the customer in terms of order cancellations, refunds, etc?

- Product/Service Differentiation and Customization—What is unique about the services provided by the online website? Online users are primarily looking for convenience. How does the store offer "maximum" convenience to its customers? That may include offering customized products or services i.e., electronic books or publishing. How timely is the delivery of products and services to the user? And what features in this website are not attainable from competitors whether in physical or virtual operations? These are the unique qualities that make the online service standout as a leader to be benchmarked by others.

- Web store policies—How customer-oriented are the web store policies? Are users given comparable policies that are available in major department stores for example? For example, charging excessive restocking fees for returned items, not providing effective warranty programs available in local areas, could dissuade users from online purchases since the cost becomes excessive and may outweigh the value of convenience.

- Reputation—the perception of quality will be affected by past experiences, perception of the website's performance, and other unexplainable intangibles that the customer may perceive. The goal of virtual operations should be to exceed the performance expectations of users and thereby, develop satisfied customers that will repeat their visits to the site and enable the site to survive and continue to provide valuable services to its customer base.

- Assurance—Virtual operations need to ensure that their employees are very knowledgeable about their operation, courteous in their responses, and able to convey trust and confidence to users. Since many virtual operations rarely encourage any direct communication except through email services, they need to provide impeccable service to avoid creating a mass of disenchanted users who have failed to get adequate responses from the online service.

- Empathy—Even though there is no direct human interaction in virtual operations however, certain elements of human contact are involved say through the email communications.

Providing individualized attention to customer concerns and requests rather than a generic auto reply shows empathy. Responses must be cognizant of the needs of the user and show concern and understanding of their needs.

We have identified fifteen dimensions for virtual operations. While this list may appear long, it is again a synthesis of the dimensions that influence product and service quality as well as new factors that affect only virtual operations. It must be mentioned that virtual operations often comprise both the tangible product side, the intangible service side, along with its unique virtual side.

Of all these dimensions, we would like to discuss further the performance and the security dimensions. We have already provided supporting statistics on the role of security and trust on web usage. It is also clear that E-commerce can only thrive as the business model becomes profitable. Creative Group dot.com points out that about $19 billion are lost annually by online retailers due to poor customer experience [Creative Good dot.com, 2000]. Another study by the Boston Consulting Group showed that 48 percent of web users abandoned their transactions due to the web site's poor performance especially in the form of site downloads. This point to the fact that users do not have the patience and the time to deal with poorly designed websites. Further, 45 percent of the users abandoned websites with confusing contents or are difficult to navigate [Lake 2000 and Sovish 2000]. We live in an era of instant gratification and if the web site does not fall in line then the customer is dissatisfied. It is therefore, important to further explore these dimensions.

Web Usability and Performance Issues

A study from Wharton School of Business notes that consumer behavior is the principal determinant of cooperate e-commerce strategy [Knowledge@Wharton, December 6, 2000]. Users often come to a web site with preconceived expectations based on their prior experiences with other platforms [Shubin and Meehan, 1997]. The conflict between these platforms may therefore lead to confusion and unpleasant experiences. Shubin and Meehan note for example that the model of navigation on the Web is different from non-Web applications. Web designers must therefore understand these differences and integrate the user's perspectives and worldviews in their design strategies. They identified six potential problems in web design that must be given serious attention. These are:

1. Basic navigation—it is important to know where you are and where you are going.
2. Offering too many choices—too many choices may not necessarily mean a good thing and could lead to confusion.
3. Separating the browser and application—this relates to problems often caused by the Back button.
4. Lack of context
5. Delays caused by network connections
6. Lack of organization of information.

A popular Internet site defined web usability as "the ability of web users to locate information on site, whether or not they know exactly what they're looking for; to understand what they're reading; and to use interactive features required to take full advantage of the site as designed -- searching for information, downloading software, completing e-commerce transactions." [Web Usability, downloaded August 6, 2001]. This definition is based on the concept of user interface design, which is rooted in understanding the human-computer interaction. This requires a user-centered design approach that is capable of integrating multidisciplinary teams that will continually seek users input and design websites that will lead to enriching experiences. In order to achieve this goal, Cornell University's Common Front Group has identified eight user interface design (UID) concepts [Web Usability, downloaded August 6, 2001]. These concepts are briefly discussed below:

1. Learnability vs usability—the designer needs to be aware of its target audience and the task to be performed in order to make the decision on whether to design for learnability or usability.
2. Metaphors and idioms—while the use of metaphors and idioms may help improve the usability of web sites, however, they do not cure poorly designed websites.
3. Intuitiveness—this is often vague and what is intuitive to one may not be to the other. Clarity should therefore be emphasized.
4. Consistency—there is a need to maintain consistency in the use of text labels and icons. They must be standardized and mean the same thing at all times.
5. Simplicity—obviously, the more tasks the user is required to complete in order to get the job done, the more complex the site becomes and the more disenchanted the user may

become. It is important to simplify tasks and reduce the number of steps required to accomplish a task.

6. Prevention—it is equally important to focus on the user's productivity. Time is of the essence and efforts should be made to keep users away from performing unwanted or inappropriate tasks.
7. Forgiveness—the site must be designed to ensure that users have a way of exiting sites or pages they do not want to be in.
8. Aesthetics—the more the user appreciates the site, the more productive it becomes and the more satisfied it would also be. It is important to design sites that will attract and retain the user's interest. Poorly designed sites will only turn them off and away from visiting again.

In line with these concepts, Morkes and Nielson [1997] in a more scientific research found that people rarely read web pages but rather, scan the pages to find information. They recommend that web pages should therefore, use easily identifiable keywords, meaningful sub-headings, bulleted lists, and one idea per paragraph. In other words, web sites need to be concise, succinct and direct since users do not have the leisure of reading a verbose website. They also found that credibility of the web site was often tied to the writing style or what they refer to as "marketese." Users are more likely to distrust sites that appear exaggerated or tend to over emphasize promotional materials.

It is imperative from these discussions that web designers need to pay attention to the needs of the customers. It is only when their needs are included at the design stage that the performance expectations of users can be met. Performance and usability are tied together and drive all the other dimensions. It is the starting point of getting the user's confidence, trust and support for the web site. It must therefore, be considered seriously.

Privacy and Security

We have discussed the importance of privacy and security of online transactions. Keen [2000] however, identified ten points that should be considered in designing a safe web site that users can trust. We shall briefly outline these points, which could further help to achieve user satisfaction. We have maintained the sub-headings provided by Keen but adapted the discussion to suit our own perceptions of how privacy and security can be achieved through the web sites.

1. Have a privacy policy—the web site must have its privacy policy in simple language that will detail privacy protection for all customers or user interaction and interface with the site. This has to be clear and unambiguous and convey trust in the system.

2. Don't ask for too much—users want privacy and are reluctant to relinquish personal information. Soliciting too much personal information becomes intrusive and may turn off potential users. Big brother need not know everything all the time.

3. The Customer's perspective—in this relationship, the customers' safety needs to be assured and they must be protected by the legal structure and policies that are developed. Contradictory policies may affect their trust in the system.

4. Security technologies—it is important to clearly state the security technologies that are in use and how such could help protect the user's privacy and security of information even if it may not offer a one hundred percent guarantee. It however, shows a genuine interest to work and protect the interests of the user.

5. Privacy organizations—Web sites should affiliate or associate with trusted and responsible organizations such as TrustE, BBBOnLine (Better Business Bureau), CPA Web Trust and other industry-based groups that certify and recognize sites for their performance.

6. Let users opt out—users should be given the option on whether their personal information can be shared with others. However, the problems with opting out of sharing information such as loss of convenience, service and customized service should be made known to them.

7. Stay away from deceptive practices—customers or users should not be coerced or deceived into services they probably would not have selected. Such act will affect customer's trust and confidence in the business.

8. Between privacy and security—the site must have policies to deal with breaches of privacy and security. Often times, such breaches may occur outside the web site and through third parties that may have access control to the information

provided on the web site. There must be clearly outlined procedures, rules and legal protections for information use. Procedures to deal with situations where this is undermined should be well established.

9. Not as simple as a firewall—there is a growing emphasis on the use of firewalls for protecting unwarranted access to information. Firewalls however, can still be breached. It is important to evaluate the system of providing the firewalls to ensure that adequate protection can be attained.

10. Look on the bright side—protecting one's privacy requires that the user take some precaution and use common sense to know when informed consent is provided. Users should be educated on how to take part in protecting their confidential records and how to participate in ensuring that the system works.

These points are some of the important issues that must be integrated in designing web sites so they meet the privacy and security needs of the user.

Disaster Recovery and Management

Disaster recovery and management is a crucial element in assessing the quality of websites or online stores. In other words, how resilient will these operations be to the acts of nature, crisis, or tragedies that may not be predicted before hand? The ability of the web sites to continue operating when such events occur will help to provide timely information to customers and users regarding the status of the organization in light of these events. Many organizations currently maintain backup systems. However, these backup systems should be maintained in multiple remote centers so that any breakdown in the main portal unit will not automatically disarm the organization. The recent terrorist attacks on the World Trade Center brought to light the failure of some organizations that did not have remote portals to backup the system at the WTC. As a result, many of the websites were dislodged and communication with users and customers were significantly affected. The WTC incident highlights the need for a web-based operation to have a crisis management system that will enable it resume normal operation in the event of a catastrophic failure in the site.

A summary and a contrast of the dimensions for products, service, and virtual operations are presented in Table 5.1 below:

Products	Service	Virtual Operation
Performance	Tangibles	Performance
Features	Reliability	Features
Reliability	Responsiveness	Structure
Durability	Assurance	Aesthetics
Serviceability	Empathy	Reliability
Conformance		Storage capability
Perceived quality		Serviceability
Aesthetics		Security and system integrity
		Trust
		Responsiveness
		Product/service differentiation and customization
		Web store policies
		Reputation
		Assurance
		Empathy

Table 5.1: Dimensions of quality of products, service, and virtual operations

CONCLUSION

In this chapter, the dimensions of quality for virtual operations are presented. Virtual operations are online operations that often involve business transactions through the Internet. The different categories of online business operations are discussed and the trend towards online purchasing is emphasized. Although there are dimensions of quality for goods and services however, little has been said of dimensions of quality for virtual operations. The dimensions of e-quality presented here, are based on a synthesis of the two major dimensions of quality by Garvin and Berry and Parasuraman. However, it is shown that while products and services, which these two models dealt with, are often contained in online operations, there are unique distinctions with virtual operations. Unlike a pure service operation where there is an interaction between the customer and the human server, with online operation, the server component is a web site and there is rarely direct interaction between the customer and the human server component. Emerging issues that become of great concern when people interact with machines or inanimate objects become of concern in developing the dimensions of quality for virtual operations.

The identification scheme for dimensions is based on a synthesis of existing literature. There is no attempt made to identify the significance or non-significance of the dimensions identified. It is also possible that some of the dimensions may closely associate with each other thereby forming a unitary factor and thus reducing the number of dimensions currently identified. It is suggested that further research should be conducted using these dimensions to identify the significance of the dimensions as well as the mutual exclusivity of these dimensions. The outcome of such research will be valuable to online providers who may want to focus attention on the dimensions that are of high significance to their customers.

REFERENCES

1. Abels, E.G., White, M.D., and Hahn, K., "Identifying user-based criteria for Web pages*," Internet Research: Electronic Networking Applications and Policy*, Vol. 7, No. 4, p. 252-262, 1997.
2. Berry, L.L. and Parasuraman, A., Marketing Services -- *Competing Through Quality*, New York, NY: The Free Press, 1991.
3. Chase, R.B. and Stewart, D.M., "Make your service fail-safe," *Sloan Management Review*, Vol. 35, No. 3, p. 35-44, Spring 1994.
4. "Statistics for online purchases," downloaded from http://www.epaynews.com/statistics/purchases.html on 12/22/00.
5. Garvin, D.A., "Competing on the eight dimensions of quality," in Unconditional quality, Cambridge, Mass: *Harvard Business Review*, 1991.
6. Keen, P., "Designing privacy for your E-business, *PC Magazine*, May 18, 2000.
7. Pisek, P.E., "Defining quality at the marketing/development interface," *Quality Progress*, p. 28-36, June 1987.

8. "Hey flasher, stop abusing your visitors," http://www.flazoom.com, 6/20/2000, downloaded on August 6, 2001.

9. Lake, D., "Close encounters with E-commerce," http://www.thestandard.com/home/circulation/promo, April 3, 2000, downloaded on August 6, 2001.

10. "Linking customer behavior to e-commerce strategy," Knowledge@Wharton, special to CNET News.com, December 6, 2000, http://news.cnet.com/news/0-1007-201-4008764-0.html, downloaded on August 6, 2001.

11. Madu, C.N., "Introduction to quality," in Madu, C.N., *Handbook of Total Quality Management*, Kluwer Academic Publishers, Boston, MA: 1998, p. 1-20.

12. Morkes, J., and Nielson, J., "Concise, Scannable, and Objective: How to write for the Web," http://www.useit.com/papers/webwriting/writing.html, 1997, downloaded on August 6, 2001.

13. Shubin, H., and Meehan, M.M., "Navigation in web applications," *ACM in Interactions Magazine*, Issue IV. 6, November 1977.

14. Shaw, M.J., Gardner, D.M., and Thomas, H., "Research opportunities in electronic commerce," *Decision Support Systems*, Vol. 21, p. 149-156, 1997.

15. Sovish, E., "Does site performance really affect your profits," http://www.workz.com/content/1674.asp, September 29, 2000, downloaded on August 6, 2001.

16. "Web usability," http://unclenetword.com/articles/writeweb2.html, downloaded on August 6, 2001.

CHAPTER 6

●————————————————————————————●

SUSTAINABLE MANUFACTURING

Earth's resources are limited. With the explosion in world population and the increasing rate of consumption, it will be increasingly difficult to sustain the quality of life on earth if serious efforts are not made now to conserve and effectively use the earth's limited resources. It is projected that the current world population of 5.6 billion people would rise to 8.3 billion people by the year 2025 [Furukawa 1996]. This is an increase of 48.21% from the current level. Yet, earth's resources such as fossil fuel, landfills, quality air and water are increasingly being depleted or polluted. So, while there is a population growth, there is a decline in the necessary resources to sustain the increasing population. Since the mid-1980s, we have witnessed a rapid proliferation of new products with shorter life cycles. This has created tremendous wastes that have become problematic as more and more of the landfills are usurped. Increasingly, more and more environmental activist groups are forming and with consumer supports, are putting pressures on corporations to improve their environmental performance. These efforts are also being supported by the increase in the number of new legislatures to protect the natural environment. Thus, responsible manufacturing is needed to achieve sustainable economic development. Strikingly, studies have linked economic growth to environmental pollution [Madu 1999]. Thus, there is a vicious cycle between improved economic development and environmental pollution. This traditional belief on a link between environment pollution and economic growth often is a hindrance to efforts to achieve sustainable development. Sustainable manufacturing is therefore, a responsible manufacturing strategy that is cognizant of the need to protect the environment from environmental pollution and degradation by conserving the earth's limited resources and effectively planning for the optimal use of resources and safe disposal of wastes. In the past, manufacturers have been lukewarm about any strategy to develop sustainable manufacturing. They viewed such strategies as expensive and therefore, not economically viable. However, this mood is gradually changing as more and more big companies are developing environmentally conscious manufacturing strategies through their entire supply chain. Many have also; seen that environmentally conscious manufacturing can become an effective competitive strategy. Thus, sustainable manufacturing can lead to improved bottom-line and therefore, makes wise business sense. We shall in this chapter, trace the origins of sustainable development, which gave rise to sustainable manufacturing. Further, we shall identify different strategies to sustainable manufacturing and then present cases of successful implementation of sustainable manufacturing by multinational corporations such as Kodak and Xerox.

Sustainable Development

The origins of sustainable development can be traced to the United Nations publication in 1987 titled the Brundtland Report. This report is named after Mrs. Brundtland, Prime Minister of Norway who chaired the UN World Commission on Environment and Development. The report focused on the problems of environmental degradation and states that "the challenge faced by all is to achieve sustainable world economy where the needs of all the world's people are met without compromising the ability of future generations to meet their needs." This report received an international acclaim as more and more people are concerned with the theme of the report on environmental degradation. Since its publication, the world community has convened several conferences on how to achieve sustainable development. In 1992, the UN organized the Earth Summit in Rio de Janeiro, Brazil with a focus on how to get the world community to cut down on the use of non renewable resources in order to achieve sustainable development. This conference highlighted the disparate views between the industrialized and the developing countries on how sustainable development could be achieved with those from the Southern Hemisphere seeing dependence on the use of natural resources as a prerequisite to their economic growth. Several publications have emerged on sustainable development since the conference.

Duncan [1992] defined sustainable development as an "economic policy which teaches that society can make the appropriate allocation of resources between environmental maintenance, consumption, and investment." However, such balance is difficult to achieve when a nation becomes completely dependent on the exploitation of natural resources to satisfy its social and economic needs [Madu 1996]. Furthermore, with the absence of a developed private sector, countries faced with harsh economic realities such as poverty and over population, are more likely to focus on exploitation of natural resources and deployment of inappropriate technologies for manufacturing. Such attempts may hinder the global efforts to achieve sustainable development. Following this debate, Singer [1992] argues that sustainable development is akin to a "New Economic Order" that may not encourage reasonable and realistic development from the Southern Hemisphere. Rather, it could be seen as an attempt to make the South financially dependent on the North. This he refers to as a Robin Hood effect which may result in the transfer of funds from the poor in the rich countries to the rich in the poor countries. Clearly, achieving sustainable development is a goal for the entire world otherwise; marginal efforts by each country will be ineffective. Fukukawa [1992] pointed out that "current global environmental problems may bring about a crisis that could never have been anticipated by our predecessors. Since the very inception of history, humankind has been pursuing technological development to protect itself from the threats and constraints of nature. However, economic activities triggered by these technological developments have grown large enough to destroy our vital ecosystem." This view is shared by many around the world and has been a motivating force in seeking for responsible manufacturing through sustainable manufacturing. While many companies in the industrialized countries have embarked on the road to sustainable development, it is important to achieve environmental conformance throughout the world. After all, noncompliance may affect the supply chain especially since some of the raw materials may be generated from the poorer nations. Getting these countries to participate in sustainable development will requires understanding their perspectives on economic and social development and how they could be assisted by the more affluent nations. The problems in developing countries are better explained by Mr. Kamal Nath, India's Minister of the Environment when he noted in the Rio de Janeiro conference that "Developed countries are mainly responsible for global environmental degradation and they must take the necessary corrective steps by modifying consumption patterns and lifestyles; developing countries can participate in global action, but not at the cost of their development efforts ... On climate change and greenhouse gases, India's stand is that global warming is not caused by emissions of the gases per se but by excessive emissions. The responsibility for cutting back on the emissions rest on countries whose per capita consumption is high. India's stand is that emission in developed countries be reduced to tally with the per capita emission levels of developing countries." This view obviously, is controversial in industrialized countries. However, what it points out is the link or the perception of a link between environmental pollution and economic growth. In fact, as Figure 6-1 shows, the emission levels of carbon tend to support such a link. This figure, suggests a direct relationship between carbon emission and economic growth when the cases for OECD (Organization of Economic Cooperation and Development) are compared to the cases for non-OECD nations.

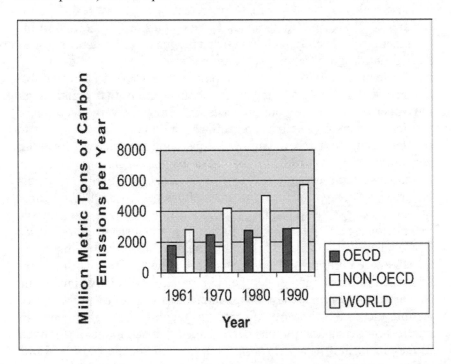

Figure 6.1: Million metric tons (2.204 lbs.) of carbon emissions per year

In 1997, the UN conference on Climate Change was held in Kyoto, Japan. This conference further raised some doubts and disagreements between member nations, non-governmental organizations, labor unions, and environmental activists. A preamble placed on the Internet states as follows, "The threat of global warming has brought more than 140 governments together in intensive negotiations to try to limit the emission of carbon dioxide and other greenhouse gases that trap heat in the atmosphere. But history, geography, economics and politics are driving them apart. Island states fear the rising oceans that warming may cause. Oil producers fear what lessening the world's dependence on fossil fuels would mean to them. Big industrial nations worry that emission limits might slow their economies. Poor nations say they should not have to bear the same burden as the rich." Obviously, sustainable development is intertwined with politics and economics and these may impede the effort to achieve sustainable development. Strategies to achieve this goal must therefore, take into consideration these concerns. Clearly, sustainable development cannot be achieved without sustainable manufacturing. Sustainable manufacturing is one of the processes or strategies to achieve the goal of sustainable development.

Sustainable manufacturing as a strategy will require the re-engineering of the organization to change design, process, work attitudes and perceptions. It will require the entire organization to be environmentally conscious and will require the support and participation of top management. More importantly, it will require investment into the future and retraining of the work force. Sustainable manufacturing is a capital venture that a company must undertake and this is a risk that some may not yet be ready for especially from the developing economies. Yet, from all indications, those corporations that have embarked on this bold step are reporting dramatic successes as we shall outline later.

The Brundtland Report was instrumental in getting the world focus on sustainable development. However, the formation of the Business Charter for Sustainable Development (BCSD) by a group of 50 business executives provided the momentum for much of businesses involvement in sustainable manufacturing. BCSD was formed in 1990 in preparation of Business activities at UNCED. This group was headed by Stefan Schmidheiny and published a book titled "Changing Course." This book detailed with case studies, challenges facing business in a sustainable environment. In January 1995, BCSD merged with another influential group with strong business ties known as the World Industry Council for the Environment (WICE). WICE is an initiative of the International Chamber of Commerce (ICC) based in Paris while BCSD was based in Geneva. These two groups shared common goals and attracted executives from similar organizations although BCSD was an executive-based group. The result of this merge is the World Business Council for Sustainable Development (WBCSD). WBCSD is presently, a coalition of 125 international companies that share a commitment to environmental protection and to the principles of economic growth through sustainable development. Its membership is drawn from 30 countries and more than 20 major industrial sectors. The aims of WBCSD as listed in its web page are stated below as follows (http://www.wbcsd.ch/whatis.htm):

1. Business leadership—To be the leading business advocate on issues connected with the environment and sustainable development;
2. Policy development—To participate in policy development in order to create a framework that allows business to contribute effectively to sustainable development;
3. Best practice—To demonstrate progress in environmental and resource management in business and to share leading-edge practices among our members;
4. Global outreach—To contribute through our global network to a sustainable future for developing nations and nations in transition.

The participation and support of many executives and major industrial sectors in sustainable development issues gave the momentum to corporate focus on sustainable manufacturing or environmentally conscious manufacturing.

Schmidheiny in his 1992 article discusses the term ecoefficiency. He defines it as "companies which add the most value with the least use of resources and the least pollution." This definition clearly linked industrial production to achieving sustainable development and shows that ecoefficiency or sustainable development can be achieved only when limited natural resources are optimized and environmental waste and pollution are minimized. Thus, corporate responsibility for sustainable development is obvious and corporations and their executives by participating in WBCSD are leading the way to achieving sustainable manufacturing. Sustainable manufacturing is therefore, synonymous to ecoefficiency. We shall therefore, define sustainable manufacturing as a means for manufacturers to add the most value to their products and services by making the most efficient use of the earth's limited resources, generating the least pollution to the environment, and targeting for environmental clean production systems. Although we emphasize on sustainable manufacturing, it should be apparent that the goal of environmental clean production can not be achieved if the service component of the manufacturing system is not environmentally conscious. The service sector must contribute by ensuring that its services are environmentally efficient. For example, can the purchasing and receive department conserve its use of paper for placing orders? Obviously, such a simple case can be achieved by using recycled papers and packaging, and by placing most orders through the Internet in a paper-less environment. Thus, our focus is on both the manufacturing and the service sector working in harmony to achieve the goal of environmentally conscious manufacturing.

Strategies for Sustainable Manufacturing

Several strategies have been developed to achieve sustainable manufacturing. We shall briefly discuss the different strategies. The aim of each of these strategies is to find a better way to make more efficient use of the earth's limited resources, minimize pollution and waste. Some of these strategies may appear in more details in subsequent chapters.

- Inverse Manufacturing—This strategy is based on prolonging the life of a product and its constituent components. Umeda [1995] refers to this as a closed-loop product life cycle. Simply stated, the life of any product can be extended by disassembling the original product at the end of its original life into components that could be reused, recycled, maintained or up-graded. Focus is on limiting the amount of components that are disposed or discarded as wastes. When this is done, environmental costs are minimized [Yoshikama 1996]. Inverse manufacturing gets its name from the reverse approach to recovery of the components that make up a product. Due attention is given at the conception of the product to the ease of disassembly. This will make it possible to reclaim component parts for future use thereby prolonging the life of the product. There are many examples of Inverse Manufacturing. For example, older computers are frequently upgraded to give them more capabilities by retaining much of the computer unit and adding only the needed features, its life is further extended. Also, important precious metals present in some older computer units such as silver, platinum and gold can be extracted and reused in building newer models when it is no longer economical or feasible to upgrade the unit. These activities reduce waste through recovery, recycling and reuse of materials. In the paper industry also, the use of recycled paper rather than virgin pulp in new paper production prolongs the life of the original virgin pulp. Inverse manufacturing has obvious advantages in extending the life of the product, minimizing waste of materials and conserves the landfills. The goal however, should be to keep waste to a bare minimum.

- Recycling—Recycling is one of the better-known strategies for sustainable manufacturing. In most communities, it is mandatory to participate in recycling programs. Many people identify with recycling of newspapers, packages, soda cans, bottles, and in fact, are required to separate them from other garbage for recycling purposes. Although there are arguments about the weaknesses of the current day recycling policies, however, the aim of recycling is to focus our attention to the finite resources available to mankind. The earth is composed of about 30% land and the rest is water. Our landfills are gradually filling up. If we continue to discard and dump wastes, the landfills will be filled up. We depend on the limited earth's resources for economic growth and if we are not able to thoroughly recycle and extend the lives of these resources, the future will be blink. Thus, a recycling policy that is efficient is needed. Such policy should be efficient and encourage more people and industries to participate in the program.

- Re-manufacturing—is the process of rebuilding a unit or machinery to restore its condition to "as good as new." This may involve reuse of existing components after overhaul, replacement of some component parts, and quality control to ensure that the remanufactured product will meet new product's tolerances and capabilities. The remanufactured product will normally come with a new product warranty. To make remanufacturing effective, the following steps are normally taken:

1. Collection of used items—This could be achieved through a recycling program where used or expired original products are collected from the customer and reshipped to the manufacturer. Some examples of these are drum and toner cartridges for computer printers and photocopying machines, auto parts, etc.
2. These items on receipt are inspected based on their material condition and a determination can be made on the economic feasibility of remanufacturing them.
3. Subsequently, the items are disassembled. If the full unit cannot be remanufactured, some components may be recovered for use in other components. Otherwise, the original item can be restored to a condition as good as new through repair and servicing. The recovery process must be efficient and focus on strategies that are conducive to the environment.

It is important that new products are designed for ease of disassemble and recovery of parts. This will make it more economical to conduct remanufacturing activities since it will be easier to determine which parts need repair or replacement. This will also help in effective planning of the master production scheduling by minimizing the production planning time and parts inventory levels.

- Reverse logistics—requires that manufacturers take a "cradle-to-grave" approach of their products. This management of a product through its life cycle does not end with the transfer of ownership to the consumer and the expiration of warranty. Rather, the manufacturer is forever, responsible for the product. This is often referred to as "product stewardship." [Dillion and Baram 1991]. Roy and Whelan [1992] noted that this is a "systematic company efforts to reduce risks to health and the environment over all the significant segments of a product life cycle." Product stewardship is driven by public outcry about the degradation of the environment. This has led to new legislatures making manufacturers responsible for the residual effects of their product on the environment with no time limit. As a result, more and more companies are responding by developing environmentally responsible strategies. Some are also seeing that such strategies are good for business and may lead to competitive advantages. The concept of product stewardship as outlined by Roy and Whelan [1992] requires a focus on the following:

1. Recycling
2. Evaluation of equipment design and material selection
3. Environmental impact assessment of all manufacturing processes
4. Logistics analysis for the collection of products at the end of their lives
5. Safe disposal of hazardous wastes and unusable components
6. Communication with external organizations—consumer groups legislature, and the industry at large.

This focus is embodied in the reverse logistic strategy. It is a new way for manufacturers to view their products and develop a business model that could enable them profit from developing a product stewardship approach. Obviously, by using remanufacturing strategy, the manufacturer can save significantly from the cost of labor and materials. About 10 to 15 % of the gross domestic product may be affected by reverse logistic strategy [Giuntini 1997]. Furthermore, about 50 to 70 percent of the original value of an impaired material can be recovered from customers. In addition, the cost of sales (direct labor, direct material, and overhead) which currently, averages 65 percent to 75 percent of the total cost structure of a manufacturer can be reduced by as much as 30 percent to 50 percent through reverse logistics. He identified the by-products of reverse logistics as follows:

1. Industrial waste throughout the manufacturing supply chain, would be reduced by as much as 30 percent
2. Industrial energy consumption would be noticeably reduced
3. Traditionally under-funded environmental and product liability costs would be better controlled and understood.

He went further to offer the following 10 steps for a manufacturer to implement a reverse logistics business strategy:

- Products must be designed for ease of renewal, high reliability, and high residual value.
- Financial functions must be restructured to cope with different cash-flow requirements and significant changes in managerial accounting cues.
- Marketing must reconfigure its pricing and distribution channels.
- Product support services and physical asset condition monitoring management systems must be implemented to manage manufacturer-owned products at customer sites.

- Customer order management systems must be implemented to recognize the need for the return of an impaired asset from a customer site.
- Physical recovery management systems must be implemented to manage the return of impaired physical assets.
- Material requirements planning management systems must be implemented to optimize the steps required to be taken upon the receipt of recovered impaired assets.
- Renewal operational processes must be established to add value to impaired assets.
- Re-entry operational processes must be established to utilize renewed assets.
- Removal processes must be established to manage nonrenewable assets.

Eco-labeling—The aim of eco-labeling is to make consumers aware of the health and environmental impacts of products they use. It is expected that consumers will make the right decision and choose products that will have less environmental and health risks. By appropriately labeling the product and providing adequate product information for consumers to make the choice between alternative products, it is hoped that manufacturers will move towards developing environmentally conscious production systems. Eco-labeling as a strategy is therefore, intended to identify the green products in each product category. It could be perceived as a marketing strategy that is partly driven by legislatures and partly driven by consumers concern for the degradation of the environment. Many of the eco-labeling schemes are based on the life cycle assessment (LCA) of a product and take the "cradle to grave" approach by evaluating the environmental impacts of the product from the extraction of the raw material to the end of the product's useful life. However, some of the popular eco-labeling schemes do not take this approach. The German "Blue Angel" mark which is one of the best known eco-labeling schemes focuses on the environmental impacts of the product at disposal and the Japanese EcoMark focus on the contributions of the product to recycling [Using Eco-labeling, http://www.uia.org/uiademo/str/v0923.htm].

Eco-labeling is increasingly being used in many industries and consumers are paying attention as opinion polls tend to suggest [Using eco labeling, 1999]. However, for eco-labeling to be effective, the public needs to be well informed and the labeling scheme must be credible. As has been suggested, it is important that all the major stakeholders (i.e., consumers, environmental interest groups, and producers) participate in developing the eco-labeling schemes. Also, information presented on the content of the product has to be valuable and understandable to consumers. There is a need for a standardized scheme in each product category to make it easier for comparative judgments. One of the major problems facing eco-labeling schemes is that it is voluntary and often, it is administered by third parties. Bach [1998] argued that mandatory eco-labeling schemes would be illegal within the context of the World Trade Organization and act as a barrier against international trade. He is of the opinion that regulatory measures will not reduce environmental degradation and further note that different countries have different environmental policies and standards as well as different economic policies and standards.

However, market forces and not government laws and legislatures drive eco-labeling. We operate in a global environment and without a standardized eco-labeling scheme; the entire supply chain will be affected. It is clear that many producers in industrialized countries source their raw materials and parts from different countries. If a standardized eco-labeling scheme is not developed, the entire supply chain will be affected and it will be difficult to implement an eco-labeling scheme that is based on a cradle to grave approach. Furthermore, the changes we have observed in the market economy since the 1980s as a result of the total quality movement and the subsequent development of the ISO 9000 series of product standards suggest that international standards on eco-labeling are not far from implementation. In fact, with the success of ISO 9000, the International Organization for Standards (ISO) has developed the ISO 14000 series of standards with a focus on guidelines and principles of environmental management systems. The technical committee (TC 207) charged with developing standards for global environmental management systems and tools, has environmental labeling as part of its focus. ISO 14020 deals with the general principles for all environmental labels and declarations [Madu 1998]. As expected, these standards will be widely adopted and when that happens, businesses will be expected to follow accordingly in order to compete in global markets. ISO already has classifications for eco-labeling schemes and the Type I eco-labels have the greatest impact on international trades. A third party to products that meet specified eco-labeling criteria grants certification. The issue is not to have each country develop its own plan for eco-labeling but, for world bodies such as ISO to institute a standardized scheme that will be cognizant of the limitations poorer nations may face. Indeed, ISO has four standards dealing with eco-labeling. These are ISO 14020, ISO 14021, and ISO 14024 and ISO 14025. ISO 14020 has been adopted as a standard while ISO 14021 and ISO 14024 are at the final stages of being adopted as standards. Although ISO standards are voluntary, with the worldwide acceptance of ISO, it is expected that many companies and countries will work within the guidelines of these standards. Environmental protection should be a worldwide effort and with out such an effort, the whole idea will be marginalized. Finally, some have argued that eco-labels do not boost sales [Christensen 1998] but it is too early to verify this claim since the public has to be sufficiently aware. Also, sales should not be the single criterion for environmental protection. Otherwise, many companies may find alternative ways to invest in that may be more profitable. Due concern should be appropriated to the need of the consumer being aware of the content of the product and having the ability to make a purchasing decision based on that information.

ISO 14000—is a series of international standards on environmental management. These standards are being put up by the International Organization for Standards (ISO) with the objective to meet the needs of business, industry, governments, non-governmental organizations and consumers in the field of the environment. These standards are voluntary; however, they continue to receive the great support of ISO member countries and corporations that do business in those countries. We shall not go into the details of these standards since ISO 14000 is a chapter in this book. We shall however, present a table that lists the ISO 14000 standards and other working documents at the time of writing. This is to help draw your attention to the work done by ISO on environmental management. However, the work of the ISO technical committee working on ISO 14000 standards is to address the following areas:

- Environmental management systems.
- Environmental auditing and other related environmental investigations.
- Environmental performance evaluations.
- Environmental labeling.
- Life cycle assessment.
- Environmental aspects in product standards.
- Terms and definitions.

Table 6.1 shows the listing of approved standards and drafts at their different stages of development.

Designation	Publication	Title
ISO 14001	1996	Environmental management system—Specification with guidance for use
ISO 14004	1996	Environmental management system—General guidelines on principles, systems and supporting techniques
ISO 14010	1996	Guidelines for environmental auditing—General principles
ISO 14011	1996	Guidelines for environmental auditing—Audit procedures—Auditing of environmental management systems
ISO 14012	1996	Guidelines for environmental auditing—Qualification criteria for environmental auditors
ISO/WD 14015	To be determined	Environmental assessment of sites and entities
ISO 14020	1998	Environmental labels and declarations—General principles
ISO/DIS 14021	1999	Environmental labels and declarations—Self declared environmental claims
ISO/FDIS 14024	1998	Environmental labels and declarations—Type I environmental labeling—Principles and procedures
ISO/WD/TR 14025	To be determined	Environmental labels and declarations—Type III environmental declarations—Guiding principles and procedures
ISO/DIS 14031	1999	Environmental management—Environmental performance evaluation—Guidelines
ISO/TR 14032	1999	Environmental management—Environmental performance evaluation—Case studies illustrating the use of ISO 14031
ISO 14040	1997	Environmental management—Life cycle assessment—Principles and framework

ISO 14041	1998	Environmental management—Life cycle assessment—Goal and scope definition and inventory analysis
ISO/CD 14042	1999	Environmental management—Life cycle assessment—Life cycle impact assessment
ISO/DIS 14043	1999	Environmental management—Life cycle assessment—Life cycle interpretation
ISO/TR 14048	1999	Environmental management—Life cycle assessment—Life cycle assessment data documentation format
ISO/TR 14049	1999	Environmental management—Life cycle assessment— Examples for the application of ISO 14041
ISO 14050	1998	Environmental management— Vocabulary
ISO/TR 14061	1998	Information to assist forestry organizations in the use of the Environmental Management Systems standards ISO 14001 and ISO 14004
ISO Guide 64	1997	Guide for the inclusion of environmental aspects in product standards

Table 6.1: ISO 14000 family of standards and ongoing work

NOTES:
CD = Committee Draft;
TR = Technical Report;
DIS = Draft International Standard;
FDIS = Final Draft International Standard;
Source: Adopted from "ISO 14000—Meet the whole family!" retrieved 3/11/1999 from http://www.tc207.org/home/index.html.

- Life cycle assessment— we shall adopt the definition provided by ISO for life cycle assessment (LCA). It is defined as "a technique for assessing the environmental aspects and potential impacts associated (with products and services)... LCA can assist in identifying opportunities to improve the environmental aspects of (products and services) at various points in their life cycles." This concept is often referred to as the "cradle to grave" approach. It requires that emphasis be placed on the environmental impacts of production or service activities from the product conception stage (i.e., raw material generation) to the end of the product's life (i.e., recovery, retirement or disposal of the product). Thus, the manufacturer is responsible for the environmental impacts of the product through different stages in its life cycle. Life cycle assessment often involve three major activities [Affisco 1998]:

1. Inventory analysis—this deals with the identification and quantification of energy and resource use as well as environmental discharges to air, water and land.
2. Impact analysis—is a technical assessment of environmental risks and degradation.
3. Improvement analysis—identifies opportunities for environmental performance improvement.
4. Notice also that several of the ISO standards listed in Table 6.1 deal with Life Cycle Assessment. Already, ISO 14040 on principles and framework and ISO 14041 on goal and scope definition and inventory analysis have been adopted as standards.

- Design for the environment—consequent to the growing demand for improvement in environmental performance is the growing need to change the traditional approach to designing. This strategy calls for an efficient designing of products for environmental management. Products are to be designed with ease of disassembly and recovery of valuable parts. Such design strategies will conserve energy and resources while minimizing waste. In designing for the environment, tradeoffs are made between the different environmental improvements over the product life cycle. Three main design strategies are design for recyclability; design for remanufacture; and design for disposal.

1. Design for recyclability—this involves the ease with which a product can be disassembled and component parts recovered for future use. For example, with computer units, precious metals can be easily recovered for use in new computers. For chemical compounds, the focus is on separability of materials to avoid contamination and waste of energy in recovering these materials.
2. Design for Remanufacture—This recognizes the different stages of equipment or product wears. For example, certain

parts of machinery (i.e., auto parts) could be recovered, remanufactured and restored to a state as good as new. Reusing them in newer products could further extend the lives of such parts. The challenge is how to design the original product for ease of recovery of those parts. We notice for example that newer computer systems are designed with the ease of upgrading them. Thus, new capabilities could be added to the system without having to dispose of the old unit.

3. Design for disposal—This recognizes the fact that many of the earth's landfills are filling up at an alarming rate. Further, many of the deposits are hazardous and unsafe. It is important to design the product with the ease of recycling and disposal. The final waste generated from the product should also be disposed safely.

Environmental Action Box

The case studies presented here are some of the popular success stories from leading manufacturers to show that responsible design; production and packaging that are environmentally sensitive are profitable. Many of these companies have witnessed growth in sales and revenue and attribute these successes to their environmental management programs.

Kodak Single-Use Camera:

The Kodak single-use camera (SUC) is perhaps, one of the most remarkable successes stories. Kodak first introduced this product in the U.S. in 1987 and it is now, the company's fastest growing product category. This product is now the company's centerpiece in its efforts in recycling, re-use, and product stewardship. Interestingly, the single-use camera was introduced as an inexpensive camera and not as an environmental product. It became known widely as a disposable camera and was even dubbed an environmental "ugly duckling." However, through innovation, commitment, and hard work, Kodak has transformed this product into an environmental success story. How did Kodak achieve this feat?

The product was designed for the environment and it is dubbed by some as the best example of closed-loop recycling. The recycling of Kodak single-use camera is a three-prong process that involves the active participation of photofinishers and a strategic partnership with other SUC manufacturers. In fact, Kodak credits photofinishers with most of the success achieved in recycling and reusing Kodak's SUCs. The new SUCs use 20 percent fewer parts from the design features to the actual film processing stage. Photofinishers return the camera after processing to Kodak and are reimbursed for each camera returned plus shipping cost. In the U.S., a 63 percent return rate has been achieved for recycling. This is equivalent to fifty million SUCs or enough SUCs to fill up 549 tractor-trailer loads.

The three-prong recycling process as detailed by Kodak in its web site (http://www.kodak.com/US/en/corp/environment/performance/recycling/suc.shtml, retrieved 3/2/99) is as follows:

1. Photofinishers ship the SUCs to three collection facilities around the world and Kodak maintains a recycling program in more than 20 countries. Through the strategic partnership with other SUC manufacturers such as Fuji, Konica, and others, they jointly accept each other's products even though Kodak cameras are in the majority. The products are sorted according to manufacturer and camera model. These cameras arrive at these facilities in recyclable cardboard.

2. Kodak cameras are shipped to a subcontractor facility for processing. The packaging is removed and any batteries in the camera are recovered. The camera is cleaned up and undergoes visual inspection. The process of remanufacturing the SUC has begun and the old viewfinders and lenses are replaced. New batteries are also inserted. Those parts that could be reused are retained after rigorous quality control checks.

3. The SUCs are now shipped to one of Kodak's three SUC manufacturing plants. This is the final assembly where new packaging made from recycled materials (with 35% post-consumer content) is added. The camera is now ready for use.

There are some lessons that could be learned from the Kodak experience:

1. Kodak notes that by weight, 77 to 86 percent of Kodak SUCs can be recycled or re-used. Yet, these products maintain high quality, attract huge demand and are profitable. This suggests that responsible environmental programs can be competitive and help the firm achieve its profit motives. Recycling programs such as this can help the manufacturer to save significantly by cutting down the cost of material, labor, and to achieve faster response to the market. It is estimated that it

takes about 30 days from the time of collection of an SUC to reclamation and re-introduction to the market.

2. Strategic partnership and working with vendors may be instrumental in effective recycling programs. Photofinishers have an incentive to participate and the cost of recycling can be shared through industry partnership as demonstrated in the case of Kodak's SUC.

3. Design for the environment is essential. Products for recycling, reuse, and remanufacturing must be designed for ease of disassemble and recycle. For example, with the SUC, it is easy to reclaim the packaging and recover component parts. Such design cuts down on cost and therefore, makes designing for the environment attractive.

4. Conservation of resources is achieved through effective recycling programs. For example, the equivalent of 549 tractor-trailer loads of SUCs has been recycled. This is said to be equivalent to 3,333 miles of cameras laid end-to-end. Imagine the enormous pollution this will create if these cameras are "disposables." How much landfill space will be needed to contain them? Since the recycling and reuse program began in 1990, more than 200 million cameras have been recycled. Since 1990, there has been an exponential growth in the number of cameras recycled with the number increasing from 42.1 million in 1996 to 51.9 million in 1997. This is shown in the figure below from the data presented by Kodak.

Figure 6.2 is adopted from, http://www.kodak.com/US/en/corp/environment/performance/recycling/suc.shtml.

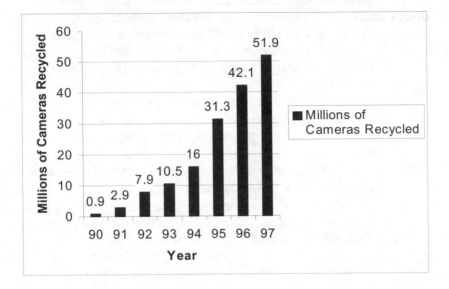

Figure 6.2: Millions of Kodak single use cameras recycled

5. The Kodak SUC is an example of a cradle-to-grave approach of a product. The manufacturer designs the product so that it has control over the life of the product. This is achieved by ensuring that the consumer ultimately, will return the camera to a photofinisher for processing and the photofinisher is given an incentive to participate in the environmental management program. The manufacturer takes the responsibility of disassemble and reuse and disposal of the product. This process ensures an effective environmental program that makes the manufacturer responsible for the life of the product.

The Kodak SUC is a success story that has helped reduce environmental degradation and has achieved tremendous economic success. Next we look at the environmental program at Xerox.

Xerox:

Xerox has a long history of developing sustainable products that dates back to 1967. Its strategy involves design for environment and life cycle product valuation. In 1967, the company embarked on a metal recovery program from photoreceptor drums and continues today to reclaim metals for reuse or remanufacturing purposes. Its design strategy today is known as "Waste-Free" design. How does this program work? Machines are recovered from customers through trade-ins and lease options. Many of the components of the xerographic machines that can still perform at their original specifications are recovered for reuse and remanufacturing. In 1997 alone, more than 30,000 tons of returned machines were used to remanufacture new equipment. Within the past five years, Xerox has more than doubled the number of machines it remanufactured. The remanufactured machines still meet Xerox's strict quality guidelines and are offered with the same Xerox Total Satisfaction Guarantee. These machines are designed for ease of disassemble, and Xerox takes the responsibility of the product's life cycle. As a result of the company's environmental efforts, natural resources are conserved and new machines are designed with fewer replacement parts.

Xerox works with its customers to carry out the recycling program. Customers of copy cartridges are provided with prepaid return labels that enable them to reuse the packaging from the new cartridge to ship the used cartridges to Xerox. The reused cartridges are then remanufactured. In 1997, Xerox achieved a return rate of 65% for print and copy cartridges. This is now the industry benchmark. Xerox also maintains a Waste Toner Return Program. This program allows customers to return waste toners for remanufacturing, reuse and recycle. This program is credited with the recovery of millions of pounds of toner which would have otherwise, been sent to landfill.

Xerox adopts a company-wide environmental program that tracks its product's life cycle and ensures environmental protection. Its recycling program works well because of the extensive network of people who participate in the delivery process to monitor the environmental and other potential impacts of the product on Xerox. A framework of its successful recycling program is shown below:

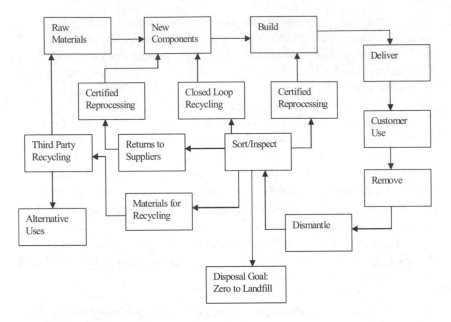

Figure 6.3: Xerox recycling program

Figure 6.3 is adapted from "Sustainable product development—The First 30 years," http://www.xerox.com/ehs/1997/sustain.htm, page 8, retrieved 3/2/99.

Notice that similar to the case of Kodak Single Use Camera, the Xerox recycling program adopts a closed-loop approach. This ensures that no waste is incurred as the material is continuously recycled, reused and remanufactured. In the end, the goal of achieving zero disposals to the landfill can be achieved. However, this can only be feasible if the product is designed for the environment. In other words, recycling will become a profitable and an economical alternative to waste.

The approaches that Kodak and Xerox are taking are innovative in that both manufacturers develop effective collection systems for their expired products. Many of the existing recycling programs depend on the garbage industry and municipalities rather than on vendors and suppliers who have stake in the recycling process. The lack of a well-designed recycling program has created displeasure and dissatisfaction that often times denigrate the value of recycling programs.

Some of the achievements of the Xerox program are outlined below http://www.xerox.com/ehs/1997/iso.htm page 2:

1   There has been a dramatic reduction in the amount of hazardous waste generated and 1997 saw a reduction of about 20% from the 1996 level.

2   There is a reduction in the amount of solvents sent off-site for recycle by about 13% in 1997.

3   Non-hazardous solid wastes designated for the landfills dropped by 20% in 1997.

4   Recycling rate of non-hazardous waste increased to 85%.

5   There is an increase in monetary savings from waste-free initiatives.

6   SARA (Superfund Amendment and Reauthorization Acts) air emission levels remain unchanged.

To add to Xerox environmental program, many of its processes are ISO 14001 certified. Xerox noted its ISO 14001 results as

- Lowered energy consumption.
- Increased recycling of various materials, including metals, plastics and cardboard.
- Reduce waste to landfill.
- Improved procedures for managing hazardous waste.
- Created an electronic document management application now being developed as a product for customers implementing their own environmental management systems.

CONCLUSION

In this chapter, we have traced the origins of sustainable development to the United Nations publication in 1987 titled the Brundtland Report. This report provided further impetus for the world community to focus on environmental protection. Since this report was presented, several conferences have been organized by several world agencies such as the United Nations to focus the world attention to the need of pollution prevention and resource conservation. However, it was the formation of the Business Charter for Sustainable Development (BCSD) by a group of 50 business executives that provided the momentum for much of businesses involvement in sustainable manufacturing. As we mentioned earlier, the publication of a book "Changing Course" by BCSD, outlined the challenges facing business in a sustainable environment. The merging of BCSD with the World Industry Council for the Environment (WICE) further expanded the industry interests in sustainable manufacturing. These two groups shared common goals and attracted several executives and industries from around the world. The new group now known as the World Business Council for Sustainable Development (WBCSD) is presently, a coalition of 125 international companies that share a commitment to environmental protection and to the principles of economic growth through sustainable development. Its membership is drawn from more than 30 countries and from more than 20 major industrial sectors.

The interest of businesses and the world community at large has spurned a lot of interests on environmental protection since the 1990s. Subsequently, several strategies have been developed to deal with environmental protection issues. We have outlined some of these strategies in this chapter. Environmental protection is increasingly seen as a competitive weapon. Companies now pride themselves for the continuous efforts they are making to protect the environment and provide consumers with environmentally clean products. We continue to see this effort expanded to include not only the content of the product but also its tertiary value such as packaging and preparation of the order. Also, the entire supply chain is now involved with environmental protection efforts. Sustainable manufacturing is in vogue now and every progressive company should have a strategy to achieve its environmental protection goals. It is important to know that with many nations adopting ISO 14001, companies that fail to follow the lead may lack access into such markets and even when granted access, may not be able to compete in an environmentally conscious market.

We ended our discussion in this chapter by presenting two classic case studies from two of the world's leading companies in sustainable manufacturing namely Kodak and Xerox. There are a host of other companies that have very good environmental strategies but the success stories of Kodak and Xerox may provide a motivation for more companies to reevaluate their environmental programs and perhaps, benchmark the leaders.

REFERENCES

1   Giuntini, R., "Redesign it + Produce it + Rent it + Support it + Renew it + Reuse it = Reverse Logistics Reinventing the Manufacturer's Business Model" APICS—The Educational Society for Resource Management, 1997 (http://www.apics.org/SIGs/Articles/redesign.htm)

2   "Kodak Recycles Its 50 Million the FUN SAVER" http://www.kodak.com/US/en/corp/environment/performance/recycling/suc.shtml, retrieved 3/2/99.

3   Furukawa, Y., "'Throwaway' mentality should be junked," The Daily Yomiuri, October 1, 1996, pp. 10.

4   Fukukawa, S., "Japan's policy of sustainable development," Columbia Journal of World Business, 27 (3 & 4), 96-105.

5   Umeda, Y., "Research topics of the Inverse Manufacturing Laboratory," http://www.inverse.t.u-tokyo.ac.jp, 1995.

6   Madu, C.N., "A decision support framework for environmental planning in developing countries," Journal of Environmental Planning and Management, Vol. 43 (2), 1999 (forthcoming).

7   Madu, C.N., Managing Green Technologies for Global Competitiveness, Westport, CT: Quorum Books, 1996.

8   Madu, C.N., "Introduction to ISO and ISO quality standards," in Handbook of Total Quality Management (ed., C.N. Madu), Boston, MA: Kluwer Academic Publishers, 1999, pp. 365-387.

9   Brundtland Commission, Our Common Future, Geneva, Switzerland: Report of UN World Commission on Environment and Development," April, 1987, p. 43.

10 Yoshikama, H., "Sustainable development in the 21st century," http://www.zeri.org/texter/ZERT_96_industries.html, 1996.

11 Singer, S.F., "Sustainable development vs. global environment -- Resolving the conflict," Columbia Journal of World Business, 27 (3 & 4), 155-162.

12 Schmidheiny, S., "The business logic of sustainable development," Columbia Journal of World Business, 27 (3 & 4), 18-24.

13 Roy, R., and Whelan, R.C., "Successful recycling through value-chain collaboration," Long Range Planning, 25 (4), 62-71, 1992.

14 Dillion, P., and Baram, M.S., "Forces shaping the development and use of product stewarship in the private sector," Conference on the Greening of Industry, The Netherlands, 1991.

15 Duncan, N.E., "The energy dimension of sustainable development," Columbia Journal of World Business, 27 (3 & 4), 164-173.

16 "Using Eco-labelling," http://www.uia.org/uiademo/str/v0923.html, retrieved 2/6/99.

17 Henriksen, A., and Bach, C.F., "Voluntary environmental labelling and the World Trade Organization," International Trade, Environment and Development, Institute of Economics, Copenhagen University, November 9, 1998.

18 Christensen, J.S., "Aspects of eco-labelling on less developed countries," International Trade, Environment and Development, Institute of Economics, Copenhagen University, December 7, 1998.

19 Affisco, J.F., "TQEM—methods for continuous environmental improvement," in Handbook of Total Quality Management (ed., C.N. Madu), Boston, MA: Kluwer Academic Publishers, 1999, pp. 388-408.

20 "Sustainable product development—The First 30 years," http://www.xerox.com/ehs/1997/sustain.htm, page 8

21 "What is the WBCSD," http://www.wbcsd.ch/whatis.htm, retrieved 3/9/99.

22 "Green business networks," http://www.epe.be/epe/sourcebook/1.14.html, retrieved 3/9/99.

23 Robinson, A., "Inverse manufacturing," March 10, 1998, http://mansci2.uwaterloo.ca/~msci723/inverse_mfg.htm

CHAPTER 7

●━━━━━━━━━━━━━━━━━━━━━━━━━━●

ENVIRONMENTALLY CONSCIOUS MANUFACTURING

In chapter 6, we introduced the concept of sustainable development and sustainable manufacturing. It is apparent that the goals of sustainable growth cannot be attained if we do not change our consumption pattern. Manufacturing plays a critical role in introducing new products to the market and also in shaping our tastes and consumption. Sustainable development cannot be achieved if adequate emphasis is not paid to sustainable manufacturing.

Environmentally conscious manufacturing (ECM) is often referred to as "ecofactory." The goal of ecofactory is to achieve optimal utilization of natural resources without harming the environment and without compromising the quality of the products. This goal can be achieved if effective utilization of natural resources is made, waste is minimized, and cradle-to-grave approach of the product is taken. In other words, the goal of ecofactory is not limited to the production process but spans through distribution, consumption and recovery and effective disposal of potential wastes. Thus, the manufacturer tracks and manages the whole product life cycle. Environmentally conscious manufacturing as a strategy adopts a systemic approach to product development and distribution. This approach starts from the design stage of the product where every effort is made to ensure that the product is environmentally friendly to an environmentally responsible disposal of the product or its waste at the end of the product life cycle. Watkins and Granoff (1992), define environmentally conscious manufacturing as "those processes that reduce the harmful environmental impacts of manufacturing, including minimization of hazardous waste, reduction of energy consumption, improvement of materials utilization efficiency, and enhancement of operational safety." Through ECM, the aim is to achieve "zero waste" through total system integration of the entire production and distribution processes. A preventive approach to environmental protection that focuses on reducing waste at the source rather than at the end-of-the-pipe treatment is commonly adopted. Manufacturers develop products for ease of disassemble, recycling, and use non-hazardous and non-toxic materials. Some of the strategies for environmentally conscious manufacturing such as inverse manufacturing, recycling, reverse logistics, re-manufacturing, and others, were introduced in chapter six. In this chapter, we explore in greater depth some of the most commonly used strategies.

Reverse Logistics— is also known, as reverse supply chain management has increasingly become popular among manufacturers. Have you ever wondered what manufacturers do with products that are returned by retailers? Well, this is the case of reverse logistics. Reverse logistics deals with the processing of goods that are returned from the customer's customer. The normal process for supply chain management involves the flow of goods and services to the consumer with little or no focus on the flow of waste back to the manufacturer. This is changing hence the term reverse supply chain management. The increasing cost of landfills, environmental laws and regulation and the economic viability of environmental strategies are pushing manufacturers to now consider reverse supply chain management. For example, localities are establishing new landfill regulations that often require separation and grouping of materials of the same type for ease of recycling. Recyclable items are no longer grouped together with all types of waste and garbage. Also communities are developing designated drop sites and manufacturers develop disposition processes. Some have also developed recycling programs for containers and cans with designated sites for ease of management of the recycled items. Here, the customer through a reverse supply chain returns goods to the manufacturer for effective disposal. For reverse logistics to work effectively, information management is critical. Manufacturers embarking on reverse logistics must be able to sort out salvageable items and separate repairable and non-repairable salvageable inventories. Effective management planning system that focuses on transportation planning, location analysis, and inventory control and management, and coordination of customer and vendor activities will be needed. Thus, it is important that in reverse logistics, not only does the product flow back to the manufacturer but also, information about the good that is being returned should flow back to the manufacturer. Manufacturers may be able to improve their bottom line if reverse logistics strategy is successfully implemented. However, before we continue, an important question in the context of environmental planning and management is why is reverse logistics an acceptable alternative to environmental protection?

Marien[1999], notes that manufacturers are developing source-reduction strategies as promising alternative to minimizing wastes and environmental pollution. This strategy is based principally on:

1. Reducing the weight and size of the product. This optimizes the logistics costs in both the supply chain and the reverse supply chain. Further, the cost of warehouse space is reduced as the size is reduced. Also, labor and material handling costs are significantly reduced when the item is trimmed in size and weight. Many organizations are embarking on this strategy. For example, the packaging industry is increasingly achieving reduction in their packaging program. Sears for example, has reported a packaging reduction program that has saved 1.5 million tons in the supply chain which is a savings of about $5 million annually in procurement and disposal costs [Marien, 1999]. Likewise, computer companies are increasingly building faster and more effective computers that are smaller in size and weigh less.

2. Minimization of production and distribution operations. There are many ways this could be achieved. First, minimizing production operation can be achieved by designing and building the right products that are highly dependable for the consumers. The high quality built in to the product means that there will be less rejects, reworks, or returns. Thus, limited resources are optimally utilized and energy consumption is reduced. Further, by doing things right the first time, labor cost is reduced. With the high quality of the product, it becomes competitive and the organization gains. Distribution operation is also optimized when quality is built into the product. Clearly, the high return rate will be avoided thus reducing the high cost of distribution through the supply chain. Also, there will be less need for inventory of replacement parts and returned goods and more efficient use of the distribution channel. The end result is that resources are optimally utilized and waste is minimized.

3. Reuse of materials and resources. The Eastman Kodak single-use-camera is a typical example of this. However, there are many more examples. Computer components are easily recycled and many of the paper products used today are recycled. It is possible to reuse some of these materials as in

the case of Kodak and Xerox because they are designed for ease of disassembly in mind. Thus, when a product is returned, it is easy to disassemble it, recover usable parts and integrate them in the production process. The concept of re-manufacturing is getting popular today because it is easier to recover useable materials from used equipment.

4. Another strategy is the substitution of materials that are environmentally friendly. This strategy is mostly utilized when a hazardous or toxic material is replaced with a more environmentally friendly substance. It could also be applied in conserving resources that are very limited in supply. One example is the replacement of the use of DDT (dichloro-diphenyl-trichloro-ethane) as a pesticide. It is known that DDT is a chlorinated hydrocarbon and it is not easily biodegradable. When used, it can be found in the tissues of living organisms that are exposed to it. It also has a disastrous influence on marine life as it reduces the rate of photosynthesis in marine phytoplankton, which is the base for most marine food chains. Since humans are at the end of this food chain, they can suffer irreparable health conditions from deposits of DDT in their tissues. Another example is the worldwide outlaw of the use of CFCs, carbon tetrachloride, and methyl chloroform. Based on the U.S. Clean Air Act of 1990, these chemicals were outlawed by the year 2002 and are to be replaced by more environmentally friendly alternatives. According to the Montreal Protocol Accord of 1987, CFCs were outlawed worldwide in 1995. CFCs are normally used as coolants and were once common in home refrigerators but is also ozone depleting. Manufacturers such as DuPont have already replaced CFCs with hydrofluorocarbon (HFC) called HFC-134a. The claim is that this new product is nonflammable, non-toxic, and non-ozone depleting, and has the same energy efficiency as CFCs.

Why Reverse Logistics?

There is limited landfill space available for dumping of wastes. Also, landfill is becoming increasingly more expensive to manage. Many organizations are realizing that reverse logistics offers the opportunity to recycle and reuse product components while cutting down the cost and the amount of waste that will normally be incurred.

In chapter 6, we presented a case of Kodak single use camera, which follows a reverse logistic strategy. We noted that in the U.S., a 63 percent return rate has been achieved for recycling. This is equivalent to fifty million SUCs or enough SUCs to fill up 549 tractor-trailer loads. Imagine the landfill requirement for disposing waste of such an enormous quantity. Not only was waste avoided, Eastman Kodak improved its bottom-line by recycling and reusing components from returned SUCs and also, reduced the cycle time for re-introducing the product into the market. While the strategy is environmentally responsible, it is also economically profitable. Eastman Kodak is not alone. Many other organizations are adopting reverse logistics. Hewlett-Packard for example refill returned printer toner cartridges and Xerox recovers used machines from customers and use them to remanufacture new ones. These actions have reduced the demand for landfill, reduced the need for excavation of new raw materials, and have reduced energy consumption from the processing and manufacturing of virgin products.

New environmental laws and regulations are clear in assigning responsibilities to manufacturers. Manufacturers must now take full responsibility of their products through the product's life cycle, or they may be subject to legal action. For example, new laws regarding the disposal of motor oil, vehicle batteries and tires assign disposal responsibility to the manufacturer once these products have passed their useful life. Thus, as Marien [1999] notes, to avoid the related supply chain complexity, it is important for manufacturers to build reusability into their products. Thus, manufacturers act by developing infrastructure to handle post-distribution and consumption activities. Hence, reverse logistics is increasingly seen as a competitive strategy that is not only designed to meet the social responsibility function of the firm but also designed to make the organization more profitable. Marien [1999] points out that the savings accruing to organizations that adopt reverse logistics are in the form of savings from "raw material and packaging procurement, manufacturing, waste disposal, and current and future regulatory compliance."

Businesses look at their bottom-line. Ultimately, the goal of environmental protection cannot succeed without the participation of business organizations. For their cooperation and participation in environmental programs to be assured, there must be potential benefits to them. In the past, businesses use to view environmental protection efforts as wasteful expenditure but not any more. They are now seeing that environmental programs offer competitive advantage.

More consumers pay attention to the environmental friendliness of the products they purchase. Also, organizations are beginning to realize that environmental strategies such as reverse logistics can cut down drastically on production and operations cost thus improving their profit margins. Some of the costs incurred from reverse logistics include the costs of refusals, reworks, recyclables, rejects, reprocessed overruns, reuse, remake, redo, residues, reorder, resale, and returnable shipping containers and pallets. However, some of these costs are controllable. For example, the cost of rejects, reworks, reprocessing can be avoided if the organization adopts a quality imperative. Thus, reverse logistics operates efficiently when the organization adopts other comparative strategies such as developing an effective quality program. Also, the benefits of reproducing a product from recyclable items may far exceed the costs associated with reverse logistics. Some of these costs such as the cost of disassembles could be seen as production costs since they replace the traditional costs of production. However, the organization can become more effective by designing its products for ease of assemble and also, by developing an efficient reverse supply chain network.

There are several logistic problems involved with reverse supply chain network. For example, what is the cost of transporting the goods back to the manufacturer? How often can the goods be returned? Is it better to use decentralized or centralized reverse logistics strategy? What is the cost of inventory? And what is the cost of processing the returns. To address some of these issues, Bunn [1999] presents factors for consideration in developing centralized logistics strategy. These factors focused mainly on costs relating to store labor processing, transportation, inventory, opportunity costs, credit terms, and operating cost of a centralized facility. These factors may play a role in negotiating better terms with vendors. By using the right logistics strategy, costs can be significantly reduced. However, each operation is different and it is important to take its uniqueness into perspective in determining the right reverse logistics strategy.

Environmental Action Box

We shall present a success story on the use of reverse logistics. Our example here is the giant name-brand cosmetics manufacturer Estee Lauder Companies Inc.

Estee Lauder Companies Inc.:

Estee Lauder Companies Inc. was founded in New York City in 1946 and is one of the world's leading manufacturers and marketers of cosmetics. Among its popular brands are Estee Lauder, Clinique, Prescriptive, Aramis, Tommy Hilfiger, Origins, and Jane. The company estimates that about $60 million worth of returned products from retainers were being dumped in landfills each year [Caldwell, 1999]. This amounts to about a third of returned goods from retailers. To cut down on this tremendous waste, the company decided to embark on developing processes and information technology. Reverse logistics became a viable alternative to consider. To develop the reverse logistics system, Estee Lauder Companies Inc. invested $1.3 million on scanners, business-intelligence tools and an Oracle data warehouse. Estee Lauder also customized the software to process returned goods. The results were encouraging. Some of the benefits derived by the company through the application of reverse logistics are outlined below [Caldwell, 1999]:

1. The company was able to evaluate 24% more returned products, redistribute 150% more of its returns, and saved $4,750,000 annually in labor costs.
2. The number of returned products destroyed because they exceeded their shelf life dropped from 37% to 27% in 1998. It is expected that this number will eventually drop to 15%.
3. The processing time for returned products was significantly reduced and the time to introduce returned goods to the market became faster.
4. Production and inventory levels reduced.
5. Better product management information system existed as data on the reasons for returns were collected.
6. Information system in place helped in developing better marketing, packaging, and production strategies.

Reverse logistics is an effective environmental management strategy. Its role in environmental protections can be outlined as follows:

1. It helps to better manage and conserve landfills as returned goods are disassembled, reused and reintroduced into the market place.
2. Information collected through the process can help in guiding the production process, quality control programs, and

marketing strategies. This will help to ensure more efficient use of resources.

3. Energy consumption is reduced, as waste management becomes more effective.

4. It complements the efforts of other environmental programs such as recycling by ensuring that valuable materials and resources are reused in the production process.

5. Reverse logistics is a win-win strategy where the organization stands to gain by making wastes profitable and the society in general stands to gain as waste disposal is minimized.

Recycling

Recycling is a process of converting materials that could have been treated as wastes into valuable resources. There are many examples of recycling such as aluminum cans, bimetal cans, glass bottles, newspapers, paper products, and composting. Recycling is one of the better-known strategies for environmentally conscious manufacturing. In fact, the concept of recycling is vogue today as many communities have adopted recycling programs. In these areas, recyclable materials are carefully separated from ordinary garbage or waste and the garbage collectors make a distinction between recyclable materials and garbage when they schedule pickups. Recycling is considered an environmental success story of the 20th century. As the Environmental Protection Agency (EPA) reports, recycling including composting has contributed to a significant reduction in the amount of material being turned over to landfills and incinerators for disposal [downloaded 11/8/99, pp. 1-4]. Based on this account, in 1996, 57 million tons of material that would have been sent to landfills and incinerators as garbage were recycled. This amounts to a 67% increase from the 34 million tons that were recycled in 1990. Likewise, the number of curbside collection programs in the United States has increased dramatically. There are reasons for the successes of recycling:

1. Consumers are increasingly concerned about the depletion of earth's limited resources and are also worried about the degradation of earth's environment through landfills, excavations, destruction of forestry, and pollution of air, water and land. They are therefore, willing to participate in protecting the environment. It is their cooperation that has attributed to the great successes of recycling programs.

Consumers are now buying recycled products and investing in companies that market recyclable products.

2. Recycling is profitable. Many organizations are now realizing that they can cut down on cost of material, reduce the cycle time for introducing new products, reduce processing time, and even become more efficient in their planning process if they recycle and reuse their products. They have better control of their recycled products and often times, may avoid complex supply chain networks when they deal with several vendors for virgin products outside their control.

3. Environmental laws and regulations that require that certain types of products be recycled have also contributed since the penalty for non-compliance may at times be severe. Apart from the legal ramifications of non-compliance, environmental activist groups can also damage the reputation of non-complying companies thus contributing to high customer dissatisfaction with the company and its products and services.

4. Apart from the profitability of recycling programs to organizations, consumers benefit directly. For example, another form of recycling is composting. Composting is the recycling of organic wastes. Many of the organic wastes can be easily recycled such as food and yard wastes and can be fed back to soils or applied in landscapes. Such applications help to reduce plant diseases and provide nutrients to soil. Further, some of the beneficial soil organism such as worms and centipedes feed of such wastes.

Palmer [2000] in his article gave a detailed discussion and definition of recycling and also identified the conflicts in current recycling programs. Noting that we live in a world endowed with finite resources, it is important to articulate and develop resource policy that can help achieve sustainable development while protecting the environment. Although this is often difficult to achieve due to several pressures on national economic programs that for some countries, often demand exploitation of these limited natural resources to generate needed capital however, it is imperative that national planning issues focus also on the needs of the future generation. Such focus will help to seek for example better alternatives to the use of landfills and encourage recycling policies that are environmentally friendly. For example, prior to recycling, all "wastes" were grouped as the same and are dumped in designated dumping sites for wastes. When a landfill has been used up, a new one is created and this process goes on and on. Little did the general public know that apart from the unsightly image of the landfill and the unbearable odor gasping out from it, it could also become a health hazard. Forty percent of the Superfund sites are municipal garbage dumps [Palmer, 2000], since all sites were for management of toxic wastes, disposal of chemicals and other hazardous wastes. For example, approximately one-third of GM 's toxic release inventory to landfill from foundry waste used to contain zinc. A new plan by GM will eliminate these land releases from GM foundries by the year 2002 [Annual report, 1997]. In 1997, GM recycled 61 percent of all these wastes. Furthermore, the separation of wastes into "recyclables" and "non-recyclables" has contributed immensely to sustainability. First, there is lesser need for landfills since the amount of wastes designated for dumpsites have declined. Second, recyclable items have extended lives and are re-used in the manufacturing and production processes. This use decreases the need for new or virgin products identical to the recycled item. Third, there is less need for energy consumption. Then, toxic compounds and chemicals were equally mixed with other wastes. This contributed to many of the environmental degradation, destruction of wildlife, and health problems. Thus, it became clear that these "wastes" needed to be separated especially from their sources. There are now several programs to avert wastes resulting from the initial processing of the raw material to the product form.

Although recycling can help conserve resources and save energy, not all materials are easily recycled. For example, cadmium and beryllium are not easy to recycle. Cadmium is widely known to the general public for its use in batteries. Its application in nickel-cadmium (Ni-Cd) batteries is one of the easiest forms to recycle. Many other applications of cadmium are in low concentrations and are difficult to recycle since much of the cadmium is dissipated. However, the growing application of cadmium in batteries and the concern for potential environmental pollution have led to regulations to limit the dissipation of cadmium into the ground [1997]. Beryllium is also difficult to recycle. Beryllium is widely dispersed in products when it is used. It dissipates and is very difficult to recycle.

Recycling Statistics

Recycling is a worldwide phenomenon. People all over the world are paying attention to recycling. Available statistics in the industrialized countries tend to support the growth in recycling programs. U.S. Geological Survey [1997] presents recycling statistics for selected metals. Generally, that survey tends to support the growth in recycling efforts. Aluminum scrap is one of the popularly recycled materials since aluminum is widely used in the manufacture of beverage cans. Thus, used beverage can (UBC) is one of the major sources of aluminum scrap. Data obtained for the survey from the Aluminum Association Inc., the Can Manufacturers Institute, and the Institute for Scrap Recycling Industries suggests that 66.8 billion of aluminum were recycled in the United States in 1997. A 66.5% recycling rate that is based on the number of cans shipped during the year was obtained. This is an increase from the 63.5% recycling rate obtained in 1996. Further, domestically produced aluminum beverage cans in 1997 had an average 54.7% post consumer recycled content. According to the Aluminum Association Inc., [1998], this is the highest recycled content percentage of all packaging materials. Statistics on other metals that were recycled between 1993 and 1997 are also presented in this survey [1997].

Aluminum cans are widely used as soft drink containers, and are perhaps, one of the oldest forms of recycling. National Soft Drink Association presents some startling statistics on the recycling of soft drink containers from 1990—1997. They present the following data [1999]:

1. Soft drink container recycling has risen from 48.7% to about 60% since 1989.
2. In 1997, a total of 51.9 billion soft drink containers were recycled.
3. Soft drink containers comprise of less than 1 percent of solid waste disposed in the U.S.
4. Beverage containers account for less than 20 percent of the materials collected through curbside recycling programs but generate about 70 percent of total scrap revenue.
5. Through packaging innovation, the weight of soft drink containers has been reduced by about 30 percent since 1972.
6. 22 percent of soft drinks are dispensed from fountains while the balance is packaged.

These data show remarkable improvement in the recycling of soft drink cans partly through cooperative recycling programs and product packaging innovations. We have also analyzed graphically, the statistics provided by the National Soft Drink Association. This data is presented below as figure 7.1.

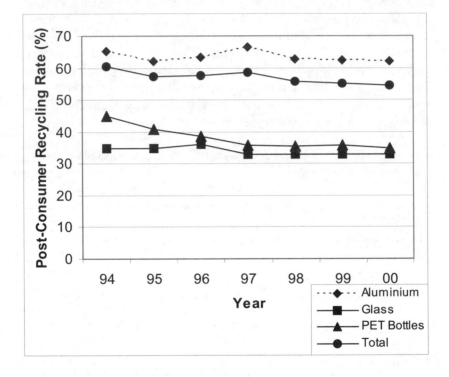

Figure 7.1: Post-consumer recycling rate (%)

As Figure 7.1 shows, even though there seems to be some gains in post-consumer recycling rate from 1996 to 1997, however, this rate is unstable over the time period considered. For example, there was a slight drop between 1990 and 1991 and then a dramatic increase to 1992 and a drop again to 1993. This up and downward swing appears to be prominent with aluminum cans. Post-consumer recycling rate for glass bottles seems to be relatively more stable. While generally, there are some gains made in improving post-consumer recycling rate, however, continuous improvement is needed to avoid the type of instability noted in the data. New studies need to identify the causes of such swings

1991-2000 Soft Drink Container Recycling Figures

Prepared by NSDA Environmental Affairs Department

Container Type	94	95	96	97	'98	'99	'00
Aluminum Cans[1]	61.2	64.6	64.3	66.1	69.6	68.9	67.8
Glass Bottles[2]	3.6	2.2	1.0	1.0	0.8	0.8	0.8
PET Bottles[3]	12.8	16.0	18.7	21.3	23.7	25.2	25.6
TOTAL	77.6	82.8	84.0	88.4	94.1	94.9	94.2

Total Units Shipped (billion units)

Container Type	94	95	96	97	'98	'99	'00
Aluminum Cans[1]	40.0	40.2	40.8	44.0	43.6	43.1	42.1
Glass Bottles[2]	1.3	0.8	0.4	0.3	0.3	0.3	0.3
PET Bottles[3]	5.7	6.6	7.2	7.6	8.4	9.0	9.0
TOTAL	47.0	47.5	48.4	51.9	52.3	52.4	51.4

Total Units Recycled (billion units)

Container Type	94	95	96	97	'98	'99	'00
Aluminum Cans[1]	65.4	62.2	63.5	66.5	62.8	62.5	62.1
Glass Bottles[2]	35.0	35.0	36.0	33.0	32.8	32.8	32.8
PET Bottles[3]	44.9	41.0	38.6	35.8	35.6	35.7	35.0
TOTAL	60.6	57.4	57.6	58.7	55.6	55.2	54.6

Post-Consumer Recycling Rate (%)

*Sources: (1) **aluminum data** – Can Manufacturers Institute, Aluminum Association, Institute of Scrap Recycling Industries, Steel Recycling Institute; (2) **glass data** – Glass Packaging Institute, U.S. Department of Commerce, Current Industrial Reports; (3) **PET data** – American Plastics Council, Container Consulting, Inc. *Reprinted with permission from NSDA Environmental Affairs Department.*

Environmental Action Box

Paper recycling is one of the most popular forms of recycling. In the Environmental Action Box, we use a giant paper manufacturer namely International Paper.

International Paper

International Paper is a leading manufacturer of paper. It is actively engaged in paper recycling programs with nearly $700 million invested. Further, the quality of its recycled paper is so high that it is indistinguishable from non-recycled paper. However, the major challenge facing IP and other paper manufacturers is that the quality of post-consumer recycled paper gradually deteriorates to the point that the recycled fibers become useless. This will eventually require virgin fibers to generate new paper products. Thus, if alternative to the use of wood pulp for paper manufacturing is not developed, sustainability cannot be achieved in the long run. International Paper has opened up the discussion and suggestion on alternatives to this problem to the general public. One alternative that is frequently alluded to is the use of annual fibers to make good paper. Although this sounds plausible, it has limitations and serious constraints that need to be considered. Some of the problems are:

1. It could lead to more environmental degradation. For example, farmers that currently manage forests because of high timber values may be tempted to mow down the timbers and harvest annual fibers if demand and price for timber drop down significantly. Thus, any alternative offered as substitute to the use of timber should be cognizant of the economic hardship forest managers may face and a plan must be in place to accommodate them.

2. Annual fibers need to be grown in large quantities to meet the current demand for paper. This will require land and perhaps, displacement of other harvested items or wildlife, which again can potentially affect the ecobalance.

3. Decisions to substitute annual fiber to timber have economic ramifications. The paper industry is one of the most capital intensive. Such decisions will require reinvestment in new technologies, equipment and material handling processes that may be different from what the industry is currently used to.

Inverse manufacturing

Inverse manufacturing has its roots from Japan where it began as a reuse and recycle project. The concept of inverse manufacturing is an extension of the recycling, reuse, and remanufacturing concept. It focuses on the pre-manufacturing process especially at the product design stage. The aim is to prolong the useful life of the product through design by designing reuse and recycling features into the product. The other feature is to design the product so that it is easy to disassemble. One way this is accomplished is by building modules into a product. For example, computers and refrigerators are made up of modules. These modules can be upgraded or replaced without replacing the entire product. For example, the functions of a personal computer can be upgraded by replacing modules such as the central processing unit (CPU) [1996]. In addition to these attributes, inverse manufacturing focuses a lot on maintenance. It envisages leaner manufacturing where companies will have to do away with the concept of mass production by creating quality products that will last longer. This vision will require transformation of many of the manufacturing outfits into life cycle companies with a focus on providing maintenance services on their products. The construction industry is actually an industry that survives well by providing mostly maintenance services on existing infrastructures. Through inverse manufacturing, product manufacturers can in fact, transform themselves to life cycle companies by providing maintenance operations and services to their products, thereby prolonging the useful life of the product. Why this concept may seem radical, it may be a desired option given the increasing problem with landfills and the limited natural resources. This closed-loop product life cycle approach leads to minimal disposal and environmental costs. According to the Inverse Manufacturing Forum Secretariat, inverse manufacturing takes a reverse process approach by focusing on the recovery of the product to disassembling to reutilization and production. This gives a complete loop of the product life cycle.

The concept of inverse manufacturing also requires a cultural transformation. The general society must be educated on the need to maintain products rather than discarding or dumping them in landfills. Further, manufacturers should also educate their customers and support the initiative to prolong the lives of these products. One factor that worries some about inverse manufacturing is that the decline in mass production may lead to loss of job as production capacity is decreased. However, the transformation to life cycle industry may absolve the excess capacity that may result from the decline in production.

In sum, inverse manufacturing involves the following:

1. Integration of reuse and recycling plans at the early stages of product design,
2. Emphasis on product maintenance and reduction in production volume through transformation to life cycle industry, and
3. Modular design strategies to make it possible to expand and upgrade product functions. Hata [1997] presents a good framework on inverse manufacturing. An adapted version is presented below:

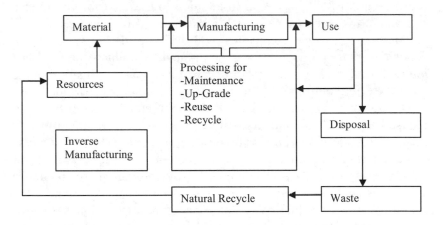

Figure 7.2: Product life cycle based on inverse manufacturing

Remanufacturing

Remanufacturing is the process of rebuilding a product from ground up utilizing new parts to return it to a condition "as good as new." This involves disassembly of each component in a product, inspection and testing of parts, evaluation of components for quality and reliability standards, replacement and upgrade of parts. Remanufactured parts possess some important attributes such as

• Appearance is as good as new
• Quality and reliability standards are satisfied
• Performance is guaranteed

- They are economical and environmentally friendly.

Remanufacturing is different from refurbishing where many of the changes are cosmetic involving rehabilitation of an older product to provide services, retrofits and upgrades. Refurbishing does not undergo the extensive process of remanufacturing a product to ensure that it is returned to a condition that is "as good as new.'

Design for Environment

The strategies discussed above consequently lead to the design for the environment. A combination of strategies must be followed in order to achieve an improvement in environmental performance. These strategies include raw material acquisition, product design, product usage and disposal. At each stage of the product life cycle, attention must be paid on how to conserve and effectively use resources. Pollution prevention and waste minimization become the driving force of strategies for designing for the environment. The product design stage pays tremendous attention on how limited resources are used, explores the use of replenishable materials and the use of substitute products to prevent pollution problems, and considers the energy demands of the product. The product design stage is critical in environmental management since problems uncovered at this stage can spread through the product life cycle and create more environmental hazards. It is at the product design stage that the decision to design for recyclability is made. If the product is not effectively designed to be easily disassemble and for component recovery or for material separability to avoid contamination, it will be difficult to treat this problem later on. Thus, a strategy at this stage to design for recyclability can help in minimizing both material and energy wastes and ensuring the conservation of limited resources. This strategy of designing for recyclability is also closely linked to the design for remanufacture. When components can be easily recovered from a malfunctioning unit, they could also be equally remanufactured, restored and reused. The extension of a component's life cycle also implies that there will be less demand for landfills for disposal of old units and there will also be less need for virgin products. These strategies therefore supplement each other. When a product is effectively designed for recyclability, it will meet the remanufacturing needs and its disposal needs.

CONCLUSION

This chapter discussed some of the strategies that are currently being adopted to achieve environmentally conscious manufacturing. It discusses how companies are designing for environment by using environmentally sound principles such as recycling, remanufacturing, inverse manufacturing and reverse logistics. It shows that these strategies are not only environmentally sound but also increasingly profitable to corporations. Recycling statistics from the National Soft Drink Association also showed that recycling is increasingly a worldwide phenomenon as more and more corporations are adopting a cradle-to-grave approach to their products. This chapter also presents an environmental action box featuring environmental activities at International Paper.

REFERENCES

1. Watkins, R.D., and Granoff, B., "Introduction to environmentally conscious manufacturing," *International Journal of Environmentally Conscious Manufacturing*, 1 (1), 5-11, 1992.
2. Bunn, J., "Centralizing reverse logistics: How to understand if it will work for you," downloaded 11/9/99, http://usserve.us.kpmg.com/cm/article-archives/actual-articles/revlogis.htm, pp. 1-3.
3. Marien, E., "Reverse logistics as competitive strategy," downloaded 11/9/99. http://www.apics.org/SIGs/articles/marien.htm, pp. 1-10.
4. Caldwell, B., "Reverse Logistics Untapped opportunities exist in returned products, a side of logistics few businesses have thought about--until now," Information Week Online, http://www.informationweek.com/729/logistics.htm, pp. 1-4, 4/12/1999.
5. "Produce less waste by practicing the 3Rs," http://www.epa.gov/epaoswer/nonhw/muncpl/reduce.htm#recycle, downloaded 11/8/99, pp.1-4.
6. Palmer, P., "Recycling as universal resource policy" in Madu, C.N., Handbook of Environmentally Conscious Manufacturing, Boston, MA: Kluwer-Academic Publishers, pp. 205-228, 2000.
7. GM Annual Report, 1997
8. U.S. Geological Survey -- Minerals Information -- 1997, "Recycling -- Metals," pp. 1-13.
9. Aluminum Association Inc., "Aluminum can recycling rate reaches 66.5 percent: Washington, DC, *Aluminum Association News*, March 6, 1998, pp. 1-4.
10. National Soft Drink Association, "Recycling," http://www.nsda.org/Recycling/facts.html, 1999, p.1.
11. Yoshikama, H., "Sustainable manufacturing in the 21st century" From ZERI (Zero Emissions Research Initiatives) Symposium, May 1996, http://www.zeri.org/texter/ZERT_96_industries.html.
12. Hata,Tomoyuki, Kimura, Fumihiko, and Hiromasa Suzuki (1997) "Product Life Cycle Design based on Deterioration Simulation," www.cim.pe.u-tokyo.ac.jp/~lcgroup/theses.htm downloaded March 2, 1999.

CHAPTER 8

●───────────────────────────────●

ENVIRONMENTAL PLANNING FRAMEWORK

A key issue in achieving sustainable development is the ability to manage human impacts on the natural environment. Clearly, the scale of environmental pollution and degradation that are of major concern is that generated by industrial wastes through the creation of products and services. If such industrial wastes are not curtailed, sustainable development will not be achieved. Strategic planning as discussed in this chapter will examine the key facts both from managerial and technical perspectives on how sustainable development can be achieved through efficient environmental management. Specifically, we explore organizational strategic planning, competitiveness and the concepts of industrial ecology to understand how they influence sustainability.

While many of us are beginning to accept the need for sustainability, we must also not lose sight of the primary objective of a business or an industrial organization. Many businesses have as the core objective to maximize shareholders' wealth. This objective may often be perceived by management to be in conflict with the goal of environmental protection. The bottom-line is what top management understands very well. Thus, to attract and sustain management's interest in environmental protection strategies, they must also be exposed to the potential benefits of such strategies. It is through thorough strategic planning of environmental issues that management would come to understand the value of environmental protection. To some companies, this is now a mute issue since they have already started to reap the benefits of sustainable development. However, more improvements can be achieved and it is necessary to continue to reinforce the value to organizations of sustainable development.

Environmental management is a corporate-level issue and demands the attention of top management. Many of the strategies required to achieve sustainable development may require organizational restructuring, adaptation to new organizational culture, capital investment, and long-term planning. These aspects of planning are beyond the horizon of middle management and will need corporate-level involvement to be successful. Furthermore, being environmentally sensitive is a responsive strategy to both the needs of the customers and to the actions of competitors. Thus, it pays to be environmentally responsible. Also, the emergence of new laws and regulations in several countries is making it much harder for polluters to operate unnoticed. Corporations that have the vision to respond proactively to environmental demands will become competitive and have early entrance into new socially responsive markets. The cost of environmental pollution is also high. Companies that pollute do not only suffer the high environmental penalty and fine costs from regulators as well as clean up costs but they also suffer loss of market share from incensed public reacting to the company's environmental record. Typical examples include Exxon Corporation during the 1990 oil spill at Prince William Sound, Alaska. Customers as a result of this accident repudiated its credit cards. Union Carbide also suffered public humiliation and discontent when its chemical plant exploded in Bhopal, India in 1989.

Strategic Environmental Management

Environmental management is a core company value and not simply a public relations ploy [Grant and Campbell 1994]. Corporations realize the business potentials that can accrue from responsible environmental management. Consumers are gradually shifting their priorities and supporting products and services that are environmentally friendly. Grant and Campbell [1994] note that the environment can be integrated into the corporate culture in several ways such as:
1. Expanded innovation and productivity,
2. Better environmental performance.
3. Improved bottom line.
4. Better handling of volatile environmental controversies.
5. Enhanced credibility and trust.
6. More employee involvement in community relations.

These approaches on how to incorporate environmental management in to the corporate culture also offer guidance on what is needed in the environmental front to achieve competitiveness in the growing environmental market. Clearly, the end result for profit making organizations will be to improve the bottom line. However, to achieve such goal, the corporation needs to develop more efficient and innovative system or processes to enable it achieve the demanding societal environmental goals. By meeting the demands on the environment, the organization builds credibility and trust and is able to deal with volatile environmental controversies. In return, market shares may be gained, cost may be reduced and the bottom line may be improved. Employees also develop a sense of pride and joy in their organization and become integral members of their communities. Responsible environmental management is a win-win strategy that benefits the business enterprise, consumers, employees, and the society as a whole.

When the company is environmentally sensitive, it enjoys the support and goodwill of its community. The company becomes more efficient and cost conscious. The cost of poor environmental quality is controlled thus enabling it to invest in innovation and Research and Development. This may lead to the generation of new and improved products and services that will have less demand on material and energy consumption. The company is also able to position itself as a leader in its industry as it continues to gain market shares.

Strategic planning requires adopting a vision for the future. Clearly, the world community has a stake in the survival of the natural environment and with new laws and regulations passed by the different nations and the world communities, businesses must heed to the need to protect the natural environment. Manufacturers are recognizing that in order to continue to be competitive, they must be environmentally conscious. Thus, the traditional manufacturing strategy and philosophy must change to respond to our changing environmental needs. There is greater desire now than ever to produce environmentally friendly products. These products must make efficient use of limited natural resources, create less waste, and have less demand on material and energy. The focus is to increase or maintain value why reducing input requirements for a product. The reduction in input results in elimination of wastes, less dependence on nonrenewable resources, less dependence on energy and material, and more efficient use of technologies. To achieve this, the entire production system must conform to the new environmental standards. The goal here shifts away from the end-of-pipe management approach where the aim is to treat waste at the end of the entire process but rather, to prevent the waste from being incurred in the first place. A cradle-to-grave approach is therefore taken starting from the idea conception stage through product design, production, usage and disposal stages. Environmental management is an ongoing process that spans through the life of the product. Environmental management and protection is supportive of business ventures. It should not be seen as a costly venture but as a means of improving the long-term profitability and survivability of the firm. Businesses must see themselves as partners in this because if the source of their input is polluted or depleted, then the future of the business will also be affected. Imagine the impact of shortage of pulp to the paper industry. However, through effective planning, the availability of the resources could be protected through effective usage and recycling efforts, replanting of the forestry, and conservation.

Environmental Planning Framework

Planning for environmental protection will take the same traditional approach as any strategic planning framework. Madu [1996] presented an environmental planning framework referred to as the strategic cycle or system transformation process. This figure is adapted and presented below.

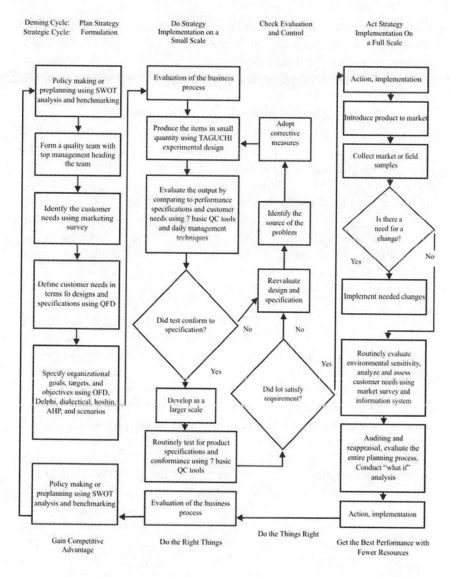

Deming Cycle: Plan Strategy | Do Strategy | Check Evaluation | Act Strategy
Strategic Cycle: Formulation | Implementation on a Small Scale | and Control | Implementation On a Full Scale

Policy making or preplanning using SWOT analysis and benchmarking

Form a quality team with top management heading the team

Identify the customer needs using marketing survey

Define customer needs in terms fo designs and specifications using QFD

Specify organizational goals, targets, and objectives using OFD, Delphi, dialectical, hoshin, AHP, and scenarios

Policy making or preplanning using SWOT analysis and benchmarking

Evaluation of the business process

Produce the items in small quantity using TAGUCHI experimental design

Evaluate the output by comparing to performance specifications and customer needs using 7 basic QC tools and daily management techniques

Did test conform to specification? No / Yes

Develop in a larger scale

Routinely test for product specifications and conformance using 7 basic QC tools

Evaluation of the business process

Adopt corrective measures

Identify the source of the problem

Reevaluate design and specification

Did lot satisfy requirement? No / Yes

Action, implementation

Introduce product to market

Collect market or field samples

Is there a need for a change? Yes / No

Implement needed changes

Routinely evaluate environmental sensitivity, analyze and assess customer needs using market survey and information system

Auditing and reappraisal, evaluate the entire planning process. Conduct "what if" analysis

Action, implementation

Gain Competitive Advantage | Do the Right Things | Do the Things Right | Get the Best Performance with Fewer Resources

Figure 8.1: System transformation process

We shall discuss each of the key steps or phases in this planning process below. It is shown in this figure, that environmental planning process is a never-ending cycle of planning that is akin to the popular Deming cycle in quality management. Dr. Edward W. Deming popularized the use of the Plan-Do-Check-Act in quality management and it is shown here that the strategic cycle for environmental management follows basically the same steps. Therefore, environmental planning can be broken down along these four major phases as we describe them below:

Plan (Strategy formulation)

Plan can be referred as the strategic formulation phase. It is a critical element of any organization's strategic formulation. The organization's vision on how to deal with its customers and its extended and external environment is made at this point. Let us take for example, the case of new product development. The company decides through its research and development that a new product to satisfy a particular need has to be developed. This new product is not without its consequences to the natural environment. Developing the product will require the use of natural resources, materials and energy and its usage may create other environmental burden such as emissions to the atmosphere or disposal to landfills. At this stage, it is important to adequately plan on how to deal with these environmental burdens. There are several things that an organization can do to minimize the environmental burden of the product. One of the approaches to be followed may include forming an environmental quality group or team that will comprise of all major stakeholders. These stakeholders will conduct a critical assessment of the product from a design, production, and disposal point of views and contrast each of the needed elements with substitutes to identify which options may have the less environmental burden. The formation of a stakeholder team brings in people with diverse worldviews and experiences and may lead to proliferation of new ideas on how to best satisfy customer needs. This approach also allows for a more thorough SWOT (strengths, weaknesses, opportunities, threats) analysis where the manufacturer does not view SWOT only internally but also externally. In other words, environmental burden and concerns of the general public about the product could be factored into the designing of the product. When the manufacturer is able to integrate the views, concerns and values of the general public in product design, it becomes more capable of seeking alternative production systems and product substitutes that may have less environmental impacts. It also becomes more capable of working with its supply chain to make sure that the entire supply chain network is adequately involved in achieving its overall goal of environmental quality. With manufacturers increasingly outsourcing different stages of their product development to different suppliers and vendors, it is important that the entire supply chain network work towards a common goal. Irrespective of whom the vendor or supplier may be the manufacturer must take a cradle to grave approach of its product.

The concept of SWOT analysis is deeper than just the manufacturer identifying its internal strengths and weaknesses or opportunities and threats from a competitive point of view. A major strength that a manufacturer can enjoy is its stakeholder's goodwill. The general perception by the stakeholder that the manufacturer is environmentally conscious by itself is a competitive weapon that could translate into increased market share. Threats could also be seen from the point that competitors have more environmentally friendly products and opportunities might rise from the fact that existing products do not meet the environmental needs of consumers. SWOT analysis could in fact, help an environmentally conscious manufacturer to identify environmental market niche that are not being satisfied by competitors.

Environmental management planning would benefit from the use of existing management tools. One of the issues involved in using stakeholder teams in planning product design and management is that an avalanche of issues may be raised regarding the interaction of the product with its natural environment. Also, several substitutes for the different components required for the product may be suggested and would need to be evaluated in terms of effectiveness, quality, cost, and environmental burden. A company could conduct a comparative assessment by using existing management tools to determine how best to satisfy customer needs through design. One of the strategies that have been effectively used in the quality management literature is to apply the quality function deployment popularly known as QFD. QFD is effective in matching customer needs to design needs. QFD drives the company by pushing the design team to identify "hidden" customer requirements and offering ways to satisfy such requirements. Its use also helps to identify those factors that are important to customers so that the design phase does not miss out on the critical feature that a product should have. Furthermore, it could help the company to conduct a competitive and technical evaluation of itself relative to its competitors and to how well it is achieving specified target values [Madu 2000]. The point is that QFD helps facilitate the planning and production of products and services that meet customer expectations and will therefore help   ensure that manufacturers adequately integrate customer concerns about environmental burden in product design and production.

Developing a product to satisfy environmental needs of the consumers is not all that easy. It requires a clear and an objective assessment of the impacts of all stages of product development on the natural environment thereby demanding that a thorough life cycle assessment should be conducted. Life cycle assessment is often difficult to conduct since it is difficult at times to prioritize different environmental impacts. For example, it is difficult to compare cotton to softwood pulp. Cotton would require more water usage while softwood pulp has higher energy requirements. It is difficult to assess which of these two creates less environmental burden. Thus, managerial expertise and input are necessary to effectively use these management tools. So, these tools offer decision support and as a guide to effective management decisions but do not preclude the direct involvement of management. Further application of management tools would require the ranking of the environmental burdens that may be identified by the stakeholder team in terms of relative importance. The use of the analytic hierarchy process to achieve this is discussed in chapter 9.

Once the planning phase is done, the next phase is to execute the plan. The execution phase is the "Do" stage.

Do (Strategy implementation on a small scale)

This phase involves the evaluation of the plan. It may involve pilot studies, developing and testing small-scale models, and computer simulations. The objective here is to mimic the real life product through modeling so to be able to address "what if" scenarios that may arise. This phase involves testing different substitutes or alternative designs and collecting samples for further analysis as regards to their environmental burden or impacts. This stage provides critical information that could be used to narrow down the potential number of substitute components for a product or the number of alternative designs that are being compared. In the end, only those components and alternative designs that meet the specified threshold are kept and further evaluated on other factors such as resource availability, cost, quality, and compatibility with other products or services provided by the manufacturer.

Check (Strategy evaluation and control)

Test marketing on a sample group could be conducted to obtain further information on how to enhance the product and its environmental quality. This is often difficult to implement since some of the environmental impacts may not be readily known and may take few years to realize. However, a full-blown implementation could be risky if proper product testing is not conducted. The testing phase is meant to see if the established environmental goals and standards are being satisfied. If not, the sources of the problem should be identified and rectified before a full implementation should be considered. Also, even when the established standards are being satisfied, it is important to match the prototype product to competitors' products to see how well it fares against them. This will help to determine market acceptability and product strengths that could be used in devising marketing strategies for competitive advantage. This testing procedure is therefore, an effective means of acquiring new information on the product through comparative assessment of its environmental features against the products of competitors.

Act (Strategy implementation on a full scale)

The product after undergoing all the necessary corrective measures should then be introduced into the market on a large scale. The stakeholder team would be supportive of the fact that adequate measures have been taken to ensure that environmental burden created by the product has been limited through effective planning. However, even with all good intents, there is no certainty that the product will not create any unwanted environmental burden. A monitoring program needs to be established to track the product through its life to detect environmental burden that could be managed. Also, with improvements in new technology and the availability of new information, it may become possible to continuously improve on the product or replace it or some of its components with more environmentally friendly substitutes. The concept of product stewardship requires the manufacturer to take responsibility of its product through its life cycle and to continuously seek methods to improve the environmental quality of its products. When significant environmental changes are needed, continuous improvement may no longer be effective and a complete overhaul and perhaps redesign of the product may be required. In this case, reengineering of the entire process from design through production and usage may be required. The key however, is that the planning process is a never ending process that constantly updates itself using new information and feedback obtained from the natural environment. It is an open system that seeks to find the best way to design and produce environmentally friendly products and services. Continuous improvement while helpful with small changes that may affect the product may become inefficient when there are significant environmental changes. When such occurs, reengineering of the entire product and production process may be required.

Understanding environmental problems

The environmental strategic planning framework presented here would be incomplete if it has no means of identifying an environmental problem or burden that may exist with a particular product. To facilitate the identification of these problems, we propose the use of a popular tool in quality management known as the fishbone diagram or the Ishikawa diagram or the 4m. Basically, this fishbone looking diagram is based on the idea that every problem can be deciphered into four parts namely man, machine, methods and material. We believe this to be also true in managing environmental problems. First, we present a hypothetical example using the fishbone diagram.

In this section, the fishbone diagram is used to identify causes and effects. The causes lead to the potential sources of environmental burden.

1. Man—The role of the labor force in creating waste and environmental pollution is rather obvious. Human error often results in the misuse of limited natural resources such as raw materials and energy in producing needed goods and services. Also, some of the major environmental accidents have been attributed to errors in human judgment, poor supervision and training, and often lack of sensitivity to environmental needs. Errors in carefully evaluating and deciding on alternative substitutes or production processes to limit environmental burden can also be attributed to management problems which are human in nature.

2. Material—Environmental burden could be created when a less efficient material is used. For example, in the paper industry, the use of virgin pulp against the use of post-

consumption paper would lead to unnecessary exploitation of forestry thereby diminishing the limited forestry resources. Likewise, the decision to use composted wastes in farms against chemically-based fertilizers will not only enrich the soil but prevent the erosion of top soil and the over buildup of nitrogen in the soil. Recycling and reuse of materials have also helped greatly in limiting environmental burden attributed to material usage. As we have illustrated in the case of Kodak single-use camera, material conservation can be achieved by remanufacturing and reuse. The use of fossil fuels can also be limited by finding renewable energy resources and by efficient manufacturing and production strategies to reduce both material and energy inputs.

3. Machine—Environmental burden may be created when equipment or machinery malfunction or fail to produce within specified tolerance limits. As a result, more scraps or rejects are incurred placing more demand on the need for both material and energy resources. Furthermore, emission to land, air and sea could be affected if the machine is improperly serviced or fails to meet emission standards.

4. Methods—The design strategy detects the technique or method of production and could significantly influence the output of wastes and energy consumption. Different design strategies such as design for environment, design for manufacturability, and design for recyclability are widely used to limit environmental burden. A diagram is presented below to illustrate the use of the 4ms in analyzing environmental impacts.

It is clear from this discussion that an efficient planning process must include consideration of man, materials, machine, and methods and how they could potentially influence environmental burden. The environmental impact of each product or service should be evaluated on the basis of these 4ms to better project its environmental burdens. This diagram should also be used to evaluate alternative or substitute products in parallel. It gives a clear view of all products and helps to better understand both the strengths and weaknesses of each design strategies. It could be used as a basis not only for selecting the product with less environmental impact but also for improving production systems by benchmarking a process that appears to be more efficient and environmentally friendly.

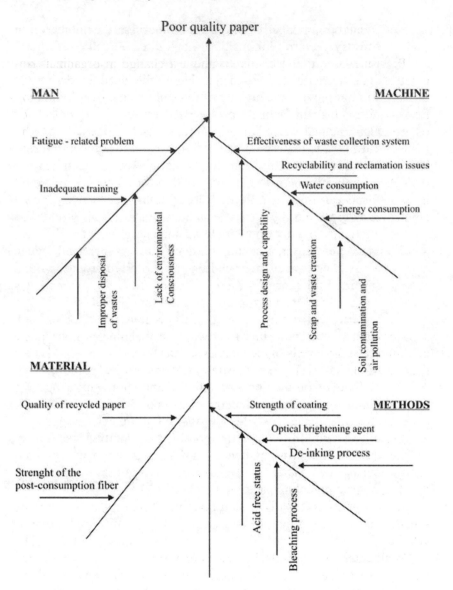

Figure 8.2: A fishbone diagram for a specific example i.e., paper production

Organizational Culture and Environmental Planning

Planning cannot be effective without a change in organizational culture. Everyone has to be intoned about the need to do things differently. This will require a total system overhaul with top management taking active part and showing support for environmental management initiatives. A total new culture has to be built and this culture will require attitude and value changes from employees. Top management must commit not only time but resources in terms of factory modernization by adopting new and more environmentally friendly processes, education and training of employees on environmental-quality standards, and their role in meeting the environmental goals of the company. Better relationship with suppliers and vendors must be fostered to ensure that they follow corporate environmental guidelines and policies. Training programs should emphasize the importance of self-regulation, governmental standards and legislation, and the influence of environmental interest groups and how to work with the different parties to achieve sustainable manufacturing practices. Employees should be acquainted on both the short- and long-term environmental forces and the role of their companies to mediate and abate some environmental causes.

When senior management is aware of the importance of environmental quality planning, they begin to analyze the buying patterns of consumers as they relate to the environment. By understanding that the buying patterns of consumers are significantly shifting from an emphasis on direct product quality to also include environmental quality, senior management realizes the necessity to develop a new organizational mission and vision for the company based on environmental goals. This is followed by the development of specific strategies and programs to meet customers' needs and to achieve the goal of company wide total environmental quality.

When senior management is aware of the importance of environmental quality, it encourages process and organizational transformation and redesign. Clearly, these actions involve not only process transformation but also cultural transformation.

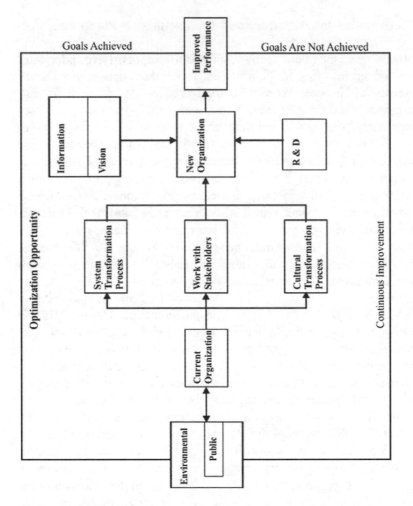

Figure 8.3: Transformation to a green organization

As shown in Figure 8.3, customers' needs are holistic and there must be a balance between environmental protection and product satisfaction. Ideally, the consumer will prefer a high-value product that is also environmentally friendly. These emerging needs of the consumer present new challenges, opportunities and threats to the company. The company would need to undergo a process of change in order to adapt to the new environment. However, these challenges pose new opportunities that could be exploited to gain new market share. If it is however ignored, it becomes a significant threat to the survival of the firm.

There are three main areas that are impacted by the process of change. The first is the system transformation process, which deals with the process of transforming inputs into outputs. Here, adequate control standards must be in place to ensure compliance with stringent environmental laws. The problem is not just producing products or services that meet environmental standards but also ensuring that the transformation process itself meets the same stringent conditions. Thus, the product or service, as well as its transformation process during every stage of production, should meet the same environmental constraints to be in full compliance.

Companies today have a large network of suppliers, distributors and vendors they work with. The concept of product stewardship requires that the manufacturer take a cradle-to-grave approach of its products through its life cycle. This requires establishing modalities to effectively work with partners or affiliates within the supply network to ensure that consistency is maintained in environmental standards and that the product is effectively monitored throughout its life.

Criteria should be established to measure the level of effectiveness of the supplier in meeting environmental standards. Inevitably, the manufacturer's environmental quality and cost of products will be affected adversely if the materials provided by the suppliers do not conform to environmental standards.

Listening to the voice of the stakeholder

In developing our planning framework, we emphasized the importance of the stakeholder team. This team would be made up of active participants with multidisciplinary background and different worldviews. The team provides valuable information to the organization on its wants and needs. A customer-focused organization can only be effective when it listens to its customers and designs and develops products and services that meet their needs. We have mentioned the importance of using the quality function deployment (QFD) tool in designing products and services that meet customer needs. It is imperative that such needs are identified by talking and working with the customer. We have purposely referred to such customer groups as stakeholders since it should be made up of not only those who purchase the product or services but all those that have a stake at the outcome of such products and services. For example, the emission of carbon and other greenhouse gases to the atmosphere affects all. It is not an issue that is left alone to the consumers of the product that is directly involved. Likewise, the filling of landfills with solid wastes that are not biodegradable affects the quality of our natural environment and therefore, concerns everyone. It is therefore more pertinent that a stakeholder rather than a customer group be used in assessing the impact of corporate activities on the environment.

It is noteworthy that many corporations are already joining the trend of involving environmental interest groups as stakeholders in their strategic plans. This partnership is helping in developing more sustainable services that will enjoy wider support from the general public. Some of the examples include the collaboration between the fast food chain McDonald's and the Environmental Defense Fund (EDF) in switching from polystyrene containers to paper wrap for its food products. Similarly, the utility company Pacific Gas and Electric Company often collaborates with the Natural Resources Defense Council. The Conservation Law Foundation also worked with New England Electric System to develop a twenty-year strategic plan that will focus on improving the use of renewable resources for power generation. This trend is continuing and shows increasingly that manufacturers are responding to the needs and wants of the general public by developing strategies to achieve sustainability.

Increasingly, visionary corporate leaders are adjusting their mission statements to include an ethical value system as their organization's social responsibility function to the society. To effectively achieve such corporate missions, organizational changes may be required and made part of the corporate environmental strategies. We shall look at some of these below:

- Top management commitment—Top management commitment is the most important factor in ensuring that corporate environmental strategies are successful. Top management takes the lead, which other employees must follow. Top management involvement highlights the importance of sustainability and good environmental practice. Furthermore, it is top management that has to allocate and commit resources to ensure that the goal of minimizing environmental burden is effectively carried out. Sound environmental practices often would require the re-engineering of the entire organization. For example, decisions would have to be made to modernize factories and replace mundane processes, training of workers would be initiated, suppliers may have to be retrained or replaced to meet environmental goals, vendors and distributors may need to be coached along, and management style may need to be changed to create more openness, sharing of ideas, and involvement of important stakeholders in environmental decision making. All these may lead to a change in organization's culture and such change need to be managed. Decisions involving such drastic changes rest with top management. Thus decisions on environmental sensitivity are strategic and can only be effectively considered at the top management layer. Any other level of management would lack the required authority to make decisions of this magnitude let alone implement them. It is also the responsibility of top management to ensure that good environmental practice is a company-wide effort that does not stop with the production of the product but also becomes part of the organization's life and involved in all its activities.

- Organizational vision and Mission—The organization needs a vision that would serve as the guiding philosophy to help it to accurately plan and predict its future. This of course is based on understanding its strengths, weaknesses, opportunities and threats (SWOT). SWOT analyses help the organization to better handle its future and understand its competitive environment. The vision articulates where the organization is and where it intends to be. Good visions require good imagination from top management and a deep understanding of its working environment. Good vision will separate better-managed organizations from their competitors as they identify new trends and market niches for the future. Vision helps the organization to plan ahead of its rivalry and position itself in its environment ready to respond to changes that might arise. It helps to restructure and redesign an organization so that it can cope with changes that may affect it. Finally, vision is based on good articulation of customer needs and wants, challenges in the market place, and understanding of competitors reactions and responses to the dynamic market environment. Being environmentally sensitive and responsive is a challenge that organizations face and must respond to in order to remain competitive.

- Change management—Clearly, introduction of cleaner, leaner and more environmentally friendly culture in an organization would require re-engineering of the organizational structure and of course, organizational cultural changes. The value system of employees as well as their perceptions of nature would have to change to align with the new vision and missions of the organization. Adherence to the new philosophy of environmental quality improvement should be obvious in their new role as the guardians of the environment and should be prevalent in all their activities within the organization and in the organization's extended environment. Employees therefore, need to be trained and sensitized to be able to identify potential sources of waste and pollution and to be able to control pollution or waste from their sources. Management of change is not easily accomplished. It would require changing life-long habits and adopting new culture that is supportive of sustainable development. Furthermore, it requires that management empower employees so they can have more leverage in making decisions and taking actions regarding their work and their role in the workplace. Top management is the key in making this transition from traditional practice to the new environmental practice culture smooth. It needs to lead by example and listen to the voices of both the customer and the employee and grant them participation in workplace decision making.
- Designing for the new environment—Effective management of the environment depends a great deal on designing. Products and services have to be designed to achieve high levels of efficiency. We have noticed increasingly the use of recycled materials or products in paper, electronic, automobile, computer industries and others. Recycling strategy helps to prolong the life of materials and substances that are used, reduce the energy demand required in excavating new materials, and yet assuring the efficiency and the effectiveness of the new product. Achieving sustainable design that meets the needs of the customer require that design engineers work with the customer to understand and design products and services that meet its needs. This approach challenges the traditional practice of engineers designing products as they see fit for use and then shoving

them down to the customer to be consumed. The customer today is an educated consumer who is often aware of his or her needs and show sensitivity to the natural environment that ultimately is involved in the systemic production process. Designing products or services to meet the challenges of today and tomorrow require that a thorough environmental impact assessment of all the components of the product or service be conducted by tracking the entire production process and the product life cycle to ensure that the final product creates the minimum environmental burden. For example, decisions on which alternative material or component to use in a product should be based on estimating each material's lifetime impacts on the natural environment and not simply on one or few direct impacts that are quite obvious. A design team that is made up of important stakeholders with multidisciplinary backgrounds should therefore be used to effectively analyze all pertinent information.

- Competitive Benchmarking—A competitive benchmarking approach needs to be adopted. In other words, the organization has to transform itself as a learning organization and be able to learn and adjust its strategies from world-class organizations. In other words, companies can learn from other organizations that have best in class sustainable manufacturing programs irrespective of their industry. For example, Kodak is a leader in product recycling as evident from its single-usage camera, Xerox is a leader in remanufacturing, and LL Bean is a leader in packaging which helps to trim waste significantly. Learning from these world-class organizations can help transform existing practices and make them more efficient. Knowledge of the corporate practice of these leading companies could help to establish achievable goals and targets on how to achieve sustainability.
- Environmental cost—A more comprehensive cost assessment methodology should be developed. One of the problems facing environmental management is that environmental costs are often undermined or underestimated. Top management should be made aware of environmental costs especially since manufacturers now must take a cradle-to-grave approach of their products. Product stewardship could create an enormous economic impact on the company since liability extends

through the entire life of the product. All the facets of cost such as internal, external, appraisal, and prevention costs must be evaluated. When top management is aware of the array of costs involved and their impact on the competitiveness of the organization, it becomes more willing to support efforts toward sustainability. One cannot overlook the importance of profitability to corporate enterprises and the need to often quantify practices to top management in terms of cost-benefit analysis. It is therefore of utmost importance that any environmental assessment program should have a major component on environmental cost analysis.

- Corporate image and social responsibility—Organizations have a stake in ensuring environmental quality. They operate to serve the general public whose perceptions of the performance of the company in their extended environment can influence their purchase decisions and reaction to the organization. Customers have demonstrated against companies such as utility and gas companies that have been perceived as polluting the environment and have even gone as far as boycotting their products. Corporate image can significantly be hampered if the company is perceived in a bad light and this perception could limit its ability to provide its intended social responsibility function to the society. Companies have important duties to their communities not just to provide jobs but also to protect and improve the quality of their natural environment. Companies that fail to deliver these important services to their communities are often entangled in litigations and poor public relations with its community. This ultimately affects its effectiveness. It is also important that the self-esteem and motivation of employees could be significantly diminished when their companies are poorly regarded in the community.

- Strategic information management system—Sharing of information is necessary in the effective management of the environment. Corporations today deal with a supply chain network of vendors, distributors, suppliers, and customers. Every group in this network participates to effectively deliver high quality goods and services to the customer. They all need to meet the established goals and standards of the organization and this can only be possible by sharing information with them and providing support to each group so the same target is achieved. The different members of the supply chain network can also obtain independent information that can be shared with any member of the network. The ultimate goal should be to improve the current level of performance using accurate and timely information. Strategic alliances should also be formed with major stakeholders with the openness and flexibility to communicate information to all groups with the intention of achieving the organizational goals.

CONCLUSION

In this chapter, we looked at the planning issues involved in environmental management. We note the importance of top management involvement and commitment in ensuring effective environmental planning. Issues evolving around environmental planning may often involve organizational restructuring or reengineering and such drastic changes can only be made by top management involvement and commitment of resources to that effect. Therefore, environmental planning is a strategic responsibility that rests with top management. We have also discussed the need of using a Plan-Do-Check-Act cycle as a means to effect a new organizational change to achieve sustainability. This systematic approach to planning will diffuse the influence of sporadic changes without adequate planning. It is also important to note that in planning for environmental management, the root causes of environmental pollution, material waste and consumption should be identified as well as their potential effects. We noted that this could be done by classifying all causes into what we refer to as "4ms" notably man, machine, methods, and material. Understanding these 4ms will help to isolate all the problems in any particular system. Finally, the need to listen to the customer and organizational cultural changes are underscored. We have identified several areas that top management must focus on to achieve its corporate environmental missions

REFERENCES

1. Grant, A.J., and G.G. Campbell, 1994 "The Meaning of Environmental Values for Managers," Total Quality Environmental Management, 3(4): 507-512.r
2. Madu, C.N., Managing Green Technologies for Global Competitiveness, Westport, CT.: Quorum Books, 1996.
3. Madu, C.N., House of Quality, Fairfield, CT.: Chi Publishers, 2000

CHAPTER 9

LIFE CYCLE ASSESSMENT

Introduction

LeVan [1995] traced the history of life cycle assessment (LCA) to 1969 and noted that the first life cycle analysis was conducted on beverage containers. The aim of this analysis was to determine the type of container that had the least impact on natural resources and the environment. This led to the documentation of the energy and material flows although the environmental impact was not determined. Since this initial work, LCA has been broadened to focus on inventorying of energy supply and demand for fossil and renewable alternative fuels. Thus, the focus of LCA is no longer inward with a concentration on the direct influence of the product but also outward to consider the energy and natural resources input during the product's life cycle as well as potential impacts of its usage on the environment. Also, the increasing concern about limited landfill spaces and the health risks associated with pollution have generated the need for a more holistic view of environmental impact assessment.

Definition

There are two major definitions of life cycle assessment. These definitions are provided by the Society of Environmental Toxicology and Chemistry (SETAC) and the International Organization for Standards (ISO) who have been active in developing guidelines for LCA. SETAC defines life cycle assessment as:
"An objective process to evaluate the environmental burdens associated with a product, process or activity by identifying and quantifying energy and materials used and wastes released to the environment, to assess the impact of those energy and materials uses and releases on the environment, and to evaluate and implement

opportunities to affect environmental improvements. The assessment includes the entire life-cycle of the product, process or activity, encompassing, extracting, processing raw materials; manufacturing, transportation, and distribution; use/reuse/maintenance; recycling; and final disposal."

ISO's definition appears in the ISO 14040.2 Draft: Life Cycle Assessment - Principles and Guidelines and is defined as:

"A systematic set of procedures for compiling and examining the inputs and outputs of materials and energy and the associated environmental impacts directly attributable to the functioning of a product or service throughout its life cycle." This goal is accomplished by the following steps:

- Compiling an inventory of relevant inputs and outputs of a system;
- Evaluating the potential environmental impacts associated with those inputs and outputs;
- Interpreting the results of the inventory and impact phases in relation to the objectives of the study.

There are three major components of life cycle assessment. These are: inventory analysis, impact assessment, and improvement assessment. LCA is a way of making the manufacturer to take responsibility for its products. It induces a design discipline that aims at achieving more value for less where the definition of value is expanded to include the potential impacts of the product or service on the environment. The designer focuses on design option that is environmentally sensitive by evaluating the product's demand for limited resources, energy, and disposal requirements at every stage of the product's life. Emphasis is on potential environmental burdens, energy consumption, and environmental releases. The manufacturer also takes a product stewardship or cradle-to-grave approach in evaluating the product, process, or activity. Environmental impacts include the expedition and use of limited natural resources, the pollution of the atmosphere, land, water or air, ecological quality (i.e., noise), ecological health, and human health and safety issues at each stage of the product's life cycle. We shall now, discuss the three stages of LCA.

THREE COMPONENTS OF LIFE CYCLE ASSESSMENT

As we mentioned above, there are three major parts to life cycle assessment. These three parts are discussed below:

Life Cycle Inventory Analysis

The aim of life cycle inventory analysis is to quantify energy and raw material requirements, atmospheric emissions to land, water and air (environmental burdens), generation of solid wastes, and other environmental releases that may result throughout the life cycle of the product, process or activity within the system boundary. These environmental problems affect the quality of the environment and in many ways, the public pays the cost of environmental burdens. The costs of these environmental burdens are often difficult to estimate since they are not all direct costs. Some of the costs may not even be detected until several years after the damage has been done. There are both economic and social costs that are involved. In order to conduct life cycle inventory analysis, we must associate the environmental burdens with functional units. In other words, it should be measurable. For example, we need to use a standardized measurement to quantify waste or raw material and energy consumption. We can for example, measure the carbon emission to the atmosphere in metric tons or the per unit weight of solid waste from a particular geographical location. The functional unit should provide information on the composition of waste both in terms of material type and relative weight [Kirkpatrick, 1999].

Inventory analysis is the thrust of LCA. The normal production process involves actually three main steps: inputs, transformation, and outputs. Each of these steps is a major source of environmental burden and environmental releases. By looking at each of these steps, the process of data collection for inventory analysis can be enhanced:

- Input - The input stage involves the acquisition of raw materials and energy resources. Inputs can also come in the form of transfers from other processes. For example, a recycled product can be a source of raw material for producing new product or semi-finished product from a different production source.
- Transformation - The transformation process normally deals with the process to convert the input into a desired output. The transformation process also involves energy consumption

as well as information flow. Further, wastes could be created through the process as a result of systemic problems with the process itself.

- Output - Output may be in the form of finished product, which is shipped out to the consumer, or semi-finished product that becomes input in another process. Also, at the output stage, two types of outcomes can be expected: products that meet the quality guidelines and those that fail the quality requirements. There is therefore, the potential that waste may be generated at this stage both in terms of raw material consumption and energy that is used to generate such wastes.

It is therefore important that these three stages of the production process be evaluated in order to generate an inventory of raw material usage and energy consumption as well as environmental releases.

In the quest for environmentally conscious manufacturing, one of the popular strategies today is to seek for better environmental alternatives. For example, polyethylene and glass, which one is more environmentally friendly? Or, should cloth diapers replace disposable diapers? One important information that is generated in life cycle inventory analysis is known as the *table of impacts*. This is a table that presents the impacts from the possible production of two materials. For example, we can look at the emissions and solid wastes generated in the production of 1kg of polyethylene and compare it to that for the production of 1kg of glass. However, such evaluation can not really suggest to us which alternative is better without taking a systemic view of the entire production process. For example, in a study by Johnson [1994], he noted that cloth diapers will require more chemical releases and water usage for cotton while softwood pulp for disposable diapers will require more energy. These two options: cloth diapers and disposable diapers create environmental burdens and it is difficult to compare these environmental burdens. So, how does one make a trade-off between these two fibers? There are therefore, a number of problems that make it difficult to conduct life cycle assessment. Some of these problems as they relate to inventory analysis were identified by Product Ecology Consultants [1999] and are discussed below:

Problems with Life Cycle Inventory Analysis

- Boundary conditions - It is difficult to define the system's boundary. For example, how far should one go in identifying inputs and outputs that relate to a particular product or process? Based on SETAC guidelines, components that comprise less than 5 percent of the inputs should be excluded. This is however, problematic since it is based on the assumption that the 5 percent component in a product will not have a significant environmental burden. If we go by the ABC rule, there is the potential that a very small fraction of the components may indeed, contribute to the majority of the environmental burden observed. LeVan [1995] presented a good example by noting that the electricity used for particular activity may be a small part of the input. However, if such electricity is generated from a high sulphur coal plant, its environmental burden could be enormous.

- System boundary condition - There is also the possibility that the links to certain products may be traced infinitum. Kirkpatrick [1999] notes for example, that the production of polyethylene involves the extraction of crude oil which is transported in a tanker. The tanker is made of steel, and the raw material required for steel is extracted. If we continue, we can see a long product chain that grows larger and larger and becomes more complex to analyse. Thus, a line must be drawn on what constitutes the system's boundary. This will generally not include capital goods.

- Multi-product processes - Some processes are designed to generate multiple products. In such cases, it is not easy to allocate and assign environmental burdens and releases to the different products.

- Avoided impacts - When materials are incinerated, energy is normally generated. Such energy is considered an impact but also, saves impacts, as it will no longer be necessary to produce the energy or the material. These avoided impacts are similar to the impacts that would have occurred in the production of material or energy. They are also, deducted from the impacts caused by other processes.

- Geographical variations - This recognizes the fact that environmental needs may be geographically dependent. We shall present two examples one from LeVan and the other from Product Ecology Consultants. LeVan [1995] notes that in the time of draught in the U.S. Southwest, single-use disposable diapers would be preferred to home-laundered diapers. While these two create environmental burdens however, the need at the time is a prevailing reason for the choice of single-use disposable diaper. Product Ecology Consultants [1999] on the other hand note that an electrolysis plant in Sweden will create less environmental burden than in Holland because hydroelectric power is in abundance in Sweden.

- Data quality - Environmental impact data are often incomplete or inaccurate. The data can also become obsolete and the use of such data may lead to distortion. There is also a problem that some of the environmental burdens may not be known and there may in fact, exist no data on the environmental impacts.

- Choice of technology - Clearly waste, energy consumption, and material releases to the atmosphere can be linked to the type of technology as well as the maintenance of the technology. Poorly maintained vehicles emit more carbon to the atmosphere and so are poorly maintained manufacturing processes. Also, the precision of such processes may be questionable leading to more creation of wastes. Further, modern technologies meet the new environmental laws and are able to control emissions and some environmental wastes and pollution.

Life Cycle Impact Assessment

Life cycle impact assessment is a way of interpreting and aggregating the inventory data so they could be useful for managerial decision making. We mentioned above that one of the important information generated through life cycle assessment is the table of impacts. The table of impacts is however, difficult to interpret without further evaluation of the environmental impacts. It is important to evaluate the impacts by assessing their relative contributions to different environmental concerns. Kirkpatrick [1999] lists some of the impact categories that are often considered in environmental impact assessments. These are:

- Resource depletion
- Greenhouse effect (direct and indirect)
- Ozone layer depletion
- Acidification
- Nutrification/eutrophication
- Photochemical oxidant formation.

Other areas that are less well defined were also identified as

- Landfill volume
- Landscape demolition
- Human toxicity
- Ecotoxicity
- Noise
- Odor
- Occupational health
- Biotic resources
- Congestion

All these areas pose environmental hazards and need to be considered in assessing environmental impacts. There are however problems with assessing environmental impacts. One problem is the fact that data is often non-existent and even when data may be available, it may be difficult to accurately determine the extent of the damage to the environment. Another reason is that there is no standardized method of estimating or measuring environmental damages.

The aim of life cycle assessment is pollution prevention rather than pollution control. By identifying the major sources of pollution and their effects on the environment, efforts could be made through product design or product development to prevent waste and reduce the risks to the environment.

Measuring Environmental Impacts

- It is difficult to measure environmental impacts. One of the beginning steps is to first identify a complete chain of cause and effect. But as we noted in the system boundary condition, this could become very cumbersome making it difficult to effectively analyze the problem. We recommend here, the use of Fishbone diagram to graphically identify the potential causes and effects. However, we must point out that there will be series of such diagrams since some of the causes or effects will need to be further analyzed. The use of Fishbone diagram offers great opportunity in breaking down the potential causes in to 4 parts or what is known as *4ms*: man, machine, material, and method. The fishbone diagram named because of its shape was introduced by Kaoru Ishikawa a Japanese professor of management and it is often referred to as Ishikawa diagram, is an effective tool in organizing problem solving efforts by identifying several factors that may cause a problem. The 4ms listed in the diagram are potential sources of environmental burden and were discussed in chapter 8.

The fishbone (cause-and-effect) diagram is a good way of completely analyzing a problem by asking who, what, when, why, and how questions about factors that appear to be likely sources of environmental burden. A generic cause-and-effect diagram is presented below as figure 9.1.

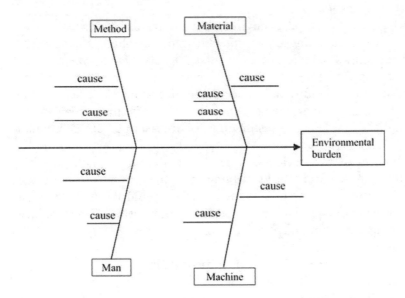

Figure 9.1: Fishbone diagram for environmental impact assessment

A similar method to the Fishbone diagram is used in Sweden to check cause and effect [Product Ecology Consultants 1999]. This is known as the EPS (Environmental Priority Strategy). The Swiss government on the other hand, uses the Ecopoint method, which measures the distance between the current impact and the target level. This is used to determine the level of seriousness of the impact to the environment.

SETAC presents the procedure for environmental impact assessment that involves three steps:
- Classification and characterization
- Normalization
- Evaluation.

However, only the classification and characterization stage has actually been implemented in practice. We shall discuss them with insight on how they may be improved.

Classification and Characterization

The fishbone diagram provides a good way of identifying causes and effects. This stage calls for classification of all impacts based on their effects on the environment. Impacts could be grouped based on their contributions to the different environmental burdens such as Resource depletion, Greenhouse effect (direct and indirect), Ozone layer depletion, Acidification, Nutrification/eutrophication, and photochemical oxidant formation. Also, an impact can be classified in more than one area. Thus, an effect table may be generated that will be in the form shown below:

Emission	Nitrogen dioxide	Sulphur dioxide	Carbon dioxide	Carbon monoxide	Nitrogen monoxide	Effect score
Quantity (kg)						
Greenhouse						
Ozone layer						
Acidification						
Nutrification / eutrophication						
Photochemical oxidant formation						

Table 9.1 Effect table for impact assessment

The contribution of each emission to each environmental burden is assessed and its effect score computed. As the intensity of effects may vary among the different chemical compounds, it is important to use a weighting factor. We suggest the use of a systematic weighting scheme such as the Analytic Hierarchy Process (AHP). A pairwise comparison of these chemicals could be conducted to determine their relative contributions to each of the environmental burdens. For example, carbon dioxide and sulphur dioxide, which has the most effect on greenhouse effect? Such weighted factors or priority indices obtained through the AHP could be used to obtain the effect scores. Thus, each quantity will be multiplied by the priority indexes generated through AHP and added up to obtain an environmental burden effect score. Clearly, there are many effect scores that may be generated. Emission for example is one area of environmental burden. Others are resource depletion, landfill usage, etc. The effects could all be compared as well as the relative importance of the different environmental burdens to a particular geographical area. This may form the basis for an informed decision on an environmental policy.

SETAC Workgroups have developed frameworks for life cycle impact assessment (LCIA). They identified the elements for conducting LCIA as classification, characterization, normalization, and valuation. Since SETAC is championing the effort in developing the methodology for life-cycle impact assessment, we shall briefly discuss the work of its two work groups from North America and Europe. The group proposed four major elements for life cycle impact assessment framework. These are classification, characterization, normalization, and valuation.

The *classification* phase involves creating different categories for inventory results. This will help distinguish and group impacts for planning purposes.

The *characterization* phase involves the conversion of inventory results in a category into a category indicator. Equivalent categories are aggregated into a category indicator. The category specific models are constructed using a cause-effect diagram.

The *normalization* phase involves normalizing the category indicators by dividing them by a reference value. This helps broaden the scope of the interpretation of the data by comparing the different category indicators.

The *valuation* phase is based on developing a formal ranking of category indicator results across impact categories. The weights or rank order are subjectively determined.

The use of AHP can also provide an alternative approach to LCIA. We shall therefore, discuss the AHP concept below.

Analysis of the Use of AHP

The Analytic Hierarchy Process (AHP) has three main components: goal, criteria, and alternatives. The goal is what is to be accomplished which in this example, is to select the most environmentally friendly product (i.e., glass or polyethylene). However, this decision depends on several factors denoted as criteria. These factors include the contribution of these products in creating environmental burden such as greenhouse effect, ozone layer depletion, energy consumption, and others. With each of these environmental burdens, there are several other sub-criteria to consider (i.e., emission of gasses that affect the ozone layer or cause the greenhouse effect). All these affect the decision on which of the two products to select. Figure 9.2 shows the hierarchical network structure of this decision making process.

The use of AHP as a decision tool has been widely published [Saaty 1987, Madu & Georgantzas 1991, Madu 1994, and Madu & Kuei 1995]. The AHP is defined by its founder Saaty as "a multi-criteria decision method that uses hierarchic or network structures to represent a decision problem and then develops priorities for the alternatives based on the decision makers' judgments throughout the system" (Saaty, 1987, p.157). The features of AHP that makes it applicable for application in life cycle impact assessment are the following:

- It allows for a systematic consideration of environmental problems by identifying all the major environmental impacts such as the greenhouse effect, depletion of the ozone layer, eutrophication, human or ecological toxicity as well as the factors that may influence them such as the emission of certain types of gases to the atmosphere, use of technology, consumption patterns, etc.
- There are many players when it comes to environmental issues. Environmental policies are not purely technical but also cognizant of the fact that there are many interest groups whose views must be aligned to develop sustainable environmental policies. The AHP makes it easier to consider all these different stakeholders in developing environmental policies.
- Its technique is novel as it deals with issues of consistency in decision making. AHP helps to measure the consistency of the decision-maker. Although consistency does not guarantee

      quality decisions, however, all quality decisions are consistent.

- Also, priorities generated through AHP can offer a good guide in reaching decisions on the relative importance of the different environmental options.
- Non-technical information can be combined with the more quantitative and scientific information on the environment to reach a decision.
- It helps to breakdown complex problems into levels of complexity that are manageable. As Figure 9.2 shows, the impact assessment problem can be broken down into the following parts: goal, criteria, sub-criteria and decision alternatives. This makes it easier to systematically analyze the problem.

Madu [1999] applied the AHP in analyzing the allocation of carbon emission to inter-dependent industries. The use of AHP as a decision support can help to clarify problems when comparing alternative choices since it will attach relative importance to different environmental impacts.

Life Cycle Improvement Analysis

    Life cycle improvement analysis is akin to the use of continuous improvement strategies. The goal in environmentally conscious manufacturing should be to achieve "zero pollution." This can only be achieved if the entire system processes are continuously improved on. For example, the process of managing the life cycle of a product is a long and an arduous task that starts from raw material acquisition through manufacturing and processing to distribution and transportation, then, recycling, reusing, maintenance, and waste management. Each stage of the product life cycle involves creation of waste, energy consumption, and material usage. A life cycle improvement strategy is needed to identify areas where improvements can be achieved such as a product design that has less demand on material requirement i.e., the reduction in the size of automobiles, replacement of 8 cylinder engines with 4 or 6 cylinder engines; enhanced consumer usage of products by reusing products or creating alternative uses for products; cutting down consumption of fossil fuels; participation in recycling programs; and so on. Life cycle improvement analysis will require the tracking and monitoring of the product through its life cycle to detect areas for continuous improvement. Life cycle improvement analysis has led to a lot of changes in design thus, the design for environment.

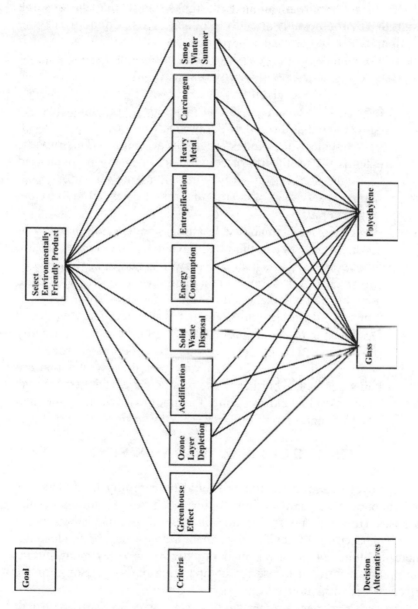

Figure 9.2: An example for selection of environmentally friendly product with AHP

Design for Environment

Design for environment is a design strategy that ensures the design of environmentally friendly products. This is done by paying attention to the importance of recycling, waste minimization, and reduction in energy consumption. We shall briefly discuss the popular design strategies in designing for environment.

- Designs for recyclability - products are now being designed for ease of disassemble so that materials and components can be recovered at the end of the product's life cycle and reused. An example is the Kodak single-usage camera. This process extends the useful life of components in many products and limits the demand for virgin items. This may therefore, lead to the conservation of energy that may be needed to excavate new materials.

- Design for maintainability/durability - increased reliability of products ensures that they will have extended operational life thus reducing the demand for newer generation of products. However, if it is difficult to maintain or repair products, there may be more demand on landfills for disposition of such items. Solid wastes will be created as well as energy wastes.

- Designs for pollution prevention - environmentally friendly products are now widely used in the production process to eliminate the amount of toxic and hazardous wastes that are being generated. Further, since products are designed for ease of disassemble and recycling, the amount of wastes generated is significantly reduced.

THE USE OF LIFE CYCLE ASSESSENT

Life cycle assessment studies should be carefully used. There is the tendency for manufacturers to use such results for marketing purposes. However, any such claims as to which product is better than the other based on life cycle assessment studies may be misleading. There are inherent problems in doing life cycle assessment studies that makes it difficult to use for comparative purposes. Some of the reasons are identified below:

- Life cycle assessment studies can not definitively state that one product is better than the other if we follow through the product's chain and study all the potential interactions of the product with the environment. It is difficult to make a decision on which form of pollution is better or preferred to another. For example, is the emission of toxic gases preferred to the use of fossil fuels? No form of pollution should be encouraged. Thus, our target should be to achieve "zero pollution." Until that goal is achieved, it will be incomprehensible to suggest that one form of pollution is better than the other.

- Life cycle assessment will be incomplete without the consideration of both quantitative and qualitative data. Further, there are cases where either data does not exist or may be incomplete. When we start integrating managerial perceptions and other non-quantitative issues in the decision making process, it becomes difficult to come up with a non-subjective decision.

- Life cycle assessment is limited by both boundary conditions and system boundary conditions. Thus, results generated may be geographically dependent rather than universal. So, a claim that one product is better than the other may depend on where the product is being used and may therefore, provide misleading information to consumers.

- Recycling is also a major source of complexity in life cycle assessment studies.

- The systemic structure of life cycle assessment makes it difficult since environmental processes vary spatially (i.e., geographically) and temporally (i.e., in time frame and extent) [SETAC Workgroup].

- There are also assumptions in life cycle assessment studies that there are no thresholds and that there exists a linear response between the system loading and the environment [Fava et al. 1991].

- Other potential problems include the fact that a solution to one form of environmental pollution may actually lead to another form of pollution. Typical example is the attempt to reduce the dependence on landfills for solid wastes. While this may reduce the pollution of air and groundwater supply, however, the burning of such wastes may lead to emission of energy to the atmosphere.

- Like the example we presented earlier, can one conclude that the use of cloth diapers is more environmentally friendly than the disposable paper diaper? Each of these presents an environmental burden.

- Data collection problems can plague the effectiveness of life cycle assessment. Sometimes, it may be difficult to correctly assess and collect information on all the inputs and outputs from a process. Further, the life cycle analysis is greatly affected by the quality of the life cycle inventory analysis. The life cycle inventory analysis is the foundation for life cycle analysis and must be done right.

These drawbacks therefore, make it difficult to use LCA in certain ways. Many have suggested that the adoption of eco-labelling schemes may standardize the comparison of products in terms of their environmentally friendliness. Eco-labelling standards are currently popular in Europe and the Nordic countries as well as Japan but the US does not have a national program for eco-labelling. Eco-labelling is however, not without problems. A major concern is that third-party certification bodies may adopt different and confusing appraisal methods. LCA however, can be used as a strategic planning tool in the following ways:

- It helps to identify which areas to focus on in order to achieve the environmental protection strategy. It is a proactive and a systemic way of looking at the company's products and services.
- The cradle-to-grave approach helps to ensure that manufacturers innovate on how to minimize wastes and eliminate environmental pollution. Further, by adopting a cradle-to-grave approach, emphasis is placed on the evaluation of multiple operations and activities throughout a product's life cycle to explore and manage potential sources of environmental pollution.
- The systemic framework adopted enables a functional analysis of the potential impacts of pollution on the environment. Thus, the different effects of energy consumption, material resources utilization, and emissions to the different environmental media such as air, water, and land, and waste disposals can be normalized in order to reach an effective decision on environmental protection.
- Emphasis is in optimization rather than sub-optimization. This is done by looking at a product in its totality by checking the consequences of its interaction and interface with the

global environment. A product is therefore seen as interacting with the outer system, receiving and providing feedback and information to it. Thus, a product's quality is not simply measured by its ability to deliver its intended function but its ability to deliver such function at a minimum social cost to the society.

- Life cycle impact assessment can be extended as a means of benchmarking competitors by developing more environmentally friendly substitutes and improving the design for environment.
- Eliminating wastes, cutting down on pollution, and increasing the recyclability of components used in product design can reduce production costs.
- Customer satisfaction and loyalty can be improved by designing and producing products that meet their environmental needs.

STRATEGIC PLANNING FOR LIFE CYCLE ASSESSMENT

Life cycle assessment can be seen as a strategic tool. It is a tool that will enable the manufacturer to understand the nature of his business and the needs of his customers. Critical questions that are asked in strategic planning include: What business are we in? Who are our customers? And who are our competitors? A well-designed life cycle assessment can enable a manufacturer to address these questions. First, what business are we in? Every business exists for a purpose and one common purpose for manufacturers is to provide goods and services. These goods and services must provide value to customers otherwise; there will be no demand for them. But, what is value? Customers' needs are ever changing. Few years back, there was not much concern about the degradation of environment. Once a product meets high "quality" standards, it is expected to do well in the market place. Today's needs are different. Customers are worried about environmental degradation resulting from depletion of limited natural resources, emissions to the different environmental media such as air, water, and land, and the influence of this entire environmental burden on their quality of life. The pressure is on manufacturers to take a cradle-to-grave approach of their products and services. Hence the need for life cycle assessment. As manufacturers grapple with life cycle assessment, they must also come to understand that environmental issues are systemic in nature and are far reaching. Focusing on direct customers alone is too narrow. As a result, manufacturers should be concerned with stakeholders rather than customers. Stakeholders are active participants who are affected by the environmental burden and whose action can also affect the role of the manufacturer in contributing to the environmental burden. The issue is who are our competitors and what are they doing? Clearly, manufacturers must strive to be the best or world-class performers in all their operations. This gives them competitive edge. Being the best is a selling point. As we noted earlier, sometimes, LCA is misused by manufacturers who tend to advertise claims that their products may be better than that of competitors based on life cycle assessment. However, there are obvious cases where a manufacturer may be making serious efforts to innovate and reduce its products' contributions to the environmental burden and the other sees no need to embark on environmental protection programs. Further, some manufacturers or service providers have achieved remarkable results like in the packaging industry or in digital rather than paper invoicing that they have become companies to be benchmarked. A holistic view of the environmental component of a product or service is not only economical in the long run as it reduces liability costs and other associated costs, but it is also strategic as it positions the manufacturer to compete effectively and expand its market base. While we have discussed the technical aspects of life cycle assessment such as life cycle inventory analysis, life cycle impact assessment, and life cycle improvement analysis, it is also important to look at the non-technical aspects that are strategic in nature.

It is crucial that life cycle assessment is an integral part of any organizational decision making process. The framework presented below has a focus on environmental management which life cycle assessment is a major part of.

Strategic Framework for Life Cycle Assessment

This framework is broken into three major parts preplanning, evaluation or impact assessment and action implementation/ improvement analysis.

Preplanning

The starting point for the framework is the formation of stakeholder team. Although most components of life cycle assessment may be scientific and objective in nature however, there are environmental perceptions and concerns that may not be effectively addressed. People are often concerned about potential impacts. Local conditions such as political and economic issues may influence perceptions. The use of stakeholders in decision making helps to ensure that the concerns of the stakeholders are considered and perhaps, integrated into the decision-making process. This will make it easier for the stakeholders to accept the final outcome of this process thus making it easier to adopt and implement the final decision. It also helps the manufacturer to expand its scope by considering environmental impacts that may have been neglected internally. For example, stakeholders may take issue with the recycling program or location of landfills.

Participation of the stakeholder team will help the manufacture to hear directly from the "voice of the stakeholder." Thus, the needs and concerns of the stakcholders are better defined and aligned with organizational goals. By working with the stakeholder team, the different environmental media of concern to the stakeholders can be identified and the relationship of the product manufacturing strategies to these media can be better understood through a life cycle inventory analysis of each product strategy. The Analytic Hierarchy Process discussed above can be used to evaluate the different product strategies or scenarios based on the life cycle inventory analysis and the concerns of the stakeholders. This will help to develop a portfolio of product strategies through which an informed decision could be made on potential strategies for adoption. However, there is the issue of cost and feasibility of some strategies. For example, some product alternatives may not be technologically or economically feasible. All these have to be taken into consideration in narrowing down the choices of effective product strategies. The AHP allows establishing priorities for the different product strategies. A systematic consideration of product strategies for implementation can be based on their priority assignments. Once a product strategy is selected, it is matched with design requirements. This phase is accomplished by using the quality function deployment (QFD) as a tool. The QFD if effectively used, will enable the manufacturer to effectively match its capabilities to stakeholders need and also benchmark its design capabilities to that of competitors [Madu 2000].

Evaluation or Impact Assessment

This stage involves the evaluation of the product design to ensure that all the significant needs of the stakeholders have been considered in the product design. A prototype or simulated product may be developed in a simulated environment and its potential impacts on the environment and product performance estimated. The simulated impacts will be compared to established standards and targets from the preplanning stage. If the estimated impact from this stage does not conform to expectations, the product design and specifications need to be re-evaluated to identify the source of the problem. Corrective actions are then taken. If however, the simulated impacts conform to expectations, the product could be developed and a random sample of the product may be used for environmental test marketing. However, the problem with this stage is that environmental impacts are often not measured in the short term and may take a long time to show up. However, the use of expert analysis could be helpful in evaluating the potential impacts of the products although there is no guarantee that these potential impacts may be actualized.

Action Implementation/Improvement Analysis

The product is now introduced into the market after it has been certified as meeting the established standards. While the product is in the market, the process of data collection continues. Routine tests are conducted to ensure that the product continues to meet the environmental requirements. Further, the availability of new scientific information may suggest new and more environmentally friendly components that could lead to redesigning of the product to conform to such changes. Also, new legislatures may impose limits on emissions or other environmental burden that may demand a change in product design. Once the product is out in the market place, information gathering must continue to create an ongoing process of improving the environmental quality of the product.

The life cycle assessment framework presented here is a continuous loop where feedback is frequently being fed into the system. The importance of this feedback loop is to ensure that the framework is timely and able to respond quickly to environmental changes. It is a dynamic framework and regards the availability of new information as a necessity in improving the quality of life cycle assessment.

The framework is shown as figure 9.3 below:

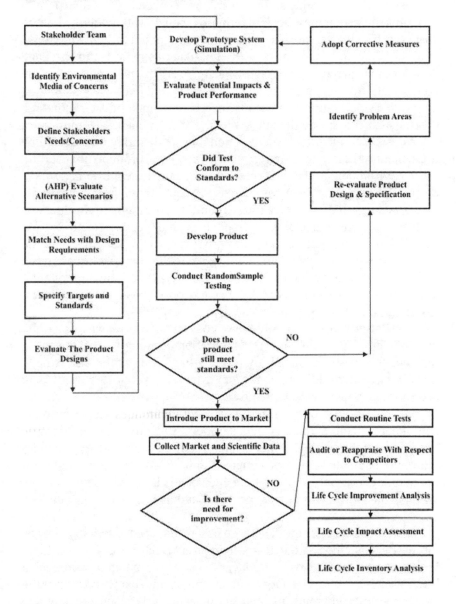

Figure 9.3: *Strategic framework for life cycle assessment*

Life Cycle Cost Assessment

Life cycle assessment models must address the cost issues. Manufacturers are expected to actively take a cradle-to-grave approach of their products. However, if life cycle assessment is not economical and cannot translate to improvement in the bottom-line, it will be difficult to assure the compliance of manufacturers. One must therefore learn to speak in the same language as manufacturers. That is, cost and profitability issues must be frequently addressed in conducting life cycle assessment studies.

Life cycle assessment cost is therefore, a method of evaluating costs that are associated with achieving environmental compliance. Such costs may include the conventional costs that may be incurred in implementing warranty programs (i.e., recalls of products that fail to meet environmental standards), social cost to the environment (i.e., costs of clean up and costs of decreased productivity from health and safety factors), liability costs (penalty and legal costs), environmental costs (i.e., environmental pollution costs and health-related costs), costs associated with loss of customer goodwill as well as cost associated with negative campaigns against the manufacturer. These costs can also be grouped into the four types of cost of quality accounting system introduced by Dr. Joseph Juran namely: internal, external, preventive and appraisal costs [Madu 1998].

Prevention costs - involve the cost incurred by ensuring that environmental pollution is prevented. Some examples of this cost include the costs incurred by conducting life cycle assessment include, training, designing for environment, product review and preplanning, vendor selection and so on.

External failure costs - these costs are incurred after the product has been manufactured and shipped out to the consumer. Environmental problems found are rectified and the product is returned back to the consumer. Such costs include costs of maintaining warranty, liability, recall, social, loss of customer good will, penalty/fines, complaints, personal and property damages and so on.

Internal failure costs - These costs are incurred internally before the product is shipped out to the end user. Such costs include high levels of emission in the production process, material usage and wastes such as scraps, energy consumption and expenditure, 100% inspection tests and retesting, and so on.

Appraisal costs - This cost is incurred by ensuring that the process and the product meet the target environmental standards or compliance. Such costs include inspection, equipment calibration, product audit and design qualifications, conformance analysis, and monitoring programs to track wastes and pollution, and environmental quality audits.

When top management understands the cost of poor environmental quality, it will take seriously the effort to improve environmental quality and will therefore, pay attention to life cycle assessment.

A CASE STUDY ON LIFE CYCLE ASSESSMENT

The case study presented here is adapted form LeVan [1995]. In her article, she discussed the work done by Franklin Associates Ltd. [1992], for the American Paper Institute and Diaper Manufacturers Group as well as the work by Johnson [1994]. These results provide insight for developing the case. However, we use the AHP to analyze the problem. The data used here are partly hypothetical and partly estimated from the figures presented by Franklin Associates Ltd. in its studies. The focus of this case study is to conduct a comparative assessment of energy consumption, water requirements, and environmental emissions associated with the three prominent types of children's diaper systems: single-use diapers containing absorbent gels, commercially laundered cloth diapers, and home-laundered cloth diapers. The comparison is based on a usage of 9.7 cloth diapers per day and 5.4 single-use diapers per day. Environmental emissions here are an aggregation of atmospheric, wastewater particulates, and solid waste.

Ultimately, any LCA study should offer a decision support to either decision or policy makers. While there are obvious limitations in some of the conclusions that may be derived such as determining whether energy consumption is more important than environmental emissions, however, a study that is vague and offers no direction to decision or policy makers will only compound the problem.

The work of Franklin Associates Ltd., compared the three diaper systems based on six criteria namely net energy requirements (using LCA method), net energy requirements (using closed thermodynamic balance), water volume requirements, atmospheric emissions, solid waste, and waterborne wastes. Johnson [1994] on the other hand, reported on the input requirements for cloth and paper diapers.

Johnson notes that there is more chemical and water usage for cotton while softwood pulp had higher energy requirements. In this case study, we consider only the factors derived in the study by Franklin Associates Ltd., although Johnson's findings can be easily integrated in the framework of AHP. The analytic hierarchy network for this case is presented in figure 9.4 below:

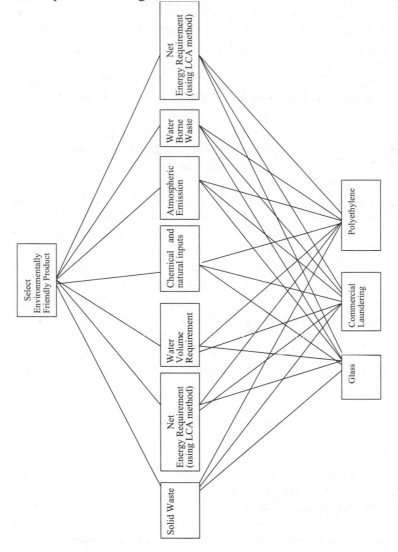

Figure 9.4: An analytical hierarchy network for type of diaper selection problem.

We use the information presented in the figures in LeVan's paper to generate a pairwise comparison ratio-scale for the six criteria and the three decision alternatives. These comparisons are shown in the Tables 9.2 to 9.7. Discussions on the applications and use of AHP are presented in Saaty (1980). Since the data we have in this problem is quantitative, rather than use weight assignments, we used ratios derived from the actual data to derive these tables. The values are then normalized using the method of AHP to obtain the priority indexes for each of the diaper type for any given environmental burden.

Type of Diapering system	Single-use diapers	Commercial laundering	Home laundering
Single-use diapers	1	.48	.40
Commercial laundering	2.083	1	.833
Home laundering	2.5	.1.2	1

Table 9.2: Pairwise comparison of the three types of diaper based on solid waste generation

Type of Diapering system	Single-use diapers	Commercial laundering	Home laundering
Single-use diapers	1	1.21	1.36
Commercial laundering	.826	1	1.12
Home laundering	.735	.892	1

Table 9.3: Pairwise comparison of diaper types based on net energy requirements using LCA methodology

Type of Diapering system	Single-use diapers	Commercial laundering	Home laundering
Single-use diapers	1	2.25	2.813
Commercial laundering	.444	1	1.25
Home laundering	.355	8	1

Table 9.4: Pairwise comparison of diaper types based on water volume requirements

Type of Diapering system	Single-use diapers	Commercial laundering	Home laundering
Single-use diapers	1	1.04	1.8
Commercial laundering	.962	1	1.731
Home laundering	.556	.578	1

Table 9.5: Pairwise comparison of diaper types based on atmospheric emissions

Type of Diapering system	Single-use diapers	Commercial laundering	Home laundering
Single-use diapers	1	6.571	7.143
Commercial laundering	.152	1	1.087
Home laundering	.140	.920	1

Table 9.6 Pairwise comparison of diaper types based on wastewater particulates

Type of Diapering system	Single-use diapers	Commercial laundering	Home laundering
Single-use diapers	1	.935	1
Commercial laundering	1.07	1	1.07
Home laundering	1	.935	1

Table 9.7: Pairwise comparison of diaper types based on net energy requirements using a closed thermodynamic balance

Applying the synthesization method of AHP we derive the priority of each diaper type given the six environmental burdens. This result is presented in Table 9.8. The weight assignments for AHP are defined as follows: 1 = equal importance; 3 = moderate importance of one customer requirement item over the other; 5 = strong importance; 7 = very strong importance; and 9 = extreme importance. The even numbers 2, 4, 6, and 8 are used for compromise, while reciprocals are used to show inverse comparisons.

	Solid waste	Net energy LCA	Water Volume Usage	Atmospheric emission	Water borne	Net energy requirement Thermo
Single-usage diaper	0.179	0.391	0.556	0.397	0.774	0.326
Commercial laundering	0.373	0.322	0.247	0.382	0.118	0.349
Home laundering	0.448	0.287	0.197	0.221	0.108	0.326

Table 9.8: Priority indexes for the three types of diapering system for each of the environmental burdens

From Table 9.8, it could be observed that the preferred choice is Home laundering if the only concern is with solid waste disposal since it has the highest priority of 0.448. However, when the concern is with water volume usage, the preferred choice will be single-usage diaper. This is also the preferred choice when concerns are with atmospheric emission and waterborne wastes.

One problem with the application of the AHP in the life cycle assessment study is to make a decision on which of the environmental burdens is more preferred to the other. As we noted earlier, such decisions may be affected by system boundary conditions since needs and requirements may vary from different geographical settings. Therefore, results derived may vary depending on where the life cycle assessment is to be applied. This will require us to compare all the six environmental burdens. This is a difficult task since none of the environmental burden should be considered an option. However, given the fact that we must reach a decision that will unavoidably contribute to environmental pollution; it is best to make choices that will lead to minimizing environmental pollution. The type of pairwise comparison conducted for this section of this chapter is described in Saaty [1980] where weight assignments ranging from 1 to 9 are used. It is recommended that a group of experts knowledgeable about this problem be used since weights assigned will affect the final recommendation. Table 9.9 is a presentation of the assignment we have made for the sake of illustration.

	Solid waste	Net energy - LCA	Water Volume Usage	Atmospheric Emission	Water -borne waste	Net energy- Thermo.
Solid waste	1	2	4	.25	.2	2
Net energy- LCA	.5	1	2	.167	.125	1
Water Volume Usage	.25	.5	1	.143	.111	.5
Atmospheric Emission	4	6	7	1	.5	3
Water-borne waste	5	8	9	2	1	4
Net energy - Thermo.	.5	1	2	.333	.25	1

Table 9.9: Pairwise comparison of environmental burdens

Based on the method of synthesization again, the following priorities were derived as shown in Table 9.10.

Type of environmental burden	Priority indexes
Solid waste	0.114
Net energy requirement - LCA Method	0.061
Water volume requirement	0.037
Atmospheric emission	0.284
Waterborne waste	0.426
Net energy requirement - Thermodynamic balance	0.078

Table 9.10: Priority indices for types of environmental burden

From the results of Table 9.10, it is clear that the three most important environmental burdens to consider in order of importance are waterborne waste, atmospheric emission, and solid waste. These results will have an effect in determining which of the different types of diaper system will be the preferred choice. We must also note that industrial policies must align with national policies on total environmental quality management. Of course, it would be ludicrous if different industrial sectors maintain different priorities on environmental burdens. Priorities generated on environmental burdens should in fact, be in conjunction with policy makers and stakeholders from the different industrial sectors and environmental interest groups.

The final phase of this analysis will be to take the product of Table 9.8 and Table 9.10. Since Table 9.8 is a 3 x 6 matrix and Table 9.10 is a 6 x 1 matrix, the product of Table 9.8 and Table 9.10 will lead to a 3 x 1 matrix that will contain the priorities for the three types of diapering system. This result is presented in Table 9.11.

Types of diapering systems	Priority indexes
Single-usage diaper	0.533
Commercial laundering	0.257
Home laundering	0.210

Table 9.11: Priority indexes for the three types of diapering systems

Our result suggests that given the six environmental burdens and the comparisons provided by experts on them, the preferred choice should be to implement a single-usage diapering system. The next preferred choice is a commercial laundering system.

We must however, point out that this case study is for illustrative purposes only. There may be other critical factors such as the input factors identified by Johnson that were excluded from our analysis. Also, the use of expert judgement in assigning some of the weights introduces subjectivity in the model. The weight assignments may change for different situations and system boundaries. However, this approach provides a guide on how important decisions on LCA studies may be reached. In this chapter, we have excluded some information on the use of AHP such as computing consistency index and how to use AHP for group decision making. However, these issues need to be explored before applying AHP. Further reading on AHP may be obtained from the following references Madu [1994, 1999], Madu and Georgantzas [1991], Madu and Kuei [1995] and Saaty [1980, 1987].

CONCLUSION

In this chapter, we have introduced the concept of life cycle assessment. We note that this requires product stewardship where the manufacturer takes a cradle to grave approach of its products. There are two main definitions of life cycle assessment that frequently appear in the literature. These two definitions provided by SETAC and ISO have also been discussed. Further, life cycle assessment consists of three main components: life cycle inventory analysis, life cycle impact analysis and life cycle improvement analysis. We have discussed all these and noted that life cycle inventory analysis is the foundation of all life cycle assessment. If that phase is incorrectly done, the entire process will be flawed. We have also identified some of the limitations and benefits of life cycle assessment and we have shown with a case study on types of diapering systems how the analytic hierarchy process (AHP) could be used in the context of life cycle assessment decision-making. We also discussed a strategic framework for LCA.

Another important topic that is discussed in this chapter is life cycle cost assessment. This is an important issue since we depend on the co-operation of businesses that have profit motives to ensure that LCA is successful. As a result, we need to speak in a language business executives will understand, by exposing them to the cost of poor environmental quality systems.

We also noted that industrial environmental goals must support national policies and in fact, derive from national policies on environmental protection. The guidelines, targets, and priorities on environmental burden should be set together by businesses working together with government agencies. Finally, life cycle assessment can help guide decision-makers to produce environmentally friendly products. It sensitizes them about the needs of their stakeholders and by listening to the voices of the stakeholders, quality decisions on environmental issues that can help improve the bottom-line of the corporation and make it competitive can be derived.

REFERENCES

1. Fava, J.A., R. Denison, B. Jones, et al., eds., (1991) A Technical Framework for Life-Cycle Assessments, SETAC, Washington, D.C. 134 pp.
2. Franklin Associates, Ltd. (1992) Energy and environmental profile analysis of children's single use and cloth diapers, Franklin Associates, Ltd., Prairie Village, Kan. 114 pp.
3. Johnson, B.W., (1994) "Inventory of Land Management Inputs for Producing Absorbent Fiber for diapers: A comparison of cotton and softwood land management," Forest Prod. J. 44(6): 39-45.

4. Kirkpatrick, N., "Life Cycle Assessment," Retrieved 12/21/99 from http://www.wrfound.org.uk/previous/WB47-LCA.html.
5. LeVan, S. L., (1995) "Life Cycle Assessment: Measuring Environmental Impact," Presented at the 49th Annual Meeting of the Forest Products Society, Portland, Oregon, June, pp. 7-16.
6. Madu C. N., (1999) "A Decision Support Framework for Environmental Planning in Developing Countries," Journal of Environmental Planning and Management, 42 (3): 287-313.
7. Madu, C.N. (1996) Managing Green Technologies for Global Competitiveness, Quorum Books, Westport, CT.
8. Madu, C.N., (1994) "A quality confidence procedure for GDSS application in multicriteria decision analysis," IIE Transactions, 26 (3): 31-39.
9. Madu, C.N., & Georgantzas, N.C., (1991) "Strategic thrust of manufacturing decisions: a conceptual framework," IIE Transactions, 23 (2): 138-148.
10. Madu, C.N., (2000) House of Quality (QFD) in a Minute, Fairfield, CT: Chi Publishers, 100 pp.
11. Madu, C.N. & Kuci, C-II., (1995) "Stability analyses of group decision making," Computers & Industrial Engineering, 28(4): 881-892.
12. Madu, C.N., (1998), "Strategic Total Quality Management," in Handbook of Total Quality Management, (ed. C.N. Madu), Boston, MA: Kluwer Academic Publishers, pp 165-212.
13. Product Ecology Consultants, "Life Cycle Assessment (LCA) Explained," Retrieved from http://www.pre.nl/lca.html on 12/21/99.
14. Saaty, T.L., (1980) The Analytic Hierarchy Process, New York, NY: McGraw-Hill.
15. Saaty, T.L. (1987) "Rank generation, preservation, and reversal in the analytic hierarchy decision process, Decision Sciences, 18: 157-162.
16. SETAC (North American & Europe) Workgroups, "Evolution and Development of the Conceptual Framework and Methodology of Life-cycle Impact Assessment," SETAC Press, Washington, D.C., 1-14.
17. Standards Council of Canada (1997) "What will be the ISO 14000 series of international standards - ISO 14000," January.

CHAPTER 10

●──●

THE INTERNET AND ENVIRONMENTAL MANAGEMENT

New technologies are gradually influencing every aspect of our lives. Notable among these technologies is the Internet. In this chapter, we explore the role of the Internet in the management of the environment. We specifically look at the influence of the Internet on consumption, supply chain, information acquisition and globalization, and life styles and marketing through electronic commerce and how that can help to achieve the goals of environmental management.

The Internet is defined as a large group of computers and network appliances that are interconnected. This Web-based technology is instrumental in driving the world towards an information-based economy. Virtually all business activities as well as consumerism have been affected by this new information technology. As Shaw et al. [1997] noted, our economy is shifting to cyberspace through globally connected electronic networks. International Data [1997] projected that Web-initiated sales will rise to the tune of US$117 billion in the year 2000 from US$1 billion in 1995 while Forrester Research [1997] estimates that Internet-related business will grow to US$196 billion by the year 2000. Aside from these predictions, we have noticed a surge in what is now dubbed the new economy businesses that are mostly information technology oriented businesses.

The growth in Internet technology has created new opportunities and challenges and has in fact transformed the modus operandi of business operations. A critical assessment of these developments shows that the Internet technology has permeated all aspects of our daily activities as well as our culture [Madu and Jacob, 1999], and may have inadvertently contributed to environmental management issues. In this chapter, we discuss aspects of environmental issues and how the Internet has influenced them.

Consumption, Life Styles and Marketing through Electronic Commerce

A major cause of environmental pollution is consumption. Consumption is influenced by life styles. Goods and services are created because there is need and demand for them. Without such needs or demand, there will be no purpose for such products or services. In our discussion in chapter 6, we quoted the Indian Minister of Environment for stating the government of India's position in the Rio de Janeiro Earth Summit conference as "Developed countries are mainly responsible for global environmental degradation and must take the necessary corrective steps by modifying *consumption patterns and life styles*; developing countries can participate in global action, but not at the cost of their *development efforts...*"

We have emphasized the key issues in this quote in Italics as they relate to this particular chapter. Clearly, consumption patterns and life styles as well as development efforts are linked to environmental degradation. In fact, the Brundtland Report and the BCSD book titled "Changing Course" recognized this linkage by challenging businesses to focus on sustainable development. Yet, it is still not easy for the world community to completely agree on strategies for sustainable development since environmental pollution can in fact, be found to be associated to economic development. With the threat of global warming and the need to limit the emission of carbon dioxide and other greenhouse gases, oil-producing nations are concerned that a lessening of the world's dependence of fossil fuels could slow down their economic growth. Apart from oil producing nations, industrialized countries are also concerned that limits placed on emission would also hurt their economies. Wealth can also be said to influence lifestyles. With wealth, there is increased demand for luxury. The number of sports utility vehicles (SUVs) in the US and Europe are on the increase even with their large capacity engines. Although these cars burn cleaner however, their share size in number means more consumption and demand for fossil fuels. Developing economies on the other, without the funds to afford newer cars, depend on the older vehicles that may be poorly maintained and likely not to meet the emission control standards. Thus, the level of pollution is also increased.

The Internet however, could help minimize waste and emission by influencing the lifestyle. The Internet offers services that can help cut down on certain trips that may require transportation thereby conserving energy. Common trips to the supermarket, shopping centers, libraries and even school can be effectively reduced through the use of the Internet. The development in the Internet technology has made it possible to conduct day-to-day business and personal activities online. Hence the popularity of electronic commerce (*e-commerce*) and online services such as electronic banking. Through ecommerce, consumers can review competitive products, shop for the better price, and place orders online without the need to drive to different stores to review the product and check on the prices. This effort significantly cuts down on gas consumption and thereby, conserves the use of limited natural resources and reduces the emission of gases to the atmosphere.

Jernelov and Jernelov [1995] identified traveling and heating as western lifestyles that have the greatest impact on the environment. In their report, they state that the classic growth philosophy of the industrialized nations contributed largely to the present environmental problems and suggest that if this philosophy is followed by the developing nations, a global environmental crisis will result. Environmental problems of large cities are often related to the transportation of goods and people. Traffic jams have often resulted to the expansion of road networks and relocation of facilities or sites that attract heavy traffic load. The impact of this has been manifold. As the road networks are expanded, more traffic follow and more pollution follow. The continued increase in traffic is also associated with demand for fossil fuel, demand for more vehicles, demand for landfills and emission control problems. Demand for more energy-efficient vehicles and traffic planning is on the rise as well as the growing emphasis on the use of mass transit system or public transportation network to cut down on traffic congestion, gas usage and emissions. Education is the key to effective environmental management and planning. Consumers of products and services that are environmentally unfriendly need to be educated and made aware of their actions and how they influence the environment. Moreover, they must be offered a reasonable alternative to help change their lifestyles. Although the use of transportation networks cannot be completely eliminated however, there are aspects that can be significantly reduced and controlled. Consumers have to also be aware of the chain reaction that results from their actions. For example, a consumer should be encouraged to use electronic mail when possible than snail mail. Electronic mail cuts down on the demand for paper, it is cost effective, and it reduces the need to travel to the post office. The same could be said of the use of electronic greeting cards. The total effect of this action will be a reduction in the loads transported by the different courier or postal services thereby, reducing the need for fossil fuel and pollution from the tail pipes of the delivery trucks. The aggregate effect of this action on the environment is significant as it not only impacts directly on transportation but also on the demand for paper, construction of new facilities for paper and ink production, less demand for delivery vehicles and less construction of postal sites. This chain reaction effect is possible only by changing a small part of ones lifestyle by switching from the use of snail mail to electronic mail. We can also go further to see that this impact will even be greater when the distance the mail has to travel is further. For example, the use of snail mail such as the delivery of international mails or the transfer of mails from the East coast to the West Coast of the United States. These will require not only road transportation but air transportation too.

The use of electronic commerce is increasingly popular today. People can now shop for almost every product from their home personal computers and even from their wireless cellular telephones or palm pilots that have access to the Internet rather than driving to the physical stores. This was instrumental to the boom enjoyed in the 1990s by the dot com companies such as Amazon.com, priceline.com and ebay.com. The advantage in terms of the environment in this case is that the services provided by these companies are convenient and are competitive. Customers can also surf the net for reasonable prices and place their orders online. Many of the orders are often times filled by warehouses that are located in close proximity to the customer thereby cutting down on shipping and transportation costs.

A more sustainable approach to development must therefore, be followed by all. This is not always possible to achieve since sustainable development is capital intensive and would require costly factory modernization, training of workers and the education of the general public. Capital funding is a limitation to developing countries involvement in sustainable development and without the requisite change in consumption patterns and lifestyles, there will continue to be dependence by poorer nations on natural resources that can be easily excavated and offer the promise of quickly generating cash flow and hard currency. To buttress our argument about the role of the Internet in achieving ecological balance, Jernelov and Jernelov [1995] further noted " the production of goods, measured in volumes, can probably continue to rise if it is the knowledge content of the goods which grows. The same applies to the production of services. Services which consume natural resources, such as transportation, cannot grow continuously without sooner or later coming into conflict with the tolerance of the ecosystem or the capacity of the Earth to supply such resources."

Clearly, the demand for goods and services must be balanced with the social costs that are involved. The Earth has finite resources and the current production and service processes must be adjusted to address the limits of the environment. But, these require not only manufacturers or service providers' decisions but also discipline on the part of the consumers. Consumers could optimize their use of the natural resources thereby protecting the environment by making a critical assessment of their decisions. It is the consumer that will make the decision on what mode of transportation to take or whether to shop on the Internet rather than drive to the store. By making such a critical decision, the consumer cuts down on the consumption of paper and the use of gasoline as well as the emission of carbon dioxide that could result from the driving. Although such efforts may appear to be minor on aggregate, they have great impact. Further, it changes our philosophy on things, as we become more environmentally sensitive. This change in attitude may contribute greatly in achieving emission targets and in reducing emission or pollution from the source rather than the end of pipe environmental management.

The Internet and Globalization

A key role of the Internet is its ability to create a virtual global environment where there are no geographical boundaries. The entire world operates in a small virtual space where members of the global community can easily interact and share their ideas and views on any matter. In the 1970s, the Club of Rome commissioned a group of researchers from Massachusetts Institute of Technology (MIT) and Boston University both in the United States, to develop a report on the environment. Their widely publicized report titled the "Limits to Growth," noted the finite nature of Earth resources by stating that the Earth can only support a certain population. This report generated a lot of concern about the limits in food supply and the exploitation of nonrenewable natural resources and raw materials. Then came the green revolution that showed that technological advances could in fact enhance farm yield and increase farm production in proportions not previously expected. A transition has now been made from "limits to growth" to "sustainable development." To make this transition requires transformation to new technology. This is not always feasible for many members of the world community thus while a portion of the world may be operating on their traditional technological practice that will lead to limits to growth, another part of the world may be focusing on sustainable development. For example, in land irrigation, without proper drainage system, large accumulation of salt will be deposited on the land and will eventually lead to a reduction in production capacity and therefore reduction in farm yield (Jernelov and Jernelov). This will create a dependency status where the poorer nations without the capital formation to modernize their production systems will eventually depend on the industrialized nations with sustainable technologies to support them.

The availability of information on the Internet is also a catch 22 in terms of environmental management. It could enhance sustainable development by making essential information and practices available to developing countries. However, it could create an array of opportunities to circumvent tough environmental laws in some countries. Companies even in the industrialized countries who cannot afford or are reluctant to adjust to new environmental laws in their home countries may easily evaluate alternative countries with lesser environmental laws and possibly relocate their operations. Further, without international policies guiding technological practices, developing countries may easily become dumping grounds for technologies that are disallowed by legislatures in industrialized countries. This is a case of buyer beware that is unheeded. For example, massive selloff of processes or technologies that do not meet emission guidelines in a particular country may find new markets in places where there are no emission laws. More importantly, the seller does not incur the huge cost of going abroad to market such products and could easily sell these products electronically. On December 20, 2000 for example, the Clinton administration approved new regulations to cut air pollution from heavy-duty trucks and buses by more than 90 percent over the next decade [Josef Hebert, 2000]. This new law requires refiners to produce sulfur-free diesel fuel. Some analysts are equating the magnitude of this new law to the removal of lead from gasoline. It is estimated that the production reduction achieved by this law will be equivalent to removing 13 million trucks from the road. This law will apply to new trucks and replacement truck engines sold beginning in late 2006. Some manufacturers and interest groups are already criticizing the law claiming that it is too stringent and that the timetable is too tight. However, it will not be unexpected to see large sell off of vehicles that do not meet these standards and demand for them in economies where emission laws are relaxed or nonexistent.

While the Internet could be a source for disseminating information globally on this and other environmental legislation, the ability to afford new technology is a major factor that will determine adherence to new environmentally sensitive technologies. In fact, for businesses in less affluent economies, it will be an opportunity to acquire a needed product at a cheap direct cost never mind the social cost to the environment. While the Internet makes information readily available, the critical issue is how such information is used given that there is no universal law enforcement on many aspects of the environment.

Perhaps, a more important aspect of this conservation of resources is in global business operations between business to business (B2B). Some of the B2B activities and operations such as enlisting new suppliers or vendors and developing new business alliances can be effectively negotiated online without a physical face-to-face meeting. This of course cuts down on the demand for travel in any form and again, reduces the demand for fossil fuels. More importantly, the operations are more efficient as just-in-time concept is introduced in every stage of the process. The essence of the just-in-time concept will be to cut down on excessive production by reducing the level of inventory. On time and online availability of information could cut down the lead-time in replenishing orders and also reduce the production cycle time. Furthermore, the availability of quality information on demand and the ability to track demand data effectively will help to reduce the size of the safety stock.

Globalization and ensuing frequent communication will help to better understand different worldviews and establish trust and security in business operations. Business partners are more able to understand each other's needs and work to accomplish the same environmental goals. The problem of miscommunication where both the vendor and supplier have different views of the same issue is significantly reduced. It will not be the case of supply exceeding demand or vice versa but the case of supply meeting exactly the demand. In any of the two adverse cases, energy and materials are expended to deal with either the excess demand or shortage in demand. For example, when supply is less than demand, higher set up cost may be incurred, as new production runs must be initiated to satisfy the extra demand. Conversely, if supply is in excess of demand, waste is incurred thus leading to sub optimization of both materials and energy that were consumed in producing the goods. Waste could also be incurred through the high cost of inventory management. Information is the key to better management of inventory and the Internet facilitates effective management of information.

Effective supply chain management can help disseminate and manage information thereby, reducing waste in both energy and material. The manufacturer works with its suppliers and internal business units through the application of Extranet and Intranet principles. Decisions made are interdependent and are thoroughly evaluated to ensure that they meet corporate goals and objectives.

Information Acquisition and Globalization

Researchers at the School of Information Management and Systems at University of California forecast that due to the Internet and the rapid global expansion of computing, humans and their machines will create more information in the next three years than in the last 300,000 years. This sentiment is also echoed by Wall Street analysts who project that spending on data storage products is approaching spending on computers and will account for 70 percent of information technology budget by the year 2005 [Feder, 2001]. EMC Corporation a major supplier of data storage devices projects that by the year 2005, an individual can easily use up a terabyte of stored information. This is equivalent to about 250 million pages of text.

There are implications to be derived from this growing demand for information. One obvious implication is the influence of information or data storage on the environment. The traditional approach to data storage is through printed-paper documents that are stored in filing cabinets and housed in warehouses or archival centers. The problem with this traditional method is its dependence on wood pulp for paper manufacturing thereby placing a huge demand on the forestry. Further when the data is archived or stored in filing cabinets, the demand for the filing cabinets also puts pressure on natural resources such as metals and again on wood and the forestry and a whole chain of other resources to build the warehouse. For example, more land is excavated for construction, more energy and material resources are used to build and maintain the warehouses. Yet, information stored in this manner is often difficult to manage, degrades overtime and may not be timely accessible for decision-making. Maintenance of physical information archives also place huge environmental burden on the society since information retrieval will often require physical transportation to the archival center and perhaps, photocopying of documents. This will utilize ink and paper. Even though paper may be recyclable however, the process of recycling often uses bleaching agents, which may place environmental burdens and may also demand energy usage. The effect of this traditional approach to data management is multifarious and its impact can only be evaluated by adopting a holistic platform.

Some of the problems encountered through the traditional data management can be curtailed by adopting a digital storage network system. Globally, more and more people are signing up to the Internet and are growing increasingly confident in using the Internet to conduct transactions. It is estimated that about 50 million new users will sign up each year for the coming decade to the Internet [Madu, 1999]. Increased use of the Internet may have also contributed to the growth in eBusiness and eCommerce and globalization. Businesses are now better able to virtually offer more features and services to customers. For example, how possible would it be without digitization for amazon.com to maintain and manage information on more than 2 million book titles? This would have required tremendous investment on warehouses and tremendous amount of paperwork if inventory is to be manually done. With the development of fast and reliable digital storage devices, the quality of stored information is not compromised and decision-making process is greatly enhanced by the timely availability and accuracy of stored information. Information is the key to effective and wise decisions. This can only be possible if the quality of information is maintained and information is timely available for decision-making. So, while digital storage of information may be environmentally sensible, it is also business-wise. For example, Linda Sanford, senior vice president for IBM storage group was quoted as stating, "Storage is becoming the heart and soul of all business. What you know about your customers, suppliers and partners will differentiate you at the end of the day." Indeed, that is true. Supply chain management is based on this concept as it strives to eliminate islands of information that are not cohesive and integrated in the decision-making framework. The maintenance of digital storage devices allow a great amount of information to be digitally stored and provide timely and multi access to users at different locations. The real globalization effect will be felt through mutual sharing of information. Thus, a supplier in Europe can digitally get purchase order from a manufacturer in the United States and confirm order fulfillment without having to printout the order or mail out any confirmation of such orders. Online electronic businesses receive the majority of their orders from customers online; provide order fulfillment and confirmation online to customers through their emails. With the rapid growth on online businesses, this is a significant saving in the demand for paper, postage and transportation. We shall therefore, discuss how supply chain network can help to accomplish these goals.

Supply Chain Management

Supply chain network involves a group of vendors, suppliers, manufacturers and distributors whose common goal is to satisfy the needs of customers by supplying them with needed products and services. While businesses have operated for centuries through this same network however, information technology helps to facilitate the supply chain network by providing timely information and reducing the cycle time to deliver products and services. There are however, many benefits to the modern application of supply chain network especially in the context of environmental protection. Through supply chain network, limited resources are more efficiently utilized, materials and energy are conserved, and production and inventory are controlled.

Beckman [2000] noted that many of the U.S. firms are highly vertically integrated but are now shifting to outsourcing some of their manufacturing operations to external vendors. She also notes that the control on the environmental impact by a company will depend on its activities along the supply chain. For example, companies such as Apple Computer and 3Com Corporation outsource most of their manufacturing operations and have minimal emission levels but may have responsibilities with the use and disposal of their products [Beckman et al 2000]. The key to environmental management through supply chain is however, not based on the direct environmental burden generated by a particular supplier or vendor in the supply chain network. Manufacturers are forced by social and environmental factors to take a cradle to grave approach of their products. They need to evaluate the entire product life cycle irrespective of whom the process is outsourced to. For example,

Apple Computer is responsible for the environmental burden generated by its products irrespective of which vendor supplied or manufactured the silicon logs that may have been used in producing the chips. As a result, the manufacturer adopts a holistic view of its product knowing that even with a vertically disintegrated setting, that the environmental supply chain management must be sound and acceptable.

It is not uncommon therefore, for manufacturers to establish standards that must be met by suppliers within its supply chain network to ensure that its final product completely satisfies environmental demands. Hence many manufacturers are requiring their vendors and suppliers to be ISO 14001 certified to participate in its supply chain management. The ISO 14000 series establishes accepted guidelines for environmental management systems and provide good guides to the manufacturer on acceptable environmental requirements. In fact, Beckman [2000] shows that even companies such as Sun Microsystems and Silicon Graphics that outsource most of their production have both developed environmental guidelines to manage supplier quality.

There are several incentives for effective management of environmental supply chain network. Some of the motivation to the focus of achieving environmental management through supply chain management can be outlined as follows:

1. Environmental prevention pays—Previously, environmental protection was perceived to be costly and burdensome to the goal of profit making. However, as corporations begin to carefully analyze the cost of environmental burdens, they perceive environmental prevention from the onset through a life cycle management approach to be cost effective. When the entire supply chain is involved in managing environmental quality, the corporation can in fact, conserve energy and resources by retrieving, recycling and reusing some of the product components without seeking the more expensive virgin components. In chapter 6, we outlined how Kodak achieved economic gains through the recycling of its single-use camera and also how Xerox has profited through remanufacturing of its products.

2. Customer focus—The pressure on companies to be environmentally sensitive is real. Consumers are now increasingly concerned about the environment and more and more people participate in recycling efforts. Environmental

activist groups are also increasingly popular and influential, and target companies perceived to be polluters. Paper manufacturers and oil companies often face demonstrations by groups opposed to their environmental records. Such demonstrations often result in disruption of operations and negative publicity to the company. The role of the environmental activist groups and the growing concern of consumers are forcing manufacturers to increasingly integrate them in the decision making framework and to develop products and services that are sensitive to environmental needs.

3. Laws and Regulations—Public concerns regarding the contamination of the environment have fueled new changes in environmental laws and regulations. Government regulations in the past focused on "end-of-pipe" management of environmental pollution [Beckman et al, 2000]. This approach often ignores the cradle-to-grave concept where the manufacturer accepts responsibility for the environmental burden created by its product and its by-products through its life cycle. As a result, the supply chain network is ignored and corrective rather than preventive action is taken. The emerging new evidences that there is a serious threat of environmental degradation influence this change in our mentality of how to best manage the environmental burden. For example, a recent report on Climate Change by the United Nations noted that global temperatures could rise by as much as 10 1/2 degrees over the next century. This is much higher than the 2 1/2 to 5 1/2 degrees previously projected. Such a sharp rise in temperature could lead to several environmental disasters such as floods, draught and shifts in weather patterns [McDonald, 2001]. A report such as this often reconfirms the growing concern for global warming and the need to enact legislatures to reduce greenhouse gases and cut atmospheric emissions of carbon dioxide.

4. The general public plays a critical role in ensuring that laws and legislatures that protect the environment by limiting industrial pollution are enacted. Environmental activist groups as well as environmental issues are increasingly important in national politics. The 2000 US presidential election where the Independent party candidate Ralph Nader a consumer advocate ran very strongly in states like Florida,

Oregon, Washington and California may have been the deciding factor for the presidential election. His support base attracted mostly environmentalists and nature conservationists. Increasingly, more politicians are declaring support for environmental causes thus also leading to development of new laws to protect the environment.

5. The cost of environmental cleanup is also significantly high. Examples include the high cost of cleanup for the Three Mile Island, the Chernobyl Chemical Plant incidence, the Union Carbide case and the Exxon Validez case [downloaded from ***http://www.iisd.ca/linkages/consume/inst-sd.html***]. In all these cases, irreparable damages were done to nature, people and wild lives thus disturbing the eco-balance and also leading to massive cost of cleanup and litigations.

6. Economic impact of environmental standards— Environmental standards and certifications are vogue today. Many nations seek environmental protections by requiring manufacturers to show evidence of ISO 14000 certification for publicly funded projects. Eco-labeling schemes are also becoming increasingly popular and are often used by manufacturers to suggest evidence of social responsibility. Consumers appear to look for some major labels as a guide on the environmental burden of the product. Popular among these labels are the blue angel eco-labeling, white swan and green seal used in Germany, Europe, Nordic Council and the United States respectively.

7. Competitiveness—Of course, if others are doing it, why not us. Manufacturers are listening to the voice of the customer. Green consumerism is strong and it is driving corporate environmental responsibility programs and profits. Auto manufacturers are increasingly designing cars that weigh less and use fewer materials, increasing mileage per gallon, and reducing requirements for oil and filter changes, and even exploring the introduction of electric cars. All these seem to position them as ready to address the environmental burdens created by their products. The recognition that there is a growing trend towards green consumerism is a backbone for gaining new market shares.

To completely address these forces that are pushing towards more environmental sensitivity requires that a cradle to grave approach be taken by implementing the environmental quality management philosophy through every step of the product design and production stages. The supply chain network is crucial to achieving this but it relies on effective information network that could be effectively offered through the Internet. In other words, the Internet will help to cut down redundancies, reduce the cycle time to implementing effective environmental policies, speed up the accessibility to information, and effectively manage and reduce waste. In the next section, we discuss some elements of environmental information management.

Environmental Information Management

Frysinger [2000] notes the complexity of environmental decision making. He states the need for environmental decision support systems to assist managers make efficient environmental decisions. However, information needs to be made available in a form that facilitates effective cognitive decision-making. Environmental problems are complex often influencing a diverse group of people and affecting domains outside its immediate environment. Also, environmental impacts and effects are far reaching and may expand well into the future. The unpredictable nature of the consequences often makes it difficult to fully access environmental impacts. Some environmental impacts are not known or even anticipated until years after they have occurred. The quality and timeliness of information could in fact, help to address some of the problems that are encountered in making environmental decisions. As stated by Frysinger, environmental decision problems can be categorized in six parts as discussed below:

- Spatial—in this case, environmental problem may be situation-dependent and may vary from place to place. For example, in most developing economies, agriculture is still the dominant economic activity. Their method of farming is primarily based on land rotation or bush fallow system that depends largely on land and labor as major inputs of production. It is therefore, important that environmental changes are contained to protect the quality of the soil, land, and forestry [Owabukeruyele, 2000]. Without decisions that recognize this need, deforestation and drilling for mineral resources could severely affect the availability of land and the quality of soil and water thus affecting the fertility of the lands. In fact, in communities such as the Niger Delta region of Nigeria where massive oil drilling has led to the pollution of once fertile lands, peasant farmers are migrating to other communities and urban areas seeking for other means of livelihood [Owabukeruyele 2000]. The issue then is the impact of such environmental decision on the economy and the health of the community. What are therefore, the cost of such social destabilization and the cost of the environmental pollution that is created?

- Multidisciplinary—environmental problems involve issues that go beyond the traditional focus on natural sciences. It is increasingly understandable now that environmental decisions involve a lot of management, economics, social, legal and political issues. Hardly any body of knowledge that is not involved in making environmental issues. Thus, environmental decision makers would benefit from interdisciplinary groups that share different worldviews of the same problem. Clearly, corporate managers are concerned with bottom-line issues and will pay more attention to environmental management issues when they perceive the benefits as outweighing the cost. Of course, cost would have to be both direct and indirect including litigation costs, clean up and malpractice costs as well as the cost of loss of customer good will for not responding appropriately and timely to environmental costs. It will therefore, behoove environmental managers to ensure that diverse teams of people that share environmental concerns participate in its advisory body. Already, this is happening. As noted in Madu [1996], collaboration between environment interest groups and corporations are increasing. For example, the Environmental Defense Fund (EDF) collaborated with McDonald's the fast food restaurant giant to switch from polystyrene containers to paper wraps for its food products thereby reducing the amount of solid waste created by the company. Pacific Gas and Electric Company often consult with the Natural Defense Council, and New England Electric System collaborated with Conservation Law Foundation in developing the company's twenty-year strategic plan. These strategic alliances suggest that corporations are not only listening to the environmental interest groups but are also benefiting from the diverse backgrounds of these groups.

- Quantitative—Frysinger suggests that since the constituent disciplines for environmental problem solving are highly quantitative, because of the consequences and significance of the costs, that objective metrics should be used. While it is important to use objective metrics, we must also state that there are several qualitative issues that may not be easily quantified. Environmental decisions involve a human side and sound and wise judgment may often not be entirely quantitative. There is also the social and political ramifications of environmental problems that often negate the value of an objective metric. We would however; recommend that any quantitative approach to solving environmental decision problems should integrate as well, the qualitative issues. This will require the use of multi-criteria decision making models that do not constrain the decision maker to only objective data.

- Uncertain—the environment we operate in is highly uncertain. We are limited by our information base and by technology. The unavailability of both could significantly affect the decisions derived. Thus, decisions may be made in the face of incomplete information. Decision models should therefore leave room for the uncertainty in the decision making environment. Further, dynamic and probabilistic models should be explored for better understanding of the decision environment. A simulated model that investigates anticipated scenarios with assigned probabilities of occurrence and adequate sensitivity analysis will enable the decision maker to better understand the decision environment even in light of these uncertainties.

- Quasi-procedural—this refers to the influence of regulatory or corporate policies on environmental decisions. There are regulatory conditions that deal with emission of greenhouse gases, and solid and toxic waste disposals that must be satisfied. There is also an avalanche of national and international standards on the environment that detect the direction a firm must follow. These standards influence corporate policies on the environment. For example, the 1990 Amendment of the Clean Air Act had a profound effect on corporate environmental policies as it stated a timetable for the different chemicals that will be outlawed such as CFC and percentage of reductions in emissions that must be achieved.

It also provided guidelines for containing urban smog within six years and limiting the emission of ground-level ozone, which is the primary cause of urban smog. Other guidelines for controlling the emissions of sulfur dioxide and nitrogen oxide in order to deal with the problem of acid rain are provided [Madu 1996]. Some of the other major legislatures on the environment include the Superfund which is an embodiment of three major environmental laws that include the Clean Air Act, the Safe Drinking Water Act, and the Comprehensive Environmental Response, Compensation and Liability Act (CERCLA), and the Montreal Protocol on CFCs—an international treaty that established timetables for worldwide phasing out of CFCs, the chemicals that destroy the ozone layer. In addition to these laws, the Emergency Planning Community Right to Know Act, 1986 known as the Title III Superfund Amendments and Reauthorization Act (SARA) mandates companies with nine or more employees to provide details of the 313 listed toxic chemicals and chemical compounds they release into the air, water, or underground wells. Its 1991 version further requires manufacturers to provide information on the chemical content per product. The importance of SARA is that it mandates public disclosure from companies thus enabling the public to scrutinize the environmental conduct of the respective companies and their industries in creating waste and pollution. Further, it makes it possible to comparatively assess the conduct of these companies on their use and emission of toxic elements. Thus, the environmental component could become a competitive factor. These laws have nonetheless, influenced corporate environmental policies and pushed more and more companies to become more environmentally responsible.

- Political—this recognizes the fact that environmental issues are intertwined with politics, economics, social impacts, and public opinion. This has become increasingly evident in international efforts to limit the emission of greenhouse gases. As stated in chapter 6, developing countries tend to perceive any cut back on emission of carbon as a hindrance to their economic growth. This is further supported by data that suggests that countries with higher emissions also have higher economic growth [Madu 1999]. The politics of economic development is also very complex and often is entangled in contradictions. While many of the industrialized nations are reluctant to offer debt relief to developing countries that owe huge sums of money to international monetary agencies and banks, they are at the same time seeking the support and participation of developing countries in reducing emission and dependence on fossil fuels. With growing economic hardship in developing countries, it is inconceivable that they will partake to cut down on drilling of raw materials or incessant destruction of their forestry for hard currency when they are strapped for cash. It is therefore, unrealistic to seek environmental protection without addressing the inherent socio-economic and political factors in many regions of the world.

Guidelines for Environmental Information System (EIS)

This discussion lays the platform for developing guidelines for information acquisition, usage and dissemination through the cyberspace. We present a model on how better environmental decisions could be made utilizing the power of the Internet or cyberspace. Environmental management requires a coordinated organizational effort and emphasis. It demands a holistic focus on the entire organizational processes and may defy the focus on small incremental continuous improvements. In fact, it demands reengineering of both the entire process of manufacturing and service delivery as well as organizational practices. One of the major problems plaguing the practice of environmental quality management is the fact the efforts to achieve environmental quality are not well coordinated to achieve a common goal. The different business units act independently rather than as a unit. Wells, O'Connell and Hochman [1993] point out "environmental information systems have not kept pace with the changes in management methods that have occurred over the past years -- they are media-specific and maintained on separate and often incompatible systems. Often, the only way to cross-media data that help to identify and prirotize pollution prevention opportunities is to download data and to crank them manually." Although this article is almost ten years old, the statement is still true. It is not uncommon for different business units in a company to have different guidelines and different sources of information on environmental pollution. The use of different environmental data and the lack of coordination by the different units lead to suboptimization. Further, the fact that an organization operates with its supply chain network demands that a cradle to grave approach be taken of its products and services. This will require sharing of the same environmental information and ensuring that environmental guidelines and standards are maintained through out the product's life cycle. It is not sufficient for a vendor to act on its part without linking it to the efforts of other vendors along the network. Otherwise, the product may be contaminated along the line and will still not meet environmental standards. There is therefore, a need to bring all these island of environmental information from different units or vendors into a cohesive whole that can be used to establish appropriate company guidelines. This systemic approach ensures that the product's stages of development may not be affected by a sub-standard practice. This is particularly important since a company may outsource some stages of its production to companies in areas with different environmental practices. For example, production in some third world nations may not be efficiently regulated for environmental purposes as in the industrialized countries. A corporate standard that meets international standards could be established as a guideline irrespective of country policies. The key to achieving these standards is information and its timely availability. The Internet in that regards will be a useful source not only to provide timely information but also to retrieve archival environmental data and coordinate the efforts and activities of vendors at multi-locations. We shall illustrate the core of the Environmental Information System using a modified version of the framework presented by Kuei [1996].

The major component of this framework is the centralization of information. All vendors, suppliers and business units have access to a common database. The database could maintain information on the inventory of substance, chemicals and toxics that could not be used in the production process. It could also maintain a record keeping of the different processes and production guidelines as well as supply sources and their environmental records. The different databases are grouped accordingly as follows:

Production Environmental Quality Assessment Database—this database maintains information on the actual production practices and their potential fallouts in terms of environmental pollution. Specific information must be provided such as the expected emission of gases and the exact levels as well as potential consequences. For example, the practice of this production process in manufacturing part product

A will lead to the generation of one million metric tons of carbon. This will exceed the requirement of 200,000 tons of carbon a year for the production of part product A. This type of information is specific. It is not sufficient to suggest that a process will emit carbon but we need to be specific on the quantity of the emission and compare it to established standards. Likewise, the consumption of resources should be clearly discussed. How much of the natural resources such as water, natural gas or fuel is used by this production process and how does it compare to standards? Even when a production plan meets an established standard, it may not be the best option available for achieving the same goal. A comparative assessment of the other production plans should be conducted before making a decision on the most appropriate production plan. It is also at this stage that a consideration of the input material is conducted.

Process Environmental Quality Assessment Database—the database contained here deal directly with the machinery of production and the human input in the production process. For example, how does the equipment used in the production process and the human interaction contribute in generating waste and creating pollution? How can such problems be avoided? Are there machinery design issues that contribute to the environmental burden that is being observed? What materials were used in designing and manufacturing the machinery? And are they environmentally friendly? A holistic approach to environmental management again will require a cradle to grave approach that treats the entire process as systemic.

Delivery Environmental Quality Assessment Database— Arguably, the delivery of products and services contribute to a lot of waste and pollution that are incurred. For example, the Kodak single-use camera illustrates how the delivery system can influence environmental protection. In that case, the entire distribution network is organized so that the product is recovered at the end of its designed useful life. Manufacturers must develop a distribution network to ensure that their products could be recovered after their intended use and may be rebuilt or remanufactured for future use. One of the strategies for recovering wastes and components include repurchase programs for toner cartridges that are refilled rather than dumped into the landfills. Many computer manufacturers also offer lease programs to major buyers while retrieving and recovering old computers and some of their component parts for future manufacturing. Packaging of materials is also another major source of pollution. Many manufacturers are now shipping their products with recycled packaging that could be recovered and reused.

Product Environmental Quality Assessment—This database deals with the product itself and its interaction with the environment. What environmental burdens does the product create to the environment? What are the sources of such burden? And how can the environmental burden be reduced? Benchmarking competitors both in terms of their product and their production and delivery practices can make product environmental quality assessment more efficient. This will also help the organization to become more competitive as it learns from its competitors and understands the needs of the customer.

Government Environmental Quality Assessment—The government maintains a huge database on the environment. For example, the United States Environmental Protection Agency maintains a huge database of toxic pollutants and their potential consequences [Madu 1996]. Further, many national governments have environmental management programs and laws and regulations guiding environmental pollution. Companies that violate environmental laws end up paying huge liability and penalty fees and their chief executive officers may get jail time. There is no excuse for ignorance of the law. The enforcement of government environmental laws will also ensure that the company does not face public outrage when a violation is noted and made public. Obviously, with many companies having multinational operations, it is perhaps more important to adopt a strict environmental guideline that will satisfy the conditions in all the nations of operation.

International Environmental Quality Assessment Database—Organizations cannot effectively chase over the avalanche of international environmental laws and regulations. However, with the adoption of common standards as in the case of ISO (International Organization for Standards) 14000 series, it will become easier to coordinate all environmental activities by private groups, nations, and international bodies as the United Nations and International Monetary Fund. ISO standards when adopted become binding to the adopting nations and can offer clear guidance and policy standards for companies operating in those nations.

These databases should be linked to a central storage device at the company referred to as Environmental Information System (EIS). Suppliers and vendors through their remote computers can hook up to the Internet and get direct access to the EIS. Once on the EIS, they can access any of the databases discussed above. The advantages of this approach to environmental management are multifold:

- Consistency of information—this method ensures that all suppliers and vendors have access to the same environmental information and are using the same information in their processes.
- Accuracy of information—it ensures that the information used is validated and acceptable to the manufacturer and removes any ambiguities.
- Centralization of information—it ensures that all scattered information is brought together into central unit for use.
- Data mining—it makes it easier to retrieve and query archival data.
- Timeliness—information is updated on timely bases and is instantly available to all users.
- Information barrier—it removes the barrier that may be created due to the multi locations of vendors. Also, misconceptions and misunderstanding of what is required is better handled.
- Efficiency of information—the efficiency of sample information is improved since quality information can easily be obtained and updated on a timely basis.
- Cross-unit efficiency—the different departments within the organization become more efficient and strive to achieve optimal environmental goals.
- Cost reduction—cost is significantly reduced since the product is now more likely to meet environmental goals. Therefore, there will be less rejects and wastes, and an early detection of environmental problems.

CONCLUSION

In this chapter, we have discussed how environmental management can benefit from the exploding use of the Internet. It is clear that using the Internet more efficiently could effectively reduce certain wastes. Some of the areas we identified include the demand on paper products and fossil fuels. We also showed that on a corporate level, that supply chain networks could help to achieve environmental quality by using a coordinated environmental information base. This will help to ensure effective participation of vendors and suppliers as well as business units in achieving organizational environmental goals.

REFERENCES

1. Shaw, M.J., Gardner, D.M., and Thomas, H., "Research opportunities in electronic commerce," *Decision Support Systems*, Vol. 21, p. 149-156, 1997.
2. International Data, Shaw, M.J., Gardner, D.M., and Thomas, H., "Research opportunities in electronic commerce," *Decision Support Systems*, Vol. 21, p. 149-156, 1997.
3. Forrester Research, Shaw, M.J., Gardner, D.M., and Thomas, H., "Research opportunities in electronic commerce," *Decision Support Systems*, Vol. 21, p. 149-156, 1997.
4. Madu, C.N., and Jacob, R.A., "The Internet and Global Cultural Transformation: A Unification of Cultures," *Foresight*, 1, 1, 1999.
5. Jernelöv, A., and Jernelöv, S., "Sustainable Development and Sustainable Consumption", Instrument to Promote Sustainable Consumption and Production Seminar, 1995. *http://www.iisd.ca/linkages/consume/inst-sd.html*
6. Herbert, J., "New Federal Pollution Rules Set for Trucks", Associated Press, 2000 *http://community.lexisone.com/news/ap/ap_b122100c.html*
7. Beckman, S., Bercovitz, J., and Rosen, C., "Environmentally Sound Supply Chain Management," in Handbook of Environmentally Conscious Manufacturing (ed. C.N. Madu), Boston, MA: Kluwer Academic Publishers, 2000.
8. McDonald, J., "Global Warming Is Getting Worse, Scientists Warn", Associated Press, 2001. *http://www.aircondition.com/wwwboard/current/22069.html*
9. Madu, C.N., Strategic Planning in Technology Transfers to Less Developed Countries, Westport, CT: Quorum Books, 1992.
10. Frysinger, S.P., "Environmental Decision Support Systems A Tool for Environmentally Conscious Manufacturing," in Handbook of Environmentally Conscious Manufacturing (ed. C.N. Madu), Boston, MA: Kluwer Academic Publishers, 2000.

11. Owabukeruyele, W.S., "Hydrocarbon exploitation, environmental degradation and poverty in the Niger Delta region of Nigeria," presented at Lund University, LUMES program, Lund, Sweden, January 2000.
12. Madu, C.N., Managing Green Technologies for Global Competitiveness, Westport, CT: Quorum Books, 1996.
13. Madu, C.N., "A decision support framework for Environmental Planning in developing countries," Journal of *Environmental Planning and Management*, 42(3), 287-313, 1999.
14. Meadows, D. et al., Limits to Growth: Report of the Club of Rome, 1972.
15. Wells, R.P., O'Connell, P.A., and Hochman, S., "What is the Difference between Reengineering and TQEM?," *Total Quality Environmental Management* 2(3), 273-282, 1993.
16. Kuei, C-H., "Reengineering Environmental-Quality Management," in Madu, C.N., Managing Green Technologies for Global Competitiveness, Westport, CT: Quorum Books, 1996.

CHAPTER 11

MANUFACTURING STRATEGIES: AGILE, LEAN AND FLOW MANUFACTURING

In this chapter, we discuss some of the new manufacturing technologies and how they could help improve quality and productivity and reduce environmental burden to the society. We shall focus specifically on agile manufacturing, lean manufacturing, and flow manufacturing. These techniques also benefit from the application of just-in-time inventory system, total quality control, and total productive maintenance. These relationships are discussed in the chapter.

Agile Manufacturing

Agile manufacturing is a new manufacturing philosophy that originated from the Japanese auto and consumer electronic industries. The aim is to inspire to achieve total flexibility with high quality at minimum costs. Agile manufacturing is intended to transform the traditional manufacturing practice to something more efficient and productive and responsive to the dynamic needs and demands of the customer. The basic thrust of agile manufacturing was identified in Keen's "Agile Manufacturing" [2001]. We shall expand the discussion to include the following:

1. Reducing dependency on the economies of scale—unlike traditional assembly line system where volume drives production, agile manufacturing encourages flexibility and therefore variations in the basic product design which counters the focus of the traditional flow shop operation. Agile manufacturing uses new adaptive manufacturing technologies such as ["Agile manufacturing," 2001]:

- Rapid prototyping (RP)—These are a class of technology that are used to develop physical and prototype parts or models and may include three dimensional computer-aided design.

- Rapid Tooling (RT)—this consists of the additive and subtractive processes. The additive processes use advanced methods of making tools based on the RP technology while the subtractive processes use the advanced methods of making tools that are based on the milling technology. Both methods rely on the use of digital database.
- Reverse Engineering (RE)—this is a hybrid of approaches to reproducing physical objects. It could use manual drawings, documentations, computer-aided approaches or a mixture of both. Reverse engineering supports the use of any method or approach that may be necessary to reproduce an item.

2. Low volumes are produced at competitive prices—this seems to encourage small orders rather than mass production operation.

3. Decentralized mini-assembly plants—the notion of maintaining a centralized assembly line system that produces basically identical products is replaced with a decentralized mini-assembly plants that are situated near demand centers. This helps to cater to the needs of the different demand centers but more importantly, satisfy the goal of just-in-time delivery. It therefore, helps to reduce inventory levels and the costs associated with inventory thus adding more value to the customer.

4. Flexibility—Flexibility is important in agile manufacturing. Different configurations of the product are encouraged and offered.

5. Worker motivation—Worker motivation is enhanced since the worker is no longer following with a routine task as defined in the traditional assembly line system. Rather, the worker offers inputs in configuring his or her work operation and is not bored by repetitive tasks.

6. Product design—the product design is based on listening to the voice of the customer. Rather than designing a product or service as perceived by the engineer, the customer is an active participant in designing the product or service to meet his or her needs. Thus, customer satisfaction is high.

7. Supply chain management—Supply chain management is emphasized, as there is need for suppliers, vendors, and distributors to share the same goals as the manufacturer and meet both its quality and environmental standards. Thus, a

transformation of the traditional type of relationship with suppliers is needed.

8. Coordination—To achieve the goals of agile manufacturing in terms of quality, speed of delivery, and flexibility, good coordination and management of information is required. Again, the use of an integrated information system.

Agility is a rapid response to the changing operating environment of the firm. Businesses operate in an atmosphere of intense competition that is subject to a lot of surprises and unpredictability. The business environment of tomorrow is unknown let alone the future. The firm is increasingly faced by many threats emanating from the following:

- Customer needs and expectations are very dynamic and evolving.
- Intense competition from new entrants into the industry and even from firms in other industrial sectors.
- Globalization of businesses while opening up new markets, has led to new competition with different rules for the game. The new competitors often come with different strategies and philosophies that are difficult to predict.
- The rapid proliferation of new technologies and new products has increased Research and Development costs and led to drastic shortening of the product life cycle. Market niches are no longer guaranteed, safeguarded or protected from competition.
- Increased number of stakeholders and interest groups with their own agendas i.e., environmental interest groups, diversity groups present new challenges that businesses must respond to.

In order to meet up with the demands of agile manufacturing, the firm must be flexible, robust, and ready to adapt. It must readily scan its environment to identify new opportunities and challenges and align its strengths to meet these rapid changes in its environment. An agile company must be in continuous movement with time to respond proactively to changes in manufacturing practices, technology, natural environment, and customer requirements. The key is to rapidly adapt to unexpected and unpredictable changes in the organization's operating environment. This is not easily achieved since rapid adaptation may often conflict with long-term organizational strategic plans and may also not align with organizational culture and climate thus disrupting the organization. However, this is the only way that the organization can remain competitive, and be able to satisfy the needs of its customers. There are five key areas that would specifically influence how the organization responds to its operating environment. These are the organization itself, management of change, product development, the natural environment, and relationship with customers and suppliers. We shall briefly discuss each of these.

The Organization As A Change System

To respond rapidly to agile manufacturing, the organization needs to adapt and change. The traditional hierarchical structure of the organization would have to be transformed into a more fluid system with openness for sharing ideas, information, and knowledge. This would require a transformation of the organizational structure to recognize the mutual dependence between the different functional and business units of the firm. More so, the firm must appreciate its operating environment and recognize the importance of the information flow and two-way relationship it has with its operating environment. This would enable it to respond rapidly to the needs of its environment.

The organizational structure must be flexible to support acquisition and use of new information to update existing knowledge. Power and authority would have to be delegated to more people so decisions can be made on a real time basis. In other words, strategizing of decisions should be spread across the firm and not rest solely with top management. Decisions regarding the different processes that interact with the firm have to be distributed and coordinated so that the firm can respond rapidly to its dynamic environment. Such decisions may include process selections, suppliers/vendor selections, partnerships with competitors and suppliers, and customer relationships. Furthermore, a more coordinated and integrated decision-making process that includes more active participants or stakeholders should be encouraged while employees are empowered to make work-related decisions.

Management of Change

To deal with agile manufacturing, a firm must develop its core competence in management of change. Change is inevitable and unpredictable and may often be clouded with uncertainties. Change is also a major threat to organization's survival and yet may provide the best opportunity for growth and competitiveness. Organizational change is complex because it deals not only with the organizational structure and processes but also the human element that is involved. It is not always easy to get people to change attitudes, values and culture that are acquired over several years. In fact, the ability to manage change will depend on how able the human processes will adapt to change. This may require a great deal of training and counseling to get employees to accept change as a necessity and vital to the survival of the organization. Agile manufacturing seeks a re-engineering of the traditional manufacturing process and such radical change cannot take place without a challenge from some traditionalists. It is therefore important to develop a proactive strategy to get everyone on board when agile manufacturing is introduced. Information sharing will be important and participatory decision-making will expose employees to the dangers of not adapting to the new process. A rapid response to change and developing strategic initiatives to manage change in the entire organization will enable the organization to respond proactively to its dynamic environment.

Product Development

Changes are needed in product development. The ultimate aim of the product is to satisfy customer needs. Therefore, the customer should be a participant in deciding how his or her needs could be satisfied through product design and development. In addition, there are several stakeholders who are influenced by the product or influence the successful introduction and marketing of the product. These stakeholders are active participants and should take part in the product design. Product development should pay attention to a host of factors including quality, price, value, and speed of delivery, mass customization, environmental content, and product stewardship. Clearly, these factors could affect the successful introduction of the product. It is important also to identify what competitors are doing and conduct a SWOT (strengths, weaknesses, opportunities, and threats) analysis to identify ways to continuously improve the product and beat competition.

Natural Environment

A major strategic issue facing organizations today is how to optimize the limited natural resources by limiting the use of nonrenewable resources and minimizing waste. Lean manufacturing strategy could help in this regard by focusing on substitute components that have or create less environmental burden, taking a product stewardship, changing consumption pattern, and focusing on environmentally conscious manufacturing. The protection of the environment and pollution prevention, are major challenges facing organizations today. Organizations need to develop socially responsible strategies to show that they care about their natural environment. We have discussed in other chapters how sustainable manufacturing may be achieved.

Customer/Supplier Relationship

The customer is the essence of any business organization. Without a customer base, the organization has no purpose and will not meet its mission. The firm must focus its strategies to listen and address the needs of the customer. Customer loyalty can only be earned when the customer is continuously satisfied. Rapid response to the changing environment is actually a response to the dynamic and the evolving needs of the customer. The firm must therefore, understand and appreciate what the customer perceives as important in satisfying his or her needs.

The supplier also plays a critical role in satisfying customer needs. As we showed in Chapter 10, the relationship between the firm and its suppliers have undergone significant transformation to building a mutual relationship that is based on trust and support for each other's activities. This mutual relationship has helped both parties to work toward a common goal to satisfy the needs and wants of the customer and should be fostered.

Agile Manufacturing vs. World Class Manufacturing

There are many other manufacturing strategies that have proliferated since the 1990s. Notable among these are mass customization and lean manufacturing. There is a tendency to log these other strategies with agile manufacturing as if they are all the same when in fact; they differ remarkably [Maskel, 2001]. Agile manufacturing can only be defined in the context of uncertainty and unpredictable changes thereby distinguishing it from the other manufacturing strategies. Mass customization on the other hand, while dissuading the notion of mass production and allowing for low volumes with different design changes to be fulfilled, relies on modular and standardized components to meet customer needs. Although it allows for a wide variety of product changes, the customer is often restricted to the list of options that are available. Outside this options list, mass customization may not respond. Dell Computers is a classical example of a company that uses mass customization. Dell Computers on its web site offers the customer the opportunity to build its own computer starting from a basic standard defined by Dell. Thus, the options open to a customer are confined within the boundaries and limits that are already established and the customer's add-ons can be applied in a modular setup. Certain changes that will be possible through agile manufacturing that would be application-specific are not easily made in a mass customization system. Agility specifically, is the ability to accommodate and manage change. It thrives on the challenges and opportunities that the dynamic environment would present.

Conversely, lean manufacturing deals with an environment with little or no uncertainty. The environment is relatively stable and predictable and the manufacturer is in full control. In fact, a major objective of lean manufacturing is to limit uncertainties and any potential variations that may exist in the production process. Lean manufacturing therefore, cannot effectively handle future events that often deal with lack of information and greater degree of uncertainty and unpredictability. While lean manufacturing may be amenable to some form of standardization, agile manufacturing is dynamic and must respond likewise to its unpredictable and uncertain environment. These uncertainties make the environment for agile manufacturing more complex and more challenging to deal with. An agile manufacturer is a futurist that has no boundary but responds rapidly to the needs of its environment. Manufacturers react accordingly to changes in demand. Because products become obsolete rapidly as a result of the rapid proliferation of new technologies, product life cycle has significantly been shortened. It will be myopic to perceive any product to last in the market for a long time without significant changes in its design and intended use. Thus, an agile manufacturer must respond by introducing new products and even entering into other business areas that may present new challenges and opportunities. For example, personal computer manufacturers facing falling demand in the PC market are shifting into the manufacture of computer storage devices and even application software programs.

Agile manufacturing can be perceived as in constant flux of change and thereby requiring re-engineering of the entire organization and its processes while the other manufacturing strategies thrive on stability and would do better with continuous improvement. The ability to adapt and manage change is the key to achieving agility and such requires radical changes in an organization's structure, culture, processes, strategy, and philosophy.

Lean Manufacturing

Lean production is a manufacturing strategy by the Toyota Production System that is based on adding value through the elimination of waste and incidental work. This strategy strives to achieve the shortest cycle time, high quality, low cost, and continuous quality improvement. It is based on the fact that the business environment is unpredictable and very dynamic. Therefore, it is important to maintain a stable production system that will provide high value at minimum cost and waste. The objective of lean production is to streamline the manufacturing process by evaluating the entire process from product design stage to the product delivery and consumption stages to identify the value added at each stage and the wastes that can be cut out at each stage. The goal is to minimize waste that may result from inventory, material, inefficiency, and quality at every stage of the production process. Lean manufacturing helps to shorten the product cycle time and to design and deliver products that are flexible and able to satisfy customer needs at the lowest possible cost with high quality and as quickly as the customer demands it. Supply chain management also plays a major role in achieving the goal of lean manufacturing since a coordinated network of suppliers is necessary to achieve the just-in-time inventory system that is maintained.

A synchronized production system is maintained to respond rapidly to customer demands. This system effectively manages work and equipment utilization and scheduling utilizing real-time information. This rapid response to customer demands, increases productivity, equipment utilization, reduces cycle times, and minimizes waste due to reduced number of scraps, rejects, and reworks. An integrative approach to information sharing between the stakeholders ensures that the system responds rapidly to customer needs and that all the business units are coordinated to achieve customer satisfaction.

Baudin [1997] identified five guiding principles for lean manufacturing. These principles could help to articulate the importance of lean manufacturing in a business enterprise. We shall expand the discussion on these principles below Baudin [1997]:

1. People are the main drivers of productivity—The main premise of this principle is to invest on people as the primary asset of an organization. With increase in automation in our world today, there is a tendency to perceive machineries as smart, intelligent, and productive. However, machineries are still easier to replace while people are indispensable. The knowledge and information embedded in people could be a major source of competitiveness for an organization. According to Baudin, people offer "both muscles and brains." A firm can achieve competitive advantage by taking advantage of what people have to offer. To achieve this, a conducive work environment that fosters trust and respect, and challenges the worker has to be created. Employee satisfaction is key. Employees have to be viewed as critical members of the business enterprise and not perceived as disposable commodities that can be easily replaced. The workers need to be motivated, allowed to achieve their self-actualization through work, and empowered to make critical work-related decisions. Their sense of belonging and association with the firm has to be enhanced and they have to perceive their self-development and growth through the organization. When employees identify with the organization, they develop pride and joy from working for the organization and are able to improve their productivity and quality.

2. The key to profits is on the shop floor—Adequate attention needs to be paid to how the shop floor is run. Many of the wastes that are incurred in lean manufacturing can be traced

to the shop floor. Wastes may be in the form of material, energy, or manpower wastes resulting from poor quality, pollution, or redundant activities. It is therefore, necessary that efforts are made to understand the tasks and activities at each stage of the manufacturing process and balance their value contributions to waste creation. Significant wastes could be trimmed by redesigning how the workplace is laid out and how activities and tasks are carried out. Furthermore, an efficient design of the shop floor may help to improve quality and productivity, cut down on scraps, rejects, and reworks, and help the organization to focus on doing things right the first time.

3. All manufacturing is repetitive—This concept is based on the premise that most manufacturing operations at least for a product or within a product family are repetitive. There are only few customized operations. Even in a mass customization system, there is a significant degree of repetitiveness. Organizations adopt flexible manufacturing systems to respond to varying customer demands that may deviate from the basic product design. Small-scale job shops may be maintained to satisfy these specialized needs. Flexibility allows the manufacturer to take advantage of these small orders without incurring the added cost.

4. The work must flow through the shop—Given the varying needs of customers and the need to customize both products and services, work must be arranged based on a job shop flow rather than on a flow shop system. In other words, people and equipment should be arranged according to the tasks they perform and work orders should be scheduled to pass through the job shops. This will help to deal with bottleneck problems encountered with the flow shop system, and will make it economically feasible to support small job orders. A "pull-driven" rather than a "push-driven" system for the transfer of parts and materials along the plant is supported. The pull system encourages the production of products according to actual orders or demand rather than based on market forecasts.

5. Improve, don't optimize—Management must begin to de-emphasize optimization and focus on achieving continuous improvement. There is no "optimum" or "best" solution when dealing in a dynamic and unpredictable environment that is

faced with a lot of uncertainties and constraints. Every effort should be made to continuously improve the process, work processes, employees, organizational processes, productivity, and quality. There is no end in achieving continuous improvement.

Lean manufacturing can be viewed as antithetic to the traditional assembly line operation that relies heavily on the ability to forecast independent demand and the use of mass production system. Lean manufacturing is based on make to order and the use of a pull-driven system. Rather than offer repetitive and monotonous tasks to employees, it empowers them to make decisions about their work. There is a high focus on flexibility, quality, and productivity improvements. However, as we have already stated, lean manufacturing should not be confused with agile manufacturing. Lean manufacturing benefits from a well coordinated management information system where both the manufacturer and the supply chain network share information on a real time basis and are able to respond swiftly to changes in the environment.

The Thrust of Lean Manufacturing

The thrust of lean manufacturing can be found in three popular manufacturing techniques namely the Just-In-Time (JIT) system, Total Quality Control (TQC), and Total Productivity Maintenance (TPM) ["Lean manufacturing,"2001]. We shall briefly discuss them.

Just-In-Time

The essence of JIT is to reduce inventory to bare minimum by delivering parts and materials exactly when they are needed. JIT ensures that parts and materials are delivered from upstream activities to downstream activities so that inventories do not accumulate at any stage. Therefore, a consumer downstream would have to signal for order before it could be delivered. These signals are known as *Kanban* signals as coined by the Toyota Production System. A fixed buffer is maintained at each workstation. When the buffer is depleted, a kanban is sent to the producer who replenishes the buffer with a new order. This process synchronizes upstream and downstream activities to ensure smooth transfer of parts and materials at minimum inventory levels at the workstations. The JIT system is known as a *pull system* or *pull manufacturing* since it is triggered by actual rather than forecast demand. The major problem in the use of a pull system can be traced to the effective coordination of all the workstations and being able to correctly calculate buffer requirements at each workstation. This system increasingly becomes complex as the supply chain network increases. However, the availability of advanced software technologies and the application of electronic commerce are helping manufacturers to better coordinate supplier's inventory system and synchronize them with the manufacturer's internal needs. This would help to achieve the JIT goal.

Total Quality Control

A major component of this book is quality management. Our modern view of quality management is shaped around total quality control. TQC is based on a company-wide strategy to achieve quality by minimizing scraps and rejects and by achieving customer satisfaction. Much has been said about quality management in the literature and how quality is directly associated to productivity improvements and cost control. The main idea behind quality practice today is that it is everyone's responsibility to aim for quality by doing things right the first time. This would not only reduce the amount of scraps and rejects from reworks but help the firm win happy customers. Ultimately, the goal of any firm should be to satisfy and maintain loyal customers. Lean manufacturing cannot foster if total quality control is nonexistent. Just like the JIT system, TQC is a strategy to minimize waste and that is a prime focus of "lean" manufacturing.

Total Productive Maintenance

The lifeblood of any manufacturing system is the process of transforming inputs into outputs or finished products. Many of the manufacturing processes today are highly mechanized and any malfunction or even inability to meet tolerance requirements would create large amounts of waste. Equipment failures can be traced to a range of causes including poor equipment design, human errors, wrong gauge settings, improper use of machine, poor maintenance operations, etc. The aim of total productive maintenance is to ensure that these problems do not occur by adopting strategies that would help minimize equipment downtime. Such strategies may include scheduled preventive maintenance programs, enhanced operator training programs, maintaining equipment backup or standbys in case of unpredicted failures, etc. However, whatever strategy is adopted should be cognizant of the type and distribution of equipment failures as well as its associated costs. Again, lean manufacturing cannot be achieved if the manufacturing process is not predictable and unable to perform within established standards and guidelines.

Flow Manufacturing

Flow manufacturing is a hybrid manufacturing strategy that exploits the strengths of other manufacturing techniques such as agile manufacturing, lean manufacturing, synchronous manufacturing, just-in-time manufacturing, and demand flow technology. It is based on a complete re-engineering of the entire manufacturing system rather than trying to achieve incremental gains or improvements. This drastic and radical approach to manufacturing relies on the premise that in order to compete in today's dynamic environment, a new manufacturing style that is proactive, flexible and dynamic must be applied. Baum [2001] notes "flow manufacturing provides the flexibility of mass customization environments with the efficiency of the classic assembly line." He further states that many of the traditional manufacturing practices such as material requirements planning (MRP), work order routings are not essential in flow manufacturing. In fact, MRP is used in flow manufacturing only to plan long-term needs and maintain vendor blanket orders and relationships. It is not needed for capacity requirements planning since flow manufacturing is based on a balanced production line.

Like the other manufacturing systems we have discussed in this chapter especially the JIT, flow manufacturing is a pull-driven system that is driven by customer orders. This contradicts the push-driven system used in the traditional assembly line operation. Furthermore, the flow manufacturing operation utilizes the good qualities of an assembly line system by ensuring smooth flows of work through the line but deviates from assembly line systems by maintaining product flexibility and using the pull system to minimize the inventory requirements. This system does not maintain work in process (WIP) inventories and ensures that high quality is maintained at a minimum cost. Flow manufacturing aims to derive maximum value from an activity while expending minimum efforts and energy. It is a value-based strategy that aims at eliminating waste and adding more value to the manufacturing operation.

This chapter's focus is on manufacturing strategy and we have specifically discussed the roles of agile, lean, and flow manufacturing in achieving competitiveness in our dynamic and highly competitive environment. One may ponder the relationship of these strategies to the goal of this book on quality and the environment. Perhaps, the relationship to quality is apparent as we have shown the relationship to JIT, TQC, and TPM and shown that these management concepts work in unison with these manufacturing styles to ensure that high level of quality is maintained, and transcends to high customer satisfaction. We should equally realize that high quality is synonymous to environmental consciousness. This results from increased productivity as more value is obtained from less input. Thus, vital and limited natural resources in the form of materials and energy may be conserved. In addition, when quality is high, the number of scraps, rejects, and reworks is reduced thereby placing less demand on the need for more resources; the number of production runs, and the demand for energy resources. The ripple effect of all these is that environmental burden is minimized. Lesser materials and wastes will be targeted for disposal at the landfills and there will be less need to excavate and exploit new natural resources. Efficient manufacturing systems can therefore, significantly help to achieve not only the quality imperative of a firm but also, the environmental needs of the society.

These new manufacturing technologies as discussed in this chapter offer effective means to meet both the firm's and the society's needs. Their application should be integrated in the framework of other environmentally conscious manufacturing strategies that have already been discussed in this book.

CONCLUSION

This chapter presents a discussion on agile, lean, and flow manufacturing. It has been shown that these new manufacturing strategies can help a firm improve its quality, minimize waste, and also remain competitive thereby improving its profits. These new strategies are gradually replacing the traditional mass production system that is push- rather than pull-driven. The push-driven system encourages large volume production, limited flexibility, quantity against quality, and large inventories. It is not robust and responsive to the dynamic changes in the environment. Given that our environment is unpredictable and very dynamic, new manufacturing strategies that are proactive and flexible to respond to uncertainties and unpredictability in the environment are in dire need. Organizations must transform themselves to adapt to these new manufacturing strategies if they intend to remain competitive and able to satisfy the changing needs and demands of their customers.

REFERENCES

1. Agile Enterprise/Next Generation Manufacturing Enterprise," http://www.CheshireHenbury.com, downloaded September 9, 2001.
2. "Agile manufacturing," http://www.technet.pnl.gov/dme/agile/index.htm, downloaded September 9, 2001.
3. Baudin, M., "The meaning of "lean."" Dated 8/11/97 http://www.mmt-inst.com/Meaning_of_lean.htm, downloaded September 26, 2001.
4. Baum, D., "Flow manufacturing," http://www.oracle.com/oramag/profit/98-May/flow.htm, downloaded September 26, 2001.
5. Keen, P.G.W., "Agile manufacturing," http://www.peterkeen.com/cmgbp003.htm, downloaded September 9, 2001.
6. Lean manufacturing, http://www.cimplest.com/leanmfg.html, downloaded September 20, 2001.
7. Maskel, B.H., "An introduction to agile manufacturing," http://www.maskel.com, downloaded September 20, 2001.

CHAPTER 12

•————————————————————•

ENTERPRISE RESOURCE PLANNING AND SUPPLY CHAIN

ERP is the short form for Enterprise Resource Planning. This name is a misnomer to what ERP actually stands for. It conjectures in this name, the feeling of resource planning which would imply some form of optimization. However, ERP is not really about resource planning in that sense but more of enterprise management. The aim of ERP is to develop an integrated enterprise—a system whereby all the functional units or departments of an enterprise are integrated onto a single computer system that will serve their different needs. This obviously will require comprehensive software that is able to integrate the functions of the different business units and departments such as finance, operations, accounting, and human resources. Prior to the concept of ERP, these departments or business units operated like scattered islands each with its own computer system and able to achieve its own departmental goals. Thus, the optimization of a department may be at the expense of the overall organizational goals. ERP therefore, helps the organization to achieve its global optimum rather than suboptimizing. The different functional units through this integrative approach are able to share a common database, share and exchange information, and shoot for the same organizational goals. With ERP, the departments are integrated and each will come to understand and appreciate each other's respective contributions towards the organization's goals and objectives.

ERP ensures lateral transfer of information to the different departments. Imagine what a simple customer order processing would be without an integrated system. That would mean that no one department can track the status of an order unless if the order during processing is specifically at that particular department. With ERP, operations department or any other department can track the status of a customer's order and be able to relay the information to the customer or in fact, use such information to better serve the customer. This approach could also be cost effective since it eliminates the need for each department to maintain its own separate database and of course cuts down on setup costs as the departments do not have to re-enter customer order information in all the different departments. There is therefore, a reduced chance of committing an error. However, this also implies that if the common database is in error, the whole system becomes error prone. It is therefore important that a high level of accuracy is maintained in entering the information in the common database.

ERP if properly implemented, will help organizations to better serve their customers by mostly cutting down on bureaucratic structures that exist in traditional organizational setup that operate as independent islands. It also will in the long run, cut down on cost, improve efficiency and productivity, and facilitate drastically information acquisition. ERP is about organizational efficiency that is based on making effective use of computer technology to reduce the structural size of organizations by integrating their functions and making them a cohesive whole. In that sense, it deals with resource planning as it makes organizations more efficient and productive and therefore, more able to effectively manage and use their limited resources. Resources conserved through ERP such as time, improved quality, and paperless services can be translated into reduced costs to customers. The organization also benefits tremendously by being able to improve customer satisfaction as it can track effectively customer orders and be able to provide valuable information on order fulfillment, production stages, and inventory levels. The ability to manage inventory effectively and timely use of accurate information could translate into significant profit margins to the organization. But remember, that ERP is based on automating an organization's business process. It is therefore, not an easy feat to accomplish given both the size of many of these organizations and the complexity of many of their business processes.

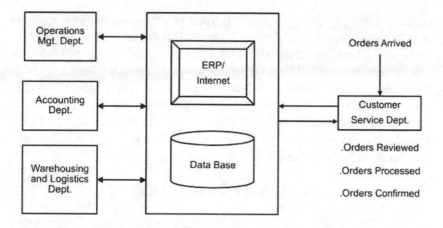

Figure 12.1: A typical ERP customer order processing

Figure12.1 presents a typical ERP customer order processing. When a new customer order arrives, it goes through a customer service representative who collects the standard customer information required by the company, evaluates customer's credit rating and makes a determination on credit if necessary. The customer service representative inputs information about this customer if a new customer or retrieves information from the database for existing customers and places an order for the customer. In placing the order, the customer service representative is able to review the company's inventory level, production lead-time, and delivery times, and appropriately informs the customer when the order will be fulfilled. The information now entered by the customer service representative to the central database system is now available to all the departments that are connected to the central unit. These departments have access to the same information through their connected computer systems and they can all track the movement of the order as they go through the different stages of processing. At any point in time, anyone within the connected systems that have authorized access to the computer unit can log in and check the status of the order. While order fulfillment is a typical function of ERP systems, its application has been applied to other areas that are internal to the organization Employees can in some cases use it to track the processing of their benefits.

An integrated system as with ERP increases accountability. The departments are now watching each other as well as evaluating the performance of the customer service representative who is the first contact point for the customer. Sources of errors in the system can now be easily tracked and specific areas for improvement identified. Communication is also significantly enhanced. The production department for example, can track the level of inventory and match it with new orders and scheduled production levels and production capacity and make a determination whether to increase production, subcontract, or use overtime to meet increased demand. ERP is therefore, a revolutionary business practice that will lead to effective management of business processes.

History and Evolution of ERP

The history of ERP can be traced to the early 1960s to the works of J.I. Case, the manufacturer of tractors and construction machinery and IBM ["ERP Background," 2001]. Their initial effort was on developing software for planning and scheduling of materials for complex manufactured products hence Material Requirements Planning or MRP. The focus therefore was primarily on effective inventory management using traditional inventory concepts. The initial program was clumsy and expensive but by the mid 1970s, MRP has gained popularity in the manufacturing industry and the concept was widely adopted in production management and control. MRP was effective in helping translate master production schedule into requirements for sub assemblies, components and raw material planning and procurement ["Introduction to ERP," 2001]. By the 1980s, MRP has evolved into MRP-II or Material Resource Planning with the objective to optimize the entire plant production process. MRP-II was extended to include shop floor and distribution management activities. This role was gradually extended in the 1990s to include other functional departments such as Engineering, Project Management, Finance, and Human Resource. This extension of MRP-II to include these areas led to the term ERP (Enterprise Resource Planning) in the early 1990s.

We should also mention that in 1972 when MRP was very difficult to use, five engineers in Mannheim, Germany formed a company known as SAP with the aim of producing and marketing standalone software for integrated business solutions. Of course, other companies are involved in marketing ERP software today. Notable among them are SAP, Oracle, PeopleSoft, JDEdwards, BAAN. ERP can be differentiated from its predecessors (i.e. MRP and MRP-II) by its inclusion of the entire range of company activities and also its integrative nature although MRP-II tried to integrate activities. ERP also addressed both system requirements and technology issues that included client/server distributed architecture, RMBMS, and object oriented programming [Shankarnarayanan, 2001].

Supply Chain Management

Supply chain management (SCM) on the other hand, deals with the integration of activities needed to procure materials, transform them into intermediate and final products, and deliver and distribute them to customers. It involves as its crucial element, the traditional purchasing function as well as other activities that relate to supplier and vendor relationship especially in the supply of materials and distribution of goods to customers. These activities include transportation, scheduling, information, and cash or credit transfers. These exchanges involve data and information sharing between the manufacturer and all the members of the supply chain network as a result, there is a need for ERP to support supply chain management. Among the common example of ERP that are used to support supply chain networks are EDI (Electronic Data Interchange) and ASN (Advanced Shipping Notice). Competitiveness is the driving force behind supply chain management. The business environment today is highly competitive and businesses must compete on the basis of speed, quality, and cost. In order to remain competitive, these organizations must define new alliance with their suppliers, vendors and customers and develop more efficient means to deliver high quality products and services on time and at reasonable costs to their customers. This requires working jointly with suppliers and vendors at each stage in the product's life cycle from design to delivery and consumption. Ultimately, more activities are encompassed including purchasing, operations, logistics and information. Further, the expansion of the network involved in managing the product or service makes management of the network more complex. Thus, the efficiency of the supply chain network will significantly influence the effectiveness of the organization, productivity and profitability.

The key to the success of supply chain network is information flow. All members of the supply chain network should have access to timely information flow and information should flow in both directions. Having an integrated information system and making it readily available is the key role of ERP in the context of SCM.

Managing The Supply Chain

A key challenge to supply chain networks is for organizations to evolve from their traditional practice to a supply chain network that will integrate more participants in its activities and sharing information with these participants in order to improve quality and delivery to customers. This will require organizational changes and top management commitment to make the supply chain work. Some of the changes the organization may perform and challenges in managing supply chain network include the following:

1. Selection of suppliers—The selection of suppliers and vendors is very important for a supply chain network to work. Suppliers have to be chosen not solely on cost but on their ability to produce items that meet the firm's quality guidelines and also deliver such items on time when they are needed and where they are needed. One of the aims in using supply chain network is to reduce inventory, improve speed in delivery and meet the high quality needs of customers. If suppliers are not able to meet the high quality needs and supply defective material, the entire network will face a bottleneck, which will ultimately, slow down the process and hamper the firm's ability to deliver high quality products to its customers on time.

2. Information sharing—The firm should form a partnership with its suppliers and share information with them on customer needs and expectations as well as the firm's standards. The problems faced by Ford Motors and Bridgestone Tires regarding the recall of tires for the Ford Sports Utility Vehicles appear to suggest an information breakdown between the supplier (Bridgestone Tires) and the manufacturer (Ford Motors). When there is breakdown of communication and lack of understanding of the expectations from both parties, such problems are bound to happen. Maintaining common database that can be easily accessible by members of the supply chain network also enhances information sharing. Integrated software systems such as provided through the ERP could be helpful.

3. Build a long-term partnership—The relationship with the supplier should be on a long-term basis. This will help in the learning process for both parties to understand the value and culture of each team member and work continuously to

improving both quality and efficiency. Also, by developing a long-term relationship, suppliers can justify the cost of changing their processes, training their workers to the new culture, and adapting their organizational structure to support the supply chain network. For example, the new Volkswagen plant in Brazil where its major suppliers such as MWM-Cummings that supplies its engines and transmission, Rockwell that supplies its suspension, IOCHPE-MAXION that supplies it chassis modules, Eisenmann that supplies its cab painting, VDO that supplies its cab finishing and upholstery, and Delga that supplies it with cab assembly, are all housed in the same plant. This arrangement shows how expensive the supply chain could be. This network as established in the case of Volkswagen requires each of these different companies to maintain its own workforce but work as a team with the other suppliers and Volkswagen to produce a finished product that meets customers needs and expectations. This obviously will require capital investment and training of the workforce to cope with this new work environment.

4. Establish liaison with suppliers—It is important that the firm's internal employees have a good relationship with the suppliers. The different functional units of the firm should coordinate their planning and activities with the suppliers especially with regards to meeting due dates, quality and environmental standards, and production scheduling. This relationship will help to ensure that all members of the supply network are in sync and working towards a common goal.

5. Product life cycle—Managing environmental burden is a new trend that is affecting manufacturers today. Manufacturers take a product stewardship or cradle-to-grave approach of their products. They are responsible for the environmental burden created by their products. Manufacturers are also benefiting from sound environmental management practices through prudent management. We have already presented examples of companies such as Kodak and Xerox in earlier chapters that have strategies for dealing with environmental burdens. It is the responsibility of the manufacturer to ensure that its suppliers do not only meet its quality requirements but also its environmental standards by ensuring that efficient environmental designs such as design for environment,

design for remanufacturing, design for disassembly, design for recyclability are followed. Also, there has to be a reclaiming or recovery strategy adopted to recover materials for safe disposal at the end of the product life cycle. A reverse logistic approach where the manufacturer and supplier trace and recover the materials and components at the end of its useful life should be adopted.

6. Total integration of the supply chain network—Although a primary objective in many supply chain networks is the value that is gained through integration in terms of reduced cost, speed in delivery, reduction in wastes and duplication of tasks and activities, and improved customer satisfaction, it is still not easy to achieve integration. This can be attributed to the different philosophies of the diverse suppliers and vendors in the network as well as the manufacturer. It is difficult for example, to share information when there is lack of trust and concern that the information may be misused or even shared with competitors or in some cases regulators. Furthermore, managing supply chain network expands the span of control to involve more people in the network who may have different worldviews and experiences. Management of people and ability to negotiate and manage conflicting views and philosophies become critical in effectively managing the supply chain. Achieving trust within members of the supply chain network will help facilitate the flow of work and materials through the network but building trust will normally require time to develop.

7. Inventory management—Many of the organization's today are focusing on lean production system that rely on Just-in-Time (JIT) inventory management system. While JIT has worked effectively in many organizations, it sometimes can breakdown especially when suppliers are globally dispersed. There are multifaceted factors that can impede efforts to achieve JIT including political problems, natural disasters, communication problems, and in-house process problems. These occurrences could in fact, make it difficult to respond to speed as a strategy in satisfying customer needs. Thus, there may still be need to maintain low levels of inventory to be able to respond to demand changes and satisfy due dates requirements. The supply chain management should therefore

be flexible enough to respond to sudden changes in the distribution network.

Supply Chain Strategies

New strategies need to be developed to deal with supply chain management. There are five types of strategies that are discussed here [Heizer and Render, 2001].

- Many Suppliers—The traditional supply strategy is to deal with many suppliers. This strategy is based on receiving quotes from suppliers and choosing the lowest bidder. This approach often plays one supplier against the other and it does not emphasize long-term relationship. The environment is less than mutual between the supplier and the manufacturer and the supplier is responsible for maintaining its processes, managing cost, quality and deliveries. The potential problem with this approach is that the supplier may not be committed to the long-term goals of the manufacturer and may not emphasize quality when cost is compromised to win the bid. Furthermore, without longterm partnership, the manufacturer may be unable to meet the long-term demands of achieving environmental standards and taking a product stewardship of its products since the supplier may not be committed to such goals.

- Partnering with suppliers—Partnership brings long-term association and interest to achieve common goals. Long term partners are not selected based on low cost advantage but based on a host of criteria that will enhance overall organizational performance. Such criteria may include cost, quality, dependability, and speed of delivery, consistency, and even the ability of the organization to adapt to the new culture. Few suppliers are maintained rather than an open-ended list of suppliers. The few suppliers selected work in a team with the manufacturer and commit their resources to ensure that a common goal is achieved. This strategy is typically followed in today's supply chain management. Lucent Technologies for example, intends to reduce its list of 7,000 suppliers in 1998 to 2,200 in the year 2000 and further down to 200 by the year 2002. The risk associated with this strategy is that once partners are selected, it is difficult to drop or change one without incurring huge costs and even disruption in the work process. Thus, both the supplier and manufacturer may become captives of each other. However, a partnership of this nature is normally based on trust, as there are more to gain through effective partnership. The trust is to ensure that trade secrets are protected, and to work collectively to improve customer satisfaction since that will in the long run benefit both the manufacturer and the supplier.

- Vertical Integration—This strategy allows the manufacturer to develop the ability to produce the goods or services that are previously subcontracted to the supplier. This ability is often achieved by buying a supplier or distributor. Vertical integration is of two forms—forward and backward integration. With forward integration, the manufacturer of parts and components end up making the final product and with backward integration, the manufacturer buys up its supplier or starts making the parts it would normally subcontract. Texas instrument is an example of forward integration since it shifted form the manufacturing of integrated circuits to manufacturing computers and calculators that use integrated circuits. On the other hand, auto manufacturers such as Ford Motors that also make parts or components such as radios that they would normally subcontract are examples of backward integration. Vertical integration can help in reducing costs, meeting due dates, and achieving both environmental and quality standards if the requisite technology and skills exist to take up such roles. However, they could be risky since attention may be diverted in investing financially and technologically in industries where the firm may not have core competence or may lack the ability to adapt to rapid changes in technology.

- Keiretsu Networks—This is popular in Japan and it is a hybrid of Partnering with suppliers and vertical integration. The manufacturer maintains partnership with few suppliers while remaining vertically integrated. A network of suppliers is developed and these suppliers may also have lower-tier supply chain networks.

- Virtual companies—This is based on establishing a more fluid and dynamic relationship with suppliers. Virtual companies are more innovative and enterprising and more able to deal with changing market needs. The supplier provides a wide variety of services that may involve conducting other services such as payroll, hiring personnel, product design, etc., for the manufacturer. Virtual companies would normally have management expertise, and the advantage of low capital investment, flexibility, and speed. They provide high level of efficiency. Relationship with virtual companies could be short- or long-term and may involve current partners or simply capable vendors and suppliers.

e-Procurement

Procurement of materials, costs, and parts is one of the most costly activities of any firm. On the average, firms spend about 50% of their sales dollar on purchasing. Thus procurement is an important activity of any supply chain network. The traditional approach to purchasing by filling out manual order forms has significantly been transformed through the use of electronic procurement system known as e-procurement. E-procurement however, is an Internet-based purchasing system that offers electronic purchase order processing and improved administrative functions for both the buyer and the seller. The system is designed to be user-friendly and it is intended to improve operational efficiencies by cutting down on costs and wastes. E-procurement has become very popular among buyers and sellers due to the rapid proliferation of Internet-based technologies and ERP systems. These technologies offer increased opportunities for competitive bidding, market collaboration, improved order and transaction processing, and information gathering thus helping to achieve cost savings. The added value to productivity through e-procurement is enormous and both buyers and sellers can save time that could be channeled to other critical activities. The purchasing function spans across all types of organizations and as we have noted, contributes to the bulk of each sales dollar. The auto industry realized the importance of this as the three major auto manufacturers namely General Motors, Ford Motor Company, and DaimlerChrysler formed an e-marketplace initiative known as Covisint in the year 2000. Covisint is an electronic marketplace where auto companies could buy and sell from their suppliers and their suppliers could also leverage the large purchasing power of these companies for all items ranging from raw materials to office products. Although this presents a big challenge in integrating the more than 30,000 suppliers that work with these companies, it also presents synergistic opportunities to participants. Ford Motor Company in July of 2001 already reported a savings of $70 million dollars attributed mainly to lower processing cost and supplier pricing [Grande, 2001].

e-Procurement vs. Paper-based Procurement

e-procurement has significant advantages over the traditional paper-based procurement system. Some of the advantages are outlined below:

- Improvement in management of information—the use of electronic or online catalogues with full information on the product including video clips, animation, and voice activation eliminates the need for mailing in catalogues thereby minimizing the tremendous waste in paper and cost of postage. Further, online catalogues have longer life span and could be viewed at any time, and has a much wider and global reach to customers and all within the supply chain network. The cost savings in terms of retrieval of paper-based information and the reduction of wastes dumped to landfills could be enormous in this quest for environmentally sensible manufacturing.

- RFQs—the tremendous effort and resources spend to develop and mail out requests for quotes (RFQs) could be significantly reduced. Members of the supply chain network can in a click of a button obtain product information and in some cases pricing system, and could negotiate orders and scheduled delivery as well as quality standards online. This helps in improving selection of suppliers based on the buyer's criteria.

- Integrated marketplace—Like the Covisint example that we mentioned, both buyer and seller can exploit the online marketplace to sell excess inventory and could also commission online bidding of such items. There is low entry barrier in this process and there is increased potential for customers and suppliers to leverage the large buying power of big companies.

- Inventory tracking system—Online purchasing system makes it possible to track orders, inventory and supply information. Just with a tracking number, updated information of where the product is in the system can be obtained. Many companies now use the tracking system offered by many of the package handlers such as UPS, FedEx and USPS. For example, Ford Motors Company uses UPS to track the movement of vehicles delivered from its plant to dealers across the country. In fact, individuals can now track the delivery of their packages to a destination using the same technology.

- Inventory reduction—Many operations now embark on Just-In-Time delivery system with a goal of keeping inventory level to a bare minimum. Maintaining an online system with suppliers will help to simplify this task as supplier's inventory system could be tracked and conferment and due dates for orders obtained.

- Elimination of maverick buying—Maverick buying deals with purchases outside negotiated supplier contract. These purchases are usually higher and often tend to reduce the firm's volume leverage with the negotiated supplier. Prices usually will go up when order sizes are small. Maverick spending is often as a result of inefficiencies in the traditional paper ordering system where the buyer may be unaware of established guidelines or frustrated by the inefficient purchasing process. With an automated system as in e-procurement, the buyer can easily search for the best negotiated price for products through on-line catalogues.

- Increase employee satisfaction—The use of e-procurement system eliminates the monotonous and routine work that is involved in filing purchasing orders and invoices as well as RFQs but also opens up order decisions to more human input through evaluation of company's criteria as they are met by the different suppliers' products. A comparative assessment of the different products can be effectively made.

Supply Chain Management and e-procurement

Logistics management is important in order to effectively manage supply chain networks. Companies that rely on a network of suppliers, distributors, vendors, and customers cannot be efficient without good coordination. Value must be added at every stage of the product delivery and waste and cost must be minimized. Given the significant role of purchasing in affecting the prices of finished products and services, it is prudent that supply chain management pay particular attention to procurement decisions. The use of e-procurement ensures that the best value is obtained for each product or service. Suppliers do not only compete on the basis of price but also on speed, quality, and environmental content of the product. Further, the elimination of maverick buying through e-procurement may lead to stability in prices and in whole, reduction in prices could lead to more efficiency and higher productivity as products and components or parts are made in the most economically feasible way. This also helps minimize waste while improving the quality of these products.

Supply chain management and e-procurement are closely linked and both the buyer and the seller should work together. Some of the costs attributed to purchasing may be due to the high level of inventory or significant downtime that the manufacturer of parts may maintain in order to meet due dates. However, with a well-coordinated network and production information shared by members of the supply chain network, such problems could be mitigated as orders schedules are shared and products and parts are delivered on just-in-time basis. This will improve the processing of sales forecasts, effectively manage inventories, optimize deliveries, and improve productivity. Supply chain management function therefore encompasses purchasing, inventory management, customer relationship, distribution and inbounds logistics.

Assessment of e-procurement Strategies

e-procurement strategies can benefit both the seller and the buyer. Both parties have a stake in ensuring that it works. Lower order and transaction processing costs can be achieved by both parties while delivering orders at higher speed thereby meeting production due dates and deadlines. The buyer also benefits from exposure to a wider choice of suppliers who may meet its stated criteria. Time and resources are conserved dealing with few qualified suppliers than receiving RFQs from a range of suppliers with many that fall below the required standards. This process may lead to better standardization of the purchasing function. Suppliers will be exposed to the standards of the buyer and try to match exactly the buyer's needs. We have already identified other advantages to the buyer such as the elimination of maverick buying, and elimination of paperwork and repetitive order filling process. The seller is also exposed to a wider audience and could expand its volume through online sales to a wider range of buyers. The improved ordering and purchasing process helps the seller to improve productivity and significantly cut down on cost.

e-procurement is not always easy to implement. It requires huge investment in both hardware and software technologies and these will require training to be effectively utilized. Furthermore, system-to-system integration would be required as well as developing security measures to limit access to members of the network. The buyer will also have to divulge some of its trade secrets to the seller in order to have its demands and product specifications fully met. Thus, maintaining trust between the buyer and the supplier is crucial in order to develop a sustainable e-procurement system and to recover the high investment cost. Training of employees is also required and most importantly, organizational culture need to adapt to this new environment.

ERP and SCM

ERP is often used synonymously with SCM as if they are the same but it is clear they aim to achieve the same goal. ERP can be viewed as an organization-wide information system that integrates key business processes to assure free flow of information between the business units of a firm. The aim is to have a centralized information system easily accessible to all the business units by reducing redundancies. ERP helps the organization to better manage by using a single source of information that is available to all its units. It helps achieve better coordination and utilization of resources for decision-making. The business units now operate as a cohesive part of the organization rather than as separate entities with different agendas. Thus in a sense, optimization rather than sub-optimization can be achieved.

ERP systems are usually software-based and these software are often very complex with long learning curves. In addition, they are very expensive and often require reengineering of the organization if they were to be effectively adopted. Thus to implement ERP, an organization needs to carefully reassess itself especially its commitment both in terms of financial and human resources to ERP. There are many vendors for ERP systems notably SAP, Oracle, BAAN, PeopleSoft and others but selecting the right ERP system for an organization is not easily accomplished. However, there are few issues that should be considered in selecting an ERP system:

1. Does the cost fit with the budget for ERP?
2. Will the organization readily adapt to the ERP system?
3. Does the ERP system adequately address the functional needs of the organization and the different business units?
4. Is the ERP system flexible and can it be adapted to the changing business environment?
5. What is the learning curve for the ERP system?
6. Is it easy to integrate the ERP with other software from different vendors?
7. Does the software cover the needs of the particular industry your organization is in?
8. Does the software come with the requisite materials such as training manuals, guarantees, and consultant services?
9. What assistance is offered by the vendor to get the program running and at what cost?
10. Does the program run through the different application system providers (ASPs)?
11. How user friendly is the system?
12. Can the system be easily customized to meet specific needs?
13. How long will it take to fully implement the ERP system?

These are few of the questions that need to be addressed in selecting an ERP platform. It must however, be mentioned that ERP implementation cannot be successful without top management commitment. It is a huge investment that has the potential of derailing the organization if it is not properly managed and implemented. It is therefore important that its implementation is taken seriously and assigned to the highest level of management. Management must be clear on what it expects to gain from ERP and have a means of measuring the performance of the system. It should also be ready for change management. As we mentioned above, it would require reengineering of the organization and a new organizational culture to support ERP. Time and resources will be needed and management must plan before hand to estimate the demands that ERP would place on the organization. It would be bad to find out midcourse that ERP is demanding resources that the organization is unable to commit. Thorough planning is therefore essential to the effective implementation of ERP. If ERP is effectively implemented, it could help the firm in the following ways:

- Information could be shared among the different departments or business units without any barrier.

- Organizational efficiency, coordination, and decision-making can be improved thereby helping to improve productivity.
- The new organization resulting from this could help to achieve efficiency and productivity.
- A cohesive business strategy is developed as the functional units and business units work toward a common goal.
- The firm is more able to respond rapidly to its changing environment.
- The organization can benefit tremendously from the use of supply chain networks and e-procurement.

ERP and E-Commerce

ERP is basically a packaged business software system [Heizer and Render, 2001] to allow a firm to

- Automate and integrate its business processes
- Share common data and practices across the entire enterprise, and
- Provide and access information in a real-time environment.

It aims to integrate the firm's back office processes and information flows. E commerce on the other hand, is the use of computer systems and packaged software applications protected by network security measures to conduct online transactions. Such transactions include mostly buying and selling of goods and services through the Internet.

ERP has faced some drawbacks because of its lack of integration of e-commerce operations. Firms adopting ERP also complain bitterly about the high cost of implementing ERP and the high failure rate due to difficulties in integrating it into the organization's processes. It is also often difficult to integrate ERP system with e-commerce packages, which firms need to adopt to participate in the growing Internet economy. Part of the problems with the integration of ERP lie on the outmoded client/server technology used for ERP that focus more on improving internal business processes rather than using the Internet to reach out to a wide range of customers and suppliers [Chen, 2001]. There is therefore, a challenge to ensure that ERP and e-commerce systems are fully integrated so information can flow directly and freely to the different application areas. Firms are increasingly seeking ERP suites that support e-commerce application rather than a stand alone package.

CONCLUSION

In this chapter, we discussed the role of supply chain management and enterprise resource planning in managing today's organization. We have identified some of the key attributes that make both SCM and ERP popular. We note in particular, the importance of the Internet in achieving these goals and the tremendous role that e-procurement occupies. We have also emphasized the problems in implementing ERP and the need to carefully evaluate the planning process before a decision on ERP platform is made. The attempt to provide products and services that are of high value to customers cannot be achieved without examining the contributions of the purchasing function and the link between the suppliers and the manufacturer in the delivery of products and services. This chapter is a primer to that and can help provide further guidelines on how we can manage quality and the natural environment through an efficient supply chain management network.

REFERENCES

1. "ERP Background", downloaded on 5/25/01. http://www.erp.computerjobs.com/site_content.asp?content_t ypeid=3
2. "Introduction to ERP," http://www.cis.ksu.edu/~arul/mgmt/Page 1.html, downloaded on 5/25/01.
3. Shankarnarayanan, S., "ERP Systems -- Using IT to gain a competitive advantage," http://www.expressindia.com/newads/bsl/advant.htm, downloaded on 5/25/01.
4. Heizer, J., and Render, B., Principles of Operations Management, Upper Saddle River, NJ: Prentice-Hall, 2001.
5. Grande, C., "Ford recoups investment in Covisint web exchange," FT.com/Financial Times, July 1, 2001.
6. Chen, A., "ERP II: Enterprises investing in extending systems for collaborative commerce," *eWeek*, May 7, 2001.

CHAPTER 13

●━━━━━━━━━━━━━━━━━━━━━━●

COMPETING ON QUALITY AND ENVIRONMENT

In this chapter, we discuss the need for a firm to focus on quality and environment to achieve competitiveness. The aim is to synchronize the information that have been presented as separate chapters to show the significance of focusing on quality and the natural environment as a firm continues with its journey towards competitiveness. We would specifically look at the evolution of both quality and environmental business strategies and how both contribute to achieving the needs of the public. We also look at the social responsibility function and how that is achieved by focusing on quality and environment as competitive weapons. Furthermore, we look at the influence of globalization and how that has helped to shape the future of the environment and affected the operating environment of firms.

The Evolution of Quality and Environmental Strategies

In this book, we have discussed the basic principles behind quality and environmental management and how both quality and environmental practices could be improved to help a firm achieve competitiveness. Today's business environment is very dynamic and complex and has changed significantly over the past twenty years. In the 1970s and into late 1980s, there was a tremendous focus on total quality management as the key to competitiveness. American companies sought to perform miracle through quality management to regain their market shares that were lost mainly to Japanese companies. In the auto industry for example, Japanese companies such as Toyota Motors and Honda took a big chunk of the auto market. US executives flocked to Japan in search of solution to their lack of competitiveness. Many found their answer in poor quality and were quick to adopt measures to make them more competitive. The late 1970s to 1980s also saw a proliferation of quality experts or "gurus" who professed to offer the magic solution to American businesses. Many of the gurus blamed the Western style of management as the major explanation for poor quality and low productivity. A significant transformation of organizational culture and practice took place to shift American companies away from the practice of Taylor's principles of management to total quality management or what some have even referred to as "Deminigism" [Nersesian 1993]. According to Nersesian, Taylorism and Demingisim are mutually exclusive. Taylor's principles which focused primarily on planning and controlling especially in using stopwatch to set slide rules to measure work done by employees contradicts the current focus on empowering workers to monitor and control their work and the quality of it. These are two opposites and it is either one or the other. The results from shifting from Taylorism to Deminigism are remarkable and America was able to get back to its feet and compete equally with the Japanese companies. Nations also offered impetus to this new direction. The United States Department of Commerce following the path of Japan that established the Deming Prize for Quality established the Malcolm Baldrige National Quality Award in honor of the former Secretary of Commerce Malcolm Baldrige. The European Quality Award was also established and many nations have followed suit recognizing the critical importance of quality in achieving competitiveness. The international community has also come together through the formation of the International Organization for Standardization (ISO) to establish set of quality standards that are now popularly known as the ISO 9000 series of standards.

With companies around the world accepting that quality or customer satisfaction is the key to remaining in business and being competitive, it became imperative that strict quality guidelines must be maintained to remain in business and gain market shares. Strategies such as "zero defects," "six sigma," etc., were adopted by many. Companies were yet to face a new feat. Globalization has set in thanks to the evolution in the information technology area and the Internet in particular. The world became much smaller and we are capable of communicating with communities thousands of miles apart yet at an intangible cost. There was a growing awareness of our natural environment and the need to protect it. The world community was mostly concerned about the quality of air, water, and land and would want to trim waste to its minimum, minimize solid waste and hazardous waste disposal, reduce the emission of poisonous and toxic gases to the atmosphere, control the emission of greenhouse gases that destroy the ozone layer, and maintain ecological balance by re-evaluating excavation and development policies. The need to protect the earth's limited natural resources became increasingly important that it was necessary to convene two international conferences—the Earth Summit held in Rio de Janeiro, Brazil in 1992, and the Global Climate conference held in Kyoto, Japan in 1997. The world business community responded to the public demand to protect the environment and conserve natural resources through the Brundtland Report of July 1987, which challenged businesses to achieve sustainable economic growth without compromising the natural environment. Many nations around the world adopted strict measures on the environment making it difficult to conduct business as usual without a focus on environmental protection. In the US, the Clean Air Act was amended in 1990 with more stringent laws and penalties for pollution. Strict laws were enacted on the use of ozone depletants such as CFCs (chlorofluorocarbons), methyl chloroform, and carbon tetrachloride, all which are to be outlawed by the year 2002. Similar laws were also being passed in other countries such as Germany and Holland. These laws do not only outline penalties for pollutants but also set guidelines and procedures to achieve environmental goals. Some of the environmental strategies encouraged include:

- The use of recyclable materials
- Designing products for ease of assemble and dismantle
- Use of reverse logistics to reclaim old equipment from users and properly disassemble them to recycle and remanufacture useful parts
- Creation of new application for used materials
- Safe disposal of unusable materials and equipment.

These requirements created new challenges and opportunities that businesses must deal with. It became clear that competing on the basis of quality alone would not help the organization to gain new markets or even maintain its existing market. Rather the new organization must compete on the basis of quality and environment. Thus, the theme of this book is competing on quality and environment. Quality and environment are not really distinct issues. It is apparent by going through this book that there is a need to have a more systemic view of quality where the definition is expanded to include the needs of the society. Thus, quality cannot be achieved if the needs of the society are not satisfied.

The Social Responsibility Function

Corporations today have to be good corporate citizens. They should be exemplary in their communities and have diverse roles to play. The business of the corporation is the business of its community and the society at large. It is not only the business of its shareholders or its direct customers. Therefore, more is expected of corporations today. They no longer provide just specialized products and services but are expected to form long-term partnership and bonding with their communities. Corporate missions must therefore be aligned with the long-term goals, missions, and vision of the community. While shareholders may be interested in maximizing their wealth, members of the community are more interested in maximizing the quality of their lives and this can only be achieved by working with the corporation to ensure that corporate goals, policies, and strategies are in line with community goals and expectations. Thus in order to achieve the social responsibility goals, business organizations must have shared mission, vision and goals with their communities or operating environment. Gone are the days when the main social responsibility function for a corporation was to provide jobs to its community. Members of the community are now more enlightened and look beyond the short-term values that a firm may offer but seek to develop a sustainable partnership that cannot only help them but also their children and the future of their natural environment. In the absence of a vision that is shared by the community, the firm stands to face increased opposition from its community, which could significantly harm the image of the organization and its ability to conduct business operations. Social responsibility can only be satisfied when the business is ethical. We have noticed in recent times, public condemnation of companies that have been involved in ecological mishaps or disorder. For example, the Exxon Valdez oil spill and the Union Carbide plant explosion in Bhopal, India not only brought litigation and large fines to these companies but public condemnation and discontent which harmed the image of these companies. There is therefore, a greater need to focus on environmental protection as a way of achieving the social responsibility function of the organization. Corporations need to start working with "stakeholders" rather than just stockholders. Stakeholders are active participants who are affected by the decisions and activities of the firm or whose activities and actions may affect the future operations of the firm. In today's litigious environment, stakeholders who feel that the quality of their lives have been compromised by the actions of firms are increasingly suing corporations and getting these firms to pay huge debts for their actions. Businesses must therefore listen to the voice of the stakeholders.

Product Stewardship

The Northwest Product Stewardship Council (NPSC) defined product stewardship as follows [Bullard, 1994]:

"Product stewardship is a principle that directs all actors in the life cycle of a product to minimize the impact of the product on the environment. The concept is unique because of its emphasis on the entire product system. Under product stewardship, all participants in the product life cycle—designers, suppliers, manufacturers, distributors, retailers, consumers, recyclers and disposers—share responsibility for the environmental effects of products."

Companies are required to take a "cradle to grave" approach in managing their products. That is, they are responsible for tracking the environmental burden of the product through its life cycle. This call for social responsibility has created huge burden to corporations that have not paid attention to the environmental content of their products. There is no time limit to the company's responsibilities when it comes to environmental burden.

Polluters are increasingly asked to take responsibility for their acts. One of the most devastating environmental pollution of the 20th century in the United States was the pollution of the Love Canal. This was a case of natural disaster of untold and unimaginable human proportion. Between 1942 and 1953, Hooker Chemical Company now part of Occidental Petroleum and Chemical Corporation dumped 20,000 to 25,000 tons of toxic chemicals in the Love Canal. Many of the chemicals dumped were pesticide waste and chemical weapons research i.e. The Manhattan Project [Allan, 1998] and are listed in the order of largest concentrations as chemical benzene hexachloride, chlorobenzenes, and dodecyl mercaptan. Although much may be known about the health effects of a single chemical, little is known about exposures to synthetic chemicals. In Love Canal, more than 200 chemicals and toxics were disposed to the soil. The impact was quite devastating as dangerous chemicals such as dioxin and mercury sipped through the soil and polluted the entire area. Women living in the area were having higher rate of miscarriages, stillbirths, crib deaths, and children were born with neurological problems and hyperactivity [Gibbs, 1999]. Bullard [1994] attributed the complacency of companies like Hooker Chemical then to the environmental policies that focused on how to manage, regulate, and distribute risks. That led to a dominant environmental protection paradigm that was according to Bullard, based on the following principles:

1. Institutionalizes unequal enforcement
2. Trades human health for profit
3. Places the burden of proof on the "victim," not on the polluting industry
4. Legitimizes human exposure to harmful chemicals, pesticides, and hazardous substances
5. Promotes "risky" technologies
6. Exploits the vulnerability of economically and politically disenfranchised communities
7. Subsidizes ecological destruction
8. Creates an industry around risk assessment
9. Delays cleanup actions
10. Fails to develop pollution prevention as the overarching and dominant strategy

History can buttress Bullard's points as we note that many industries and corporations then were anti-pollution prevention and sought end-of-pipe management of pollution problems. They adopted the "quick fix" strategy to environmental management and would then respond only when a problem occurs. For example, some of the companies that are being heralded today for championing the environmental movement were once at loggerheads with environmental protection strategies. The Exxon-Valdez Oil Spill was as a result of the single-hulled oil tanker that ran aground and spilled 11 million gallons of oil into the Prince William Sound. Prior to this disaster, the oil industry fought against legislatures that would have required the use of double-hulled oil tankers. Likewise, the fossil fuel industry used to work hard to discredit efforts on global warming by claiming it was a myth. Chemical companies such as Dupont took a long time before acknowledging that CFCs were destroying the environment, and McDonald's even filed a libel suit against London Greenpeace for criticizing McDonald's role in rainforest destruction and other practices.

The environment has however changed since Bullard made his assertions. More and more corporations are being made to take full responsibility for their acts irrespective of when it occurred and what information they had at the time. The environment today is more litigious than twenty years ago. Further, many states and countries have responded to public outcries and enacted new laws to ensure corporate responsibility towards the environment and to protect the rights of citizens and communities. These laws have made companies vulnerable to law suits from stakeholders and they are responding by taking a product stewardship approach of their products.

Product stewardship requires taking a cradle to grave approach of one's products and services. It starts from product design and involves all stages of product development, distribution, consumption, and disposal. This therefore, requires that the manufacturer works with its suppliers and vendors to ensure that this goal is achieved. Madu [1996] reported that companies and industries in Japan are already embarking on environmental friendly practices as next competitive weapon. This role is also fostered by some of their manufacturing practices such as the Just-in-time and lean manufacturing practices that are inadvertently, supportive of the goal for environmentally conscious manufacturing. Madu notes that industries ranging from auto, steel, heavy metals, and energy in Japan have already adopted environmentally friendly practices to help them compete in the new millennium. American companies are also heeding the call to be environmentally conscious. Many corporations are now integrating environmental friendly practices in their mission statements and are assigning strategic importance to them. We have given some examples of corporate actions and practices in chapters 6 and 7 and would like to refer the reader to those chapters. However, what is important here is how suppliers can help support the environmental practices of a firm. This we shall discuss in the next section.

Supplier Participation in Environmental Practice

As we have already discussed, companies today are adjusting their strategies of selecting suppliers to move away from a low bid approach and look at a whole range of other factors that may influence quality, productivity, effectiveness, and customer satisfaction. Although factors may include issues such as quality, reliability, cost, flexibility of the supplier, a critical element that is now frequently considered is the environmental practice of the supplier. Manufacturers look beyond the bidding system to develop a long-term partnership with a supplier and this long-term outlook requires that the manufacturer also evaluates the long-term costs that may be absorbed by partnering with the supplier. Such long-term costs may be related to the environmental practice of the supplier. So, the environmental issues that the manufacturer considers in selecting suppliers are far-reaching. Issues to be considered are outlined below:

1. Does the supplier have established environmental guidelines and practices? It is important to know the record of the supplier in terms of environmental practice and how that aligns with the manufacturer's and industry practices. Specific areas to look at include the nature of materials, process technologies, and energy resources that are used by supplier in its production process. In fact, is the supplier's production system efficient and can it be reasonably brought to compliance to meet the environmental goals of the manufacturer?

2. Does the supplier have the capability for reverse logistics? In other words, when it is time to disassemble and reuse a component, are the products or parts designed with ease of assemble and would they be easily reusable or recycled without creating a huge environmental burden. Thus, the environmental costs of disassemble and reuse should be lower than the cost of disposal.

3. Does the manufacturer adopt a packaging and shipping standards that are consistent with recycling and reuse efforts? And are the materials used easily recycled and biodegradable? Packaging constitute a major cost of many products today but more and more industries and companies such as LL Bean are developing efficient packaging systems that help to conserve resources such as paper products. It is important that the supplier adheres to a packaging standard that is consistent with sustainable development.

4. The supplier should also have a program for continuous improvement in its selection and use of raw materials, technological processes, and packaging. It should be involved in ongoing training activities for its employees and adopt new environmental standards as the laws and guidelines change.

5. Quality is one of the themes of this book and it has been clearly stated that when quality is achieved, rejects, reworks,

and scraps significantly diminish. Suppliers that meet the environmental targets of environmentally conscious manufacturers should be those that have world class quality performance and are able to minimize rejects, reworks, and scraps. Notice that these actions conserve energy resources by not re-running the production line to fix problems and also conserve material and natural resources by not wasting materials through rejects and scraps. Also, being a world-class supplier means that there would be a reduction in emission of gases and disposal of hazardous wastes since these are significantly cut down through efficient production system. In addition, world-class suppliers should have a means of reclaiming hazardous materials that may occur for safe disposal.

6. Product design is a critical component in selecting suppliers. Suppliers should design products based on customer needs and must integrate customers in the design stage. However, it is very important to take a holistic outlook of the entire product design phase. This would require developing a life cycle assessment of the product. We have devoted a whole chapter on life cycle assessment and this goes to ensure that the best alternative for product design and development is selected after a complete environmental impact assessment.

7. Eco-labeling is increasingly getting attention. Many countries, industries and professional associations have adopted labeling schemes. There are two classifications of eco-labeling schemes notably voluntary and mandatory. Popular among them are the German Blue Angel scheme, which became operational in 1977 and the White Swan, which is used in the Nordic countries. In the US, the Green Seal is popular although not endorsed by the government but run by a private organization. These schemes play a role in green consumerism and tend to give the impression of compliance to environmental guidelines. Although it may sometimes be misapplied and therefore misused, it could be a motivation for a supplier to meet certain environmental guidelines.

8. Distribution and logistics play a key role in selecting suppliers if there is a strong interest in minimizing environmental burden. It would therefore be important to find out how the supplier transports products and how efficient

that system of transportation and distribution is. The manufacturer may also want to know the measures that are adopted in the transportation of hazardous and toxic materials when they may be involved, the handling of such materials, and the selection and training of workers who work with those materials.

9. Finally, the supplier must show sensitivity to environmental practices in each of its activities. The culture for environmental protection must be enshrined in each worker to achieve the goal of environmentally friendly practice. For example, electronic mails may be used instead of snail mail, memos may be sent electronically rather than printed on paper, meetings may be conducted via video conferencing rather than driving to a physical site, significant amount of paper work can be trimmed by streamlining operations. It is therefore, not a simple task to select an environmentally conscious supplier.

Product Stewardship Practice

Product stewardship requires a change in attitude and manufacturing practices with a focus on conservation of materials and resources. As noted by NPSC, product stewardship practice requires that producers minimize the impacts of their activities on the environment by doing the following:

- Use renewable resources or resources that can be replenished. For example, the use of alternative energy supply such as solar energy or windmill as opposed to the use of fossil fuels. Fossil fuels are limited natural resources and are nonrenewable. Furthermore, the process of excavating and mining them create more environmental burden to the environment.
- Use of biodegradable materials. These are materials that can break down into the soil without emitting harmful chemicals or toxic materials to the entire ecosystem. For example, some of the plastic materials are biodegradable and therefore environmentally friendly.
- Use of recycled and/or recyclable materials. Paper products and packaging materials represent a large bulk of recycled and recyclable materials. Many of the paper products that are

used now contain a significant percentage of recycled material.

- Use of low or no toxic materials. This is required to avoid the emission of poisonous or toxic gases to the atmosphere and also to avoid the emission of greenhouse gases or ozone-depleting gases.
- Use of sustainable harvesting methods. Land is one of the limited natural resources on earth. There are not enough lands for landfills hence the need to conserve more land. It is also obvious that harvesting activities can erode the topsoil and deplete the quality of the land. New efforts are made to change the harvesting methods such as cutting down on the use of fertilizers and instead encouraging the use of organic biostimulants to regenerate the natural condition of the soil. Thus, the use of composting methods is getting increasingly popular.

Strategies for Product Stewardship

Some of the strategies listed here have been discussed in this book in the chapters that deal with environmentally conscious manufacturing. However, we shall elaborate further here. The list of strategies is:

1. Designs for ease of disassembly — Manufacturers are increasingly designing their products so they could be easily disassembled. This has the added advantage of making it easier to recover reusable materials that could be transferred and used in the manufacture of other products. Personal computers represent good example of products that are designed for ease of disassembly. This makes it easier to recover precious materials that could be used in manufacturing new computers.
2. Use of modular design—The use of modular design helps prolong the useful life of a product. Hardware systems that are modular designed can be upgraded at the end of their useful life by adding new components that could enhance its continuing performance. So, rather than worrying about the product becoming obsolete, it could be upgraded to continue to meet future challenges. Computer systems are increasingly designed this way.

3. Design for dematerialization—This is a process of designing that allows materials to be taken out of the product without affecting the performance of the product. Products could therefore be restructured or resized without affecting their performance.
4. Design for conservation—Emphasis of all design strategy should be on how to conserve materials and energy and minimize waste and any form of pollution.
5. Lease options—Many products are now offered by manufacturers under lease option rather than outright purchase. The effect of this is that a consumer with short-term need for the product could use the lease option and allow the manufacturer to assume responsibility for the product at the end of the lease. The manufacturer has the necessary support service and logistic network to ensure that the product finds alternative usage at the end of the lease. Also, it puts the disposal responsibility on the manufacturer who has the resources to ensure disassemble, recovery and safe disposal of the product.
6. Product take-back—Some manufacturers have designed a system of recovering the product from the consumer at the end of the product's life. This strategy ensures environmentally compliant disposal and management of the product thereafter. The example we gave about the Kodak single use cameral falls very well here.
7. Design for recycle—Corporations such as IBM has used 100% recycled plastic in all their personal computer plastic parts. Some others have used 100% recycled materials for their packaging. It is important that parts and products are designed with materials that are recyclable.

CONCLUSION

It is clear that for businesses to compete effectively in today's economy, they need to focus attention on the needs and wants of customers and in particular stakeholders. The stakeholders are active participants whose actions and reactions affect the activity of the firm. The emerging factors in achieving competitiveness today are quality and environment. These two factors are encompassing of all the other measures of productivity that the firm may introduce. A firm for example cannot effectively compete on the basis of low cost advantage if its quality is poor. Poor quality implies higher costs in the long run to the consumer. The same is also true for environment. When environmental quality is not achieved, the cost both to the consumer and the society is significantly increased. The high cost of noncompliance has made many firms to rethink their strategies and increasingly, corporations are beginning to realize that it pays to be environmentally friendly and conscious. Many have reported significant savings and increased profits as in some of the cases presented in this book. Furthermore, by focusing on environmental protection programs, they have enjoyed the trust and respect of their communities. Firms must take a product stewardship of their products. We have outlined in this chapter some of the strategies to take to accomplish that goal. We have also noted that environmental compliance is only attainable if all the major participants such as distributors, suppliers, consumers and others participate in the program. It is therefore a systemic problem that needs to be addressed by all that is involved. Organizations today must therefore compete on quality and environment.

REFERENCES

1. Allan, S., "What happened at Love Canal? Alfred, NY: Alfred University. http://cems.alfred.edu/students98/allansm/Onemoretry.html.
2. Bullard, R.D., <u>Unequal Protection: Environmental Justice & Commentaries of Color</u>, San Francisco, CA: Sierra Club Books, 1994.
3. "Defining product stewardship," Northwest Product Stewardship Council, http://www.govlink.org/nwpsc/DefiningStewardship.htm, downloaded on September 28, 2001.
4. Gibbs, L.M., <u>Love Canal: Twenty years later</u>, Harlem Adams Theatre; CSU, Chico: Associated Students Environmental Affairs Council and Environmental Studies Program.
5. Nersesian, R., "A comparative analysis of Japanese and American production management practices, pp. 37-71, in <u>Management of New Technologies for Global Competitiveness</u> (ed., C.N. Madu), 1993.
6. Madu, C.N., <u>Managing green technologies for global competitiveness</u>, Westport, CT: Quorum Books, 1996.

APPENDIX

Observations in sample, n	Factors for	
	B_3	B_4
2	0	3.267
3	0	2.568
4	0	2.266
5	0	2.089
6	0.030	1.970
7	0.118	1.882
8	0.185	1.815
9	0.239	1.761
10	0.284	1.716
11	0.321	1.679
12	0.354	1.646
13	0.382	1.618
14	0.406	1.594
15	0.428	1.572
16	0.448	1.552
17	0.466	1.534
18	0.482	1.518
19	0.497	1.503
20	0.510	1.490
21	0.523	1.477
22	0.534	1.466
23	0.545	1.455
24	0.555	1.445
25	0.565	1.435

The above table is a copy of Table 27 in *ASTM Manual on Presentation of Data and Control Chart Analysis* (1976). ASTM Publication STP15D, American Society for Testing and Materials, Philadelphia, pp. 134–135. Used with permission.

Notes: For $n > 25$,

$$A = 3/\sqrt{n},$$
$$c_4 \approx 4(n - 1)/(4n - 3);$$
$$B_3 = 1 - 3/c_4\sqrt{2(n - 1)},$$
$$B_4 = 1 + 3/c_4\sqrt{2(n - 1)},$$
$$B_5 = c_4 - 3/\sqrt{2(n - 1)},$$
$$B_6 = c_4 + 3/\sqrt{2(n - 1)}$$

Appendix B and C

Appendix Factors for determining the three-sigma control limits for X bar and
R charts

Number of observations in a subgroup (n)	A_2	D_3	D_4
2	1.88	0	3.27
3	1.02	0	2.57
4	0.73	0	2.28
5	0.58	0	2.11
6	0.48	0	2.00
7	0.42	0.08	1.92
8	0.37	0.14	1.86
9	0.34	0.18	1.82
10	0.31	0.22	1.78
11	0.29	0.26	1.74
12	0.27	0.28	1.72
13	0.25	0.31	1.69
14	0.24	0.33	1.67
15	0.22	0.35	1.65
16	0.21	0.36	1.64
17	0.20	0.38	1.62
18	0.19	0.39	1.61
19	0.19	0.40	1.60
20	0.18	0.41	1.59

Source: G.L. Grant Statistical Quality Control, 6th ed. (New York, McGraw Hill, 1988).

Appendix E_2 factors for control charts

Number of observations in subgroup	E_2
2	2.660
3	1.772
4	1.457
5	1.290
6	1.184
7	1.109
8	1.054
9	1.010
10	0.975
11	0.946
12	0.921
13	0.899
14	0.881
15	0.864

Source: Juran's Quality Control Handbook, 4th ed., 1988.

Appendix D

Appendix Areas under the standard normal probability distribution between the mean and successive values of z

Example: If z = 1.00, then the area between the mean and this value of z is 0.3413.

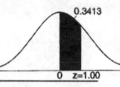

z	0.00	0.01	0.02	0.03	0.04	0.05	0.06	0.07	0.08	0.09
0.0	0.0000	0.0040	0.0080	0.0120	0.0160	0.0199	0.0239	0.0279	0.0319	0.0359
0.1	0.0398	0.0438	0.0478	0.0517	0.0557	0.0596	0.0636	0.0675	0.0714	0.0753
0.2	0.0793	0.0832	0.0871	0.0910	0.0948	0.0987	0.1026	0.1064	0.1103	0.1141
0.3	0.1179	0.1217	0.1255	0.1293	0.1331	0.1368	0.1406	0.1443	0.1480	0.1517
0.4	0.1554	0.1591	0.1628	0.1664	0.1700	0.1736	0.1772	0.1808	0.1844	0.1879
0.5	0.1915	0.1950	0.1985	0.2019	0.2054	0.2088	0.2123	0.2157	0.2190	0.2224
0.6	0.2257	0.2291	0.2324	0.2357	0.2389	0.2322	0.2454	0.2486	0.2518	0.2549
0.7	0.2580	0.2612	0.2642	0.2673	0.2704	0.2734	0.2764	0.2794	0.2823	0.2852
0.8	0.2881	0.2910	0.2939	0.2967	0.2995	0.3023	0.3051	0.3078	0.3106	0.3133
0.9	0.3159	0.3186	0.3212	0.3238	0.3264	0.3289	0.3315	0.3340	0.3365	0.3389
1.0	0.3413	0.3438	0.3461	0.3485	0.3508	0.3531	0.3554	0.3577	0.3599	0.3621
1.1	0.3643	0.3665	0.3686	0.3708	0.3729	0.3749	0.3770	0.3790	0.3810	0.3830
1.2	0.3849	0.3869	0.3888	0.3907	0.3925	0.3944	0.3962	0.3980	0.3997	0.4015
1.3	0.4032	0.4049	0.4066	0.4082	0.4099	0.4115	0.4131	0.4147	0.4162	0.4177
1.4	0.4192	0.4207	0.4222	0.4236	0.4251	0.4265	0.4279	0.4292	0.4306	0.4319
1.5	0.4332	0.4345	0.4357	0.4370	0.4382	0.4394	0.4406	0.4418	0.4429	0.4441
1.6	0.4452	0.4463	0.4474	0.4484	0.4495	0.4505	0.4515	0.4525	0.4535	0.4545
1.7	0.4554	0.4564	0.4573	0.4582	0.4591	0.4599	0.4608	0.4616	0.4625	0.4633
1.8	0.4641	0.4649	0.4656	0.4664	0.4671	0.4678	0.4686	0.4693	0.4699	0.4706
1.9	0.4713	0.4719	0.4726	0.4732	0.4738	0.4744	0.4750	0.4756	0.4761	0.4767
2.0	0.4772	0.4778	0.4783	0.4788	0.4793	0.4798	0.4803	0.4808	0.4812	0.4817
2.1	0.4821	0.4826	0.4830	0.4834	0.4838	0.4842	0.4846	0.4850	0.4854	0.4857
2.2	0.4861	0.4864	0.4868	0.4871	0.4875	0.4878	0.4881	0.4884	0.4887	0.4890
2.3	0.4893	0.4896	0.4898	0.4901	0.4904	0.4906	0.4909	0.4911	0.4913	0.4916
2.4	0.4918	0.4920	0.4922	0.4925	0.4927	0.4929	0.4931	0.4932	0.4934	0.4936
2.5	0.4938	0.4940	0.4941	0.4943	0.4945	0.4946	0.4948	0.4949	0.4951	0.4952
2.6	0.4953	0.4955	0.4956	0.4957	0.4959	0.4960	0.4961	0.4962	0.4963	0.4964
2.7	0.4965	0.4966	0.4967	0.4968	0.4969	0.4970	0.4971	0.4972	0.4973	0.4974
2.8	0.4974	0.4975	0.4976	0.4977	0.4977	0.4978	0.4979	0.4979	0.4980	0.4981
2.9	0.4981	0.4982	0.4982	0.4983	0.4984	0.4984	0.4985	0.4985	0.4986	0.4986
3.0	0.49865	0.4987	0.4987	0.4988	0.4989	0.4989	0.4989	0.4990	0.4990	
4.0	0.49997									

Source: Statistical Analysis for Decision Making, 6th ed., 1994, Morris Hamburg & Peg Young, Harcourt Brace Jovanovich, Inc.

INDEX